NGOs, Civil Society and Global Future

NGOs, Civil Society and Global Future

Dr. R. K. Pruthi

Raj Publications
New Delhi-110002 (INDIA)

NGOs, Civil Society and Global Future

First Published in 2008

ISBN: (10) 81-86208-58-5
(13) 978-81-86208-58-8

Published by : **Raj Publications**
108, 4855/24, Ansari Road
Daryaganj, New Delhi - 110 002
Tel. : 011 - 30120939, 9811010939
E Mail: rajpublications@yahoo.com

Laser Typesetting by : Tamalika Computers, Delhi

Printed at : Balaji Offset Printers, Delhi

PRINTED IN INDIA

Contents

Preface

NGO is non-profit, non commercial, non-government and legally registered body. There is plenty of excitement about new possibilities, tempered by widespread anxiety about the future. In the NGO world, this feeling of excitement stemps from the opportunities for civil action that global trends are creating, on a scale never witnessed before. The anxiety arises because more critical questions are being asked about the role NGOs will play in occupying these spaces.

Aim of this is book is to provide to our readers a unique mix of material on vital aspects of the fundamentals on the subject and its varied functions, organisational and even funding aspects. It also deals with NGOs in a global Society and NGOs and Civil Society.

In preparing this work we have incurred indebtedness of national and international authorities we record our respectful acknowledgements. Librarians have been kind and helpful we thank them.

My publisher ofcourse, deserves appreciation and patronage of my readers for publishing this rich and important material in its present form for greater intellectual persuits. Needless to say, our readers satisfaction with the book will serve as our highest reward.

1

Non - Governmental Organisation

The term non- governmental organisation (NGO) is used in a variety of ways all over the world and, depending on the context in which it is used, can refer to many different types of organisations.

In its broadest sense, a non-governmental organisation is one which is not directly part of the structure of government.

The number of internationally operational NGOs are around 40,000. National numbers are even higher: The *United States* has an estimated 2 million NGOs, most of them formed in the past 30 years. *Russia* has 400,000 NGOs. *India* is estimated to have between 1 and 2 million NGOs. In *Kenya* alone, some 240 NGOs come into existence every year.

History

International non-government organisations have a history dating back to at least the mid-nineteenth century. They were important in the antislavery movement and the movement for women's suffrage, and reached a peak at the time of the *World Disarmament Conference*.

However, the phrase "non-governmental organisation" only came into popular use with the establishment of the *United Nations Organisation* in 1945 with provisions in Article 71 of Chapter 10 of the United Nations Charter for a consultative role for organisations which are neither government nor member states.

The definition of "international NGO" (INGO) is first given in resolution 288 (X) of ECOSOC on *February 27, 1950:* it is defined as

> "any international organisation that is not founded by an international treaty".

The vital role of NGOs and other "major groups" in sustainable development was recognized in Chapter 27 of *Agenda* 21, leading to intense arrangements for a consultative relationship between the United Nations and non-governmental organisations.

Globalization during the 20th century gave rise to the important of NGOs. Many problems could not be solved within a nation. *International treaties* and international organisations such as the *World Trade Organisation* were perceived as being too centred on the interests of capitalist enterprises. In an attempt to counterbalance this trend, NGOs have developed to emphasize humanitarian issues, developmental aid and sustainable development. A prominent example of this is the *World Social Forum* which is a rival convention to the *World Economic Forum* held annually in January in *Davos, Switzerland.* The Fifth World Social Forum in *Porto Alegre, Brazil,* in January 2005 was attended by representatives from more than 1,000 NGOs.

Types

Apart from 'NGO' often alternative terms are used as for example independent sector, volunteer sector, civil society, grassroots organisations, transnational social movement organisations, private voluntary organisations, self- help organisations and non- state actors (NSAs).

NGOs are a heterogeneous group. A long list of acronyms has developed around the term 'NGO'.

These include:

⇒ *INGO* stands for international NGO, such as *Doctors Without Borders / Medecins Sans Frontieres*;

⇒ *BINGO*, is short for business- oriented international NGO;

⇒ *ENGO*, short for environmental NGO, such as *Global 2000;*

⇒ GONGOs are government-operated NGOs, which may have been set up by governments to look like NGOs in order to qualify for outside aid or promote the interests of the government in question;

⇒ *QUANGO*s are quasi- autonomous non-governmental organisations, such as the International Organisation for Standardisation (ISO), which is actually not purely an NGO, since its membership is by nation, and each nation is represented by what the ISO Council determines to be the 'most broadly representative' standardization body of a nation. Now, such a body might in fact be a non-governmental organisation--for example, the United States is represented in ISO by the *American National Standards Institute*, which is independent of the federal government. However, other countries can be represented by national governmental agencies-- this is the trend in Europe.

Classification of NGOs

There are also numerous classifications of NGOs. The typology the *World Bank* uses divides them into:

Operational NGOs

The primary purpose of an operational NGO is the design and implementation of development- related *projects*. One frequently used categorization is the division into:

* Relief Oriented Organisation
* Development Oriented Organisations

They can also be classified according to whether they stress *service* delivery or participation; or whether they are religious or secular; and whether they are more public or private-oriented. Operational NGOs can be *community*- based, national or international.

Advocacy NGOs

The Primary purpose of an Advocacy NGO is to defend or promote a specific cause. As opposed to operational project management, these organisations typically try to raise awareness, acceptance and knowledge by lobbying, press work and activist events.

USAID refers to NGOs as *private voluntary organisations*. However many scholars have argued that this definition is highly problematic as many NGOs are infact state and corporate funded and managed projects with professional staff.

Reasons for NGOs

NGOs exist for a variety of reasons, usually to further the political or social goals of their members or founders. Examples include improving the state of the *natural environment*, encouraging the observance of *human rights,* improving the welfare of the disadvantaged, or representing a corporate agenda. However, there are a huge number of such organisations and their goals cover a broad range of political and philosophical positions. This can also easily be applied to private schools and athletic organisations.

Methods

NGOs vary in their methods.

Some act primarily as lobbyists, while.

Others conduct programs and activities primarily.

For instance, an NGO such as *Oxfarm*, concerned with poverty alleviation, might provide needy people with the equipment and skills to find food and clean *drinking water*.

Public Relations

Non-governmental organisations need healthy relationship with the public to meet their goals.

Foundations and charities use sophisticated public relations campaigns to raise funds and employ standard lobbying techniques with governments. Interest groups may be of political importance because of their ability to influence social and political outcomes.

At times NGOs seek to mobilize public support.

Consulting

Many international NGOs have a consultative status with United Nations agencies relevant to their area of work.

As an example, the *Third World Network* has a consultative status with the *UN Conference on Trade* and *Development* (UNCTAD) and the UN Economic and Social *Council* (ECOSOC).

While in 1946, only 41 NGOs had consultative status with the *ECOSOC*, by 2003 this number had risen to 3550.

Project Management

There is an increasing awareness that management techniques are crucial to project success in non- governmental organisations.

Generally, non- governmental organisations that are private have either a community or environmental focus. They address varieties of issues such as religion, emergency aid, or humanitarian affairs. They mobilize public support and voluntary contributions for aid; they often have strong links with community groups in developing countries, and they often work in areas where government- to- government aid is not possible.

NGOs are accepted as a part of the international relations landscape, and while they influence national and multilateral policy- making, increasingly they are more directly involved in local action.

Management

Two management trends are particularly relevant to NGOs:

Diversity Management

Diversity management deals with different cultures in an organisation. Intercultural problems are prevalent in Northern NGOs which are engaged in developmental activities in the South. Personnel coming from a rich country are faced with a completely different approach of doing things in the target country.

Participatory Management

A participatory management style is said to be typical of NGOs. It is intricately tied to the concept of a *learning organisation*: all people within the organisation are perceived as sources for knowledge and skills.

To develop the organisation, individuals have to be able to contribute in the *decision making process* and they need to learn.

Staffing

Not all people working for non-governmental organisations are *volunteers*.

Paid staff members typically receive lower pay than in the *commercial private sector.*

Employees are highly committed to the aims and *principles* of the *organisation.*

The reasons people volunteer are not necessarily purely *altruistic,* and can provide immediate benefits for themselves as well as those they serve, including skills, experience, and contacts.

There is some dispute as to whether *expatriates* should be sent to developing countries. Frequently this type of personnel is employed to satisfy a *donor* who wants to see the supported project managed by someone from an *industrialized country.* However, the expertise these employees or volunteers may have can be counterbalanced by a number of factors: the cost of *foreigners* is typically higher, they have no *grassroot connections* in the country they are sent to, and local expertise is often undervalued.

The NGO sector is an important employer in terms of numbers. For example, by the end of 1995, *Concern worldwide*, an international Northern NGO working against poverty, employed 174 expatriates and just over 5,000 national staff working in ten developing countries in *Africa* and *Asia,* and in *Haiti.*

Funding

Large NGOs may have annual budgets in the millions of dollars.

For instance, the budget of the *American Association of Retired Persons* (AARP) was over US $ 540 million in 1999.

Human Rights Watch spent and received US $ 21.7 million in 2003.

Funding such large budgets demands significant fund-raising efforts on the part of most NGOs.

Major sources of NGO funding include *membership dues,* the sale of goods and services, grants from international institutions or national government, and private *donations.* Several *EU grants* provide funds accessible to NGOs.

Even though the term "non-governmental organisation" implies *independence* from governments, some NGOs depend heavily on governments for their funding.

A quarter of the US $ 162 million income in 1998 of the *famine- relief* organisation Oxfam was donated by the British government and the EU.

The Christian relief and development organisation *World Vision* collected US $ 55 million worth of goods in 1998 from the American government.

Nobel Prize winner *Medecins Sans Frontieres* (MSF) (known in English as Doctors Without Borders) gets 46% of its income from government sources.

Monitoring and Control

In a March 2000 report on United Nations Reform priorities then U.N. Secretary General Kofi Annan wrote in favour of international humanitarian intervention, arguing that the international community has a *"right to protect"* citizens of the world against ethnic cleansing, genocide, and crimes against humanity.

On the heels of the report, the Canadian government launched the Responsibility to Protect *R2PPDF (434 KiB)* project, outlining the issue of humanitarian intervention. While the R2P doctrine has wide applications, among the more controversial has been the Canadian government's use of R2P to justify its intervention and support of the *coup* in Haiti.

Years after R2P, the *World Federalist Movement*, an organisation which supports "the creation of democratic global structures accountable to the citizens of the world and call for the division of international authority among separate agencies," has launched Responsibility to Protect - Engaging Civil Society (R2PCS). A collaboration between the WFM and the Canadian government, this project aims to bring NGOs into lockstep with the principles outlined under the original R2P project.

NGO Monitor is a conservative pro-Israel site which aims to promote "critical debate and accountability of human rights NGOs in the *Arab- Israeli* conflict. "The organisation has successfully conducted campaigns against Oxfam and the Ford Foundation--Leading to formal apologies and changes in practice- on the grounds that organisations are too anti- Israeli.

NGO Watch is a project of the *American Enterprise Institute* which monitors NGOs. The project is primarily a negative analysis of NGOs which are considered to be on the progressive side of the political spectrum.

Indian NGOs is a portal of over 20,000 NGOs who work with the corporate sector in India. This portal offers insights into how the corporate sector is using NGOs to benefit their program.

In recent years, many large corporations have beefed up their Corporate Social Responsibility departments in an attempt to pre-empt NGO campaigns against certain corporate practices. As the logic goes, if corporations work with NGOs, NGOs will not work against corporations.

Legal Status

NGOs are not *legal entities* under *international law,* as states are.

An exception is the *International Committee of the Red Cross,* which is considered a legal entity under international law because it is based on the *Geneva Convention.*

Other Terminology for the Sector

There is a growing movement within the "non" "profit and "non"- government sector to define itself in a more constructive, accurate way. Instead of being defined by "non" words, organisations are suggesting new terminology to describe the sector.

The term "civil society organisation" (CSO) has been used by a growing number of organisations, such as The Center for the Study of Global Governance.

The term "citizen sector organisation" (CSO) has also been advocated to describe the sector - as one of citizens, for citizens - by organisations such as *Ashoka: Innovators for the Public.*

This labels and positions the sector as its own entity, without relying on language used for the government or business sectors.

2

How To Form A Society ?

The application for registration of a society (under the Societies Registration Act, 1960) should be made to the assistant registrar of societies (in Maharashtra state, the assistant registrar of societies is the assistant charity commissioner) having jurisdiction over the region / sub region in which the society is sought to be registered.

The application should be submitted together with

⇒ memorandum of association and rules and regulations;

⇒ consent letters of all the members of the managing committee;

⇒ authority letter duly signed by all the member of the managing committee;

⇒ an affidavit sworn by the president or secretary of the society on non-judicial stamp paper of Rs. 10/-, together with a court fee stamp and

⇒ a declaration by the members of the managing committee that the funds of the society will be used only for the purpose of furthering the aims and objects of the society.

In Maharashtra state, since the registrar of societies is the charity commissioner, the society also has to be registered as a trust hence an application should also be made u/s 18 of the Bombay Public Trusts Act 1950, in the prescribed form.

All the aforesaid documents which are required for the application for registration should be submitted in duplicate, together with a registration fee of Rs. 50/-. Unlike the trust deed, the memorandum of association and rules and regulations need not be executed on stamp paper. The process of registering a society generally takes a longer time than registering a trust.

Registration Act

(21 of 1860)

An Act for the Registration of Welfare, Literary, Scientific and Charitable Societies.

Whereas it is expedient that provision should be made for improving the legal condition of societies established for the promotion of literature, science, of the fine arts, or for the diffusion of useful knowledge, the diffusion of political education or for charitable purposes; It is enacted as follows:

Societies formed by memorandum of association and registration

1. Any seven or more persons associated for any literary, scientific, or charitable purpose, or for any such purpose as is described in section 20 of this Act, may, by subscribing their names to a memorandum of association, and filing the same with the Registrar of Joint-stock Companies, form themselves into a society under this Act.

Memorandum of association

2. The memorandum of association shall contain the following things, that is to say,

⇒ the name of the society

⇒ the objects of the society

⇒ the names, addresses, and occupations of the governors, council, directors, committee, or other governing body to whom, by the rules of the society, the management of its affairs is entrusted.

A copy of the rules and regulations of the society, certified to be a correct copy by not less than three of the members of the governing body, shall be filed with the memorandum of association.

Registration and fees

3. Upon such memorandum and certified copy being filed, the Registrar shall certify under his hand that the society is registered under this Act. There shall be paid to the Registrar for every such registration a fee of fifty rupees, or such smaller fee as the State Government may, from time to time, direct, and all fees so paid shall be accounted for to the State Government.

Annual list of managing body to be filed

4. Once in every year, on or before the fourteenth day succeeding the day on which, according to the rules of the society, the annual general meeting of the society is held, or, if the rules do not provide for an annual general meeting, in the month of January, a list shall be filed with the Registrar

of Joint-stock Companies, of the names, addresses and occupations of the governors, council, directors, committee, of other governing body then entrusted with the management of the affairs of the society.

Property of society how vested

5. The property, movable and immovable, belonging to a society registered under this Act, if not vested in trustees, shall be deemed to be vested, for the time being, in the governing body of such society, and in all proceedings, civil and criminal, may be described as the property of the governing body of such society by their proper title.

Suits by and against societies

6. Every society registered under this Act may sue or be sued in the name of the president, chairman, or principal secretary, or trustees, as shall be determined by the rules and regulations of the society, and, in default of such determination, in the name of such persons as shall be appointed by the governing body for the occasion.

Provided that it shall be competent for any person having a claim or demand against the society, to sue the president of chairman, or principal secretary or the trustees thereof, if on application to the governing body some other officer or person be not nominated to be the defendant.

Suits not to abate

7. No suit or proceeding in any Civil Court shall abate or discontinue by reason of the person, by or against whom such suit or proceedings shall have been brought or

continued, dying or ceasing to fill the character in the name whereof he shall have sued or been sued, but the same suit or proceeding shall be continued in the name of or against the successor of such person.

Enforcement of judgement against society

8. If a judgement shall be recovered against the person or officer named on behalf of the society, such judgement shall not be put in force against the property, movable or immovable or against the body of such person or officer, but against the property of the society.

The application for execution shall set forth the judgement, the fact of the party against whom it shall have been recovered having sued or having been sued, as the case may be, on behalf of the society only, and shall require to have the judgement enforced against the property of the society.

Recovery of penalty accruing under bye-law

9. Whenever by any bye-law duly made in accordance with the rules and regulations of the society, or, if the rules do not provide for the making of bye-laws, by any bye-law made at a general meeting of the members of the society convened for the purpose (for the making of which the concurrent votes of three-fifths of the members present at such meeting shall be necessary), any pecuniary penalty is imposed for the breach of any rule or bye-law of the society, such penalty, when accrued, may be recovered in any Court having jurisdiction where the defendants shall reside, or the

society shall be situate, as the governing body thereof shall deem expedient.

Members liable to be sued as strangers

10. Any member who may be in arrear of a subscription which according to the rules of the society he is bound to pay, or who shall possess himself or detain any property of the society in a manner or for a time contrary to such rules, or shall injure or destroy any property of the society, may be sued for such arrear or for the damage accruing from such detention, injury, or destruction of property in the manner hereinbefore provided. Recovery by successful defendant of costs adjudged. But if the defendant shall be successful in any suit or other proceeding brought against him at the instance of the society, and shall be adjudged to recover his costs, he may elect to proceed to recover the same from the officer in whose name the suit shall be brought, or from the society, and in the latter case shall have process against the property of the said society in the manner above described.

Members guilty of offences punishable as strangers

11. Any member of the society who shall steal, purloin, or embezzle any money or other property, or wilfully and maliciously destroy or injure any property of such society, or shall forge any deed, bond, security for money, receipt, or other instrument, where by the funds of the society may be exposed to loss, shall be subject to the same prosecution, and, if convicted, shall be liable to be punished in like manner, as any person not a member would be subject and liable to in respect of the like offence.

Societies enabled to alter, extend, or abridge their purposes

12. Whenever it shall appear to the governing body of any society registered under this Act, which has been established for any particular purpose or purposes, that it is advisable to alter, extend, or abridge such purpose to or for other purposes within the meaning of this Act, or to amalgamate such society either wholly or partially with any other society, such governing body may submit the proposition to the members of the society in a written or printed report, and may convene a special meeting for the consideration thereof according to the regulations of the society; but no such proposition shall be carried into effect unless such report shall have been delivered or sent by post to every member of the society ten days previous to the special meeting convened by the governing body for the consideration thereof, not unless such proposition shall have been agreed to by the votes of three-fifths of the members delivered in person or by proxy, and confirmed by the votes or three-fifths of the members present at a second special meeting convened by the governing body at an interval of one month after the former meeting.

Provision for dissolution of societies and adjustment of their affairs

13. Any number not less than three-fifths of the members of any society may determine that it shall be dissolved, and thereupon it shall be dissolved forthwith, or at the time then agreed upon, and all necessary steps shall be taken for the disposal and settlement of the property of

the society, its claims and liabilities, according to the rules of the said society applicable thereto, if any, and, if not then as the governing body shall find expedient, provided that, in the event of any dispute arising among the said governing body or the members of the society, the adjustment of its affairs shall be referred to the principal Court of original civil jurisdiction of the district in which the chief building of the society is situate and the court shall make such order in the matter as it shall deem requisite:

Assent required. Provided that no society shall be dissolved unless three-fifths of the members shall have expressed a wish for such dissolution by their votes delivered in person, or by proxy, at a general convened meeting for the purpose:

Government consent. Provided that whenever any Government is a member of or a contributor to, or otherwise interested in, any society registered under this Act, such society shall not be dissolved without the consent of the Government of the State of registration.

Upon a dissolution no member to receive profit

14. If upon the dissolution of any society registered under this Act there shall remain, after the satisfaction of all its debts and liabilities, any property whatsoever, the same shall not be paid to or distributed among the members of the said society or any of them, but shall be given to some other society, to be determined by the votes of not less than three-fifths of the members present personally or by proxy at the time of the dissolution, or, in default thereof, by such Court as aforesaid:

Court not to apply to Joint-stock Companies. Provided, however, that this clause shall not apply to any society which shall have been founded or established by the contributions of shareholders in the nature of a Joint-stock Company.

Member defined

15. For the purposes of this Act a member of a society shall be a person who, having been admitted therein according to the rules and regulations thereof, shall have paid a subscription, or shall have signed the roll or list of members thereof, and shall not have resigned in accordance with such rules and regulations.

But in all proceedings under this Act no person shall be entitled to vote or be counted as a member whose subscription at the time shall have been in arrear for a period exceeding three months.

Governing body defined

16. The governing body of the society shall be the governors, council, directors, committee, trustees or other body to whom by the rules and regulations of the society the management of its affairs is entrusted.

Registration of societies formed before Act

17. Any company or society established for a literary, scientific or charitable purpose, and registered under Act 43 of 1850, or any such society established and constituted previously to the passing of this Act but not registered under the said Act 43 of 1850, may at any time hereafter be registered as a society under this Act:

Subject to the proviso that no such company or society shall be registered under this Act unless an assent to its being so registered has been given by three-fifths of the members present personally, or by proxy, at some general meeting convened for that purpose by the governing body.

In the case of a company or society registered under Act 43 of 1850, the directors shall be deemed to be such governing body.

In the case of a society not so registered, if no such body shall have been constituted on the establishment of the society, it shall be competent for the members thereof, upon due notice, to create for itself a governing body to act for the society thenceforth.

Such societies to file memorandum, etc., with registrar of Joint-stock Companies

18. In order to any such society as is mentioned in the last preceding section obtaining registry under this Act, it shall be sufficient that the governing body file with the Registrar of Joint-stock Companies a memorandum showing the name of the society, the objects of the society, and the names, addresses and occupations of the governing body, together with a copy of the rules and regulations of the society certified as provided in section 2, and a copy of the report of the proceedings of the general meeting at which the registration was resolved on.

Inspection of documents

19. Any person may inspect all documents filed with

the Registrar under this Act on payment of a fee of one rupee for each inspection; and any person may require a copy or extract of any document or any part of any document, to be certified by the Registrar, on payment of amount prescribed for every hundred words of such copy or extract.

Certified copies. And such certified copy shall be prima facie evidence of the matters therein contained in all legal proceedings whatever.

To what Societies Act applies

20. The following societies may be registered under this Act:-

> Charitable societies, the military orphan funds or societies established at the several presidencies of India, societies established for the promotion of science, literature of the fine arts, for instruction, the diffusion of useful knowledge, the diffusion of political education, the foundation or maintenance of libraries or reading-rooms for general use among the members or open to the public, or public museums and galleries of paintings and other works of art, collections of natural history, mechanical and philosophical inventions, instruments, or designs.

3

How To Form An NGO?

The application for registration of a public charitable trust should be submitted (under section 18 of the Bombay Public Trusts Act, 1950) to the deputy/ assistant charity commissioner having jurisdiction over the region /sub region in which the trust is sought to be registered.

In Bombay, the office of the charity commissioner is situated at 83, Dr. Annie Besant Road, Worli, Bombay-400018.

The application should be made in the prescribed form which is available, at a very nominal price, from the office of the charity commissioner. In Bombay, the form is also available at Tax Print, 177 Bazargate Street, Bombay - 400001.

After providing details (in the form) regarding designation by which the public trust shall be known, names of trustees, mode of succession, etc. the applicant has to affix a court fee stamp of Rs. 2/- to the form and pay in cash, registration fee which may range from Rs. 3/- to Rs. 25/-, depending on the value of the trust property. If the value of the trust property does not exceed Rs 2,000, the registration fee levied is Rs. 3/-. If the value exceeds Rs. 25,000/- it is Rs 25/-.

The application form should be signed by the applicant before the regional officer or superintendent of the regional office of the charity commissioner or a notary. The application form should be submitted, together with a copy of the trust deed (the original may be produced, later, for verification) which is the main instrument of the trust. The trust deed is a document every trustee must turn to, whenever in doubt regarding the aims and objects of the trust, mode of succession or any issue concerning the management of the trust.

The trust deed must be executed on non-judicial stamp paper, the value of which would depend on the valuation of the trust property.

According to article 61 of schedule 1 of the Bombay Stamp Act, 1958, "where there is disposition of property" and "where the Trust is made for a religious or charitable purpose", the stamp duty is "the same duty as a Bond (article 13) for a sum equal to the amount settled or market value of the property settled". On reading the aforesaid article 61, together with article 13, of the Bombay Stamp Act, we understand that for "every rupees five hundred or part thereof the stamp duty (w.e.f. 1-5-1993) is "rupees twenty".

If one decides to start a trust with a token amount of Rs. 1,000/-, the trust deed should be executed on a non-judicial stamp paper of Rs. 40/-. It is advisable to use both sides of the paper, an the pages, other than the stamp paper, be of a variety known as "ledger paper". The trust deed should be signed by both the settlor/s and trustee/s in the presence of a witness. The witness may be a friend of relative. Some even prefer to sign before a notary.

Two other documents which should be submitted at the time of making an application for registration are

⇒ affidavit which must be sworn (by the trustees making the application) before a notary and executed on non-judicial stamp paper of Rs. 10/- and

⇒ consent letter which may be prepared on an ordinary sheet of paper and signed by the trustee/s other than the trustee making the application. In the absence of a consent letter from the remaining trustees, the deputy/ assistant charity commissioner can insist on the presence of all the remaining trustees for the hearing.

Processing the application usually takes about six to eight weeks. A notice informing the applicant about the day and time fixed for a formal hearing is dispatched usually 10 to 15 days in advance. The applicant generally has to appear in person or depute his/ her lawyer. The original trust deed should be produced for verification at the time of the hearing.

The deputy/ assistant charity commissioner before whom the enquiry is held has to ascertain:

⇒ Whether a trust exists and whether such trust is a public trust;

⇒ Whether any property is the property of such trust;

⇒ Whether the whole or any substantial portion of the subject matter of the trust is situated within his jurisdiction;

⇒ The names and addresses of the trustees and managers of such trust;

⇒ The mode of succession to the office of the trustee of such trust;

⇒ The amount of gross average annual income and expenditure of such trust;

⇒ Any other particulars as may be prescribed under sub-section (5) of section 18.

After making enquiries on the aforesaid issues, the deputy/ assistant charity commissioner makes entries in the register kept under section 17 (popularly known as schedule 1) of the Bombay Public Trust Act and issues a certificate of registration which bears the official seal and registration number of the trust.

If the certificate of registration is lost or damaged over the years, a duplicate certificate can be obtained from the department, on application and on payment of a nominal fee.

How To Form A Society ?

The application for registration of society (under the Societies Registration Act, 1960) should be made to the assistant registrar of societies (in Maharashtra state, the assistant registrar of societies is the assistant charity commissioner) having jurisdiction over the region / sub region in which the society is sought to be registered.

The application should be submitted together with

⇒ memorandum of association and rules and regulations;

⇒ consent letters of all the members of the managing committee;

⇒ authority letter duly signed by all the members of the managing committee;

⇒ an affidavit sworn by the president or secretary of the society on non-judicial stamp paper of Rs. 10/-, together with a court fee stamp and

⇒ a declaration by the members of the managing committee that the funds of the society will be used only for the purpose of furthering the aims and objects of the society.

In Maharashtra state, since the registrar of societies is the charity commissioner, the society also has to be registered as a trust hence an application should also be made u/s 18 of the Bombay Public Trusts Act 1950, in the prescribed form.

All the aforesaid documents which are required for the application for registration should be submitted in duplicate, together with a registration fee of Rs. 50/-. Unlike the trust deed, the memorandum of association and rules and regulations need not be executed on stamp paper.

The process of registering a society generally takes a longer time than registering a trust.

Societies Registration Act, 1850

{21 of 1860}

An Act for the Registration of Welfare, Literary, Scientific and Charitable Societies.

Whereas it is expedient that provision should be made for improving the legal condition of societies established for the promotion of literature, science, or the fine arts, or for the diffusion of useful knowledge, the diffusion of political education or for charitable purposes: It is enacted as follow:-

Societies Formed by Memorandum of Association and Registration

1. Any seven or more persons associated for any literary, scientific, or charitable purpose, or for any such purpose as is described in section 20 of this Act, may, by subscribing their names to a memorandum of association, and filling the same with the Registrar of Joint-stock Companies, form themselves into a society under this Act.

Memorandum of Association

2. The memorandum of association shall contain the following things, that is to say,

⇒ the name of the society

⇒ the objects of the society

⇒ the names, addresses, and occupations of the governors, council, directors, committee, or other governing body to whom, by the rules of the society, the management of its affairs is entrusted.

A copy of the rules and regulations of the society, certified to be a correct copy by not less than three of the members of the governing body, shall be filed with the memorandum of association.

Registration and Fees

3. Upon such memorandum and certified copy being

filed, the Registrar shall certify under his hand that the society is registered under this Act. There shall be paid to the Registrar for every such registration a fee of fifty rupees, or such smaller fee as the State Government may, from time to time, direct, and all fees so paid shall be accounted for to the State Government.

Annual List of Managing Body To Be Filed

4. Once in every year, on or before the fourteenth day succeeding the day on which, according to the rules of the society, the annual general meeting of the society is held, or, if the rules do not provide for an annual general meeting, in the month of January, a list shall be filed with the Registrar of Joint-stock Companies, of the names, addresses and occupations of the governors, council, directors, committee, or other governing body then entrusted with the management of the affairs of the society.

Property of Society How Vested

5. The property, movable and immovable, belonging to a society registered under this Act, if not vested in trustees, shall be deemed to be vested, for the time being, in the governing body of such society, and in all proceedings, civil and criminal, may be described as the property of the governing body of such society by their proper title.

Suits by and Against Societies

6. Every society registered under this Act may sue or be sued in the name of the president, chairman, or principal secretary, or trustees, as shall be determined by the rules

and regulations of the society, and, in default of such determination, in the name of such persons as shall be appointed by the governing body for the occasion:

Provided that it shall be competent for any person having a claim or demand against the society, to sue the president or chairman, or principal secretary or the trustees thereof, if on application to the governing body some other officer or person be not nominated to be the defendant.

Suits Not To Abate

7. No suit or proceeding in any Civil Court shall abate or discontinue by reason of the person, by or against whom such suit or proceedings shall have been brought or continued, dying or ceasing to fill the character in the name whereof he shall have sued or been sued, but the same suit or proceeding shall be continued in the name of or against the successor of such person.

Enforcement of Judgement Against Society

8. If a judgement shall be recovered against the person or officer named on behalf of the society, such judgement shall not be put in force against the property, movable or immovable, or against the body of such person or officer, but against the property of the society.

The application for execution shall set forth the judgement, the fact of the party against whom it shall have been recovered having sued or having been sued, as the case may be, on behalf of the society only, and shall require to have the judgement enforced against the property of the society.

Recovery of Penalty Accruing Under Bye-Law

9. Whenever by any bye-law duly made in accordance with the rules and regulations of the society, or, if the rules do not provide for the making of bye-laws, by any bye-law made at a general meeting of the members of the society convened for the purpose (for the making of which the concurrent votes of three-fifths of the members present at such meeting shall be necessary), any pecuniary penalty is imposed for the breach of any rule or bye-law of the society, such penalty, when accrued, may be recovered in any Court having jurisdiction where the defendants shall reside, or the society shall be situate, as the governing body thereof shall deem expedient.

Members Liable To Be Sued As Strangers

10. Any member who may be in arrear of a subscription which according to the rules of the society he is bound to pay, or who shall possess himself or detain any property of the society in a manner or for a time contrary to such rules, or shall injure or destroy any property of the society, may be sued for such arrear or for the damage accruing from such detention, injury, or destruction of property in the manner hereinbefore provided. Recovery by successful defendant of costs adjudged. But if the defendant shall be successful in any suit or other proceeding brought against him at the instance of the society, and shall be adjudged to recover his costs, he may elect to proceed to recover the same from the officer in whose name the suit shall be brought or from the society, and in the latter case shall have process against the property of the said society in the manner above described.

Members Guilty of Offences Punishable As Strangers

11. Any member of the society who shall steal, purloin, or embezzle any money or other property, or wilfully and maliciously destroy or injure any property of such society, or shall forge any deed, bond security for money, receipt, or other instrument, where by the funds of the society may be exposed to loss, shall be subject to the same prosecution, and, if convicted, shall be liable to be punished in like manner, as any person not a member would be subject and liable to in respect of the like offence.

Societies Enabled To Alter, Extend, or Abridge Their Purposes

12. Whenever it shall appear to the governing body of any society registered under this Act, which has been established for any particular purpose of purposes, that it is advisable to alter, extend, or abridge such purpose to or for other purposes within the meaning of this Act, or to amalgamate such society either wholly or partially with any other society, such governing body may submit the proposition to the members of the society in a written or printed report, and may convene a special meeting for the consideration thereof according to the regulations of the society; but no such proposition shall be carried into effect unless such report shall have been delivered or sent by post to every member of the society ten days previous to the special meeting convened by the governing body for the consideration thereof, not unless such proposition shall have been agreed to by the votes of three-fifths of the members delivered in person or by proxy, and confirmed by the votes or three-fifths of the members present at a second special meeting convened by

the governing body at an interval of one month after the former meeting.

Provision for Dissolution of Societies and Adjustment of Their Affairs

13. Any number not less than three-fifths of the members of any society may determine that it shall be dissolved, and thereupon it shall be dissolved forthwith, or at the time then agreed upon, and all necessary steps shall be taken for the disposal and settlement of the property of the society, its claims and liabilities, according to the rules of the said society applicable thereto, if any and, if not, then as the governing body shall find expedient, provided that, in the event of any dispute arising among the said governing body or the members of the society, the adjustment of its affairs shall be referred to the principal Court of original civil jurisdiction of the district in which the chief building of the society is situate and the court shall make such order in the matter as it shall deem requisite:

Assent required. Provided that no society shall be dissolved unless three-fifths of the members shall have expressed a wish for such dissolution by their votes delivered in person, or by proxy, at a general convened meeting for the purpose.

Government consent. Provided that whenever any Government is a member of or a contributor to, or otherwise interested in, any society registered under this Act, such society shall not be dissolved without the consent of the Government of the State of registration.

Upon A Dissolution No Member To Receive Profit

14. If upon the dissolution of any society registered under this Act there shall remain, after the satisfaction of all its debts and liabilities, any property whatsoever, the same shall not be paid to or distributed among the members of the said society or any of them, but shall be given to some other society, to be determined by the votes of not less than three-fifths of the members present personally or by proxy at the time of the dissolution, or, in default thereof, by such Court as aforesaid:

Court not to apply to Joint-stock Companies. Provided, however, that this clause shall not apply to any society which shall have been founded or established by the contributions of shareholders in the nature of a Joint-stock Company.

Member Defined

15. For the purposes of this Act a member of a society shall be a person who, having been admitted therein according to the rules and regulations thereof, shall have paid a subscription, or shall have signed the roll or list of members thereof, and shall not have resigned in accordance with such rules and regulations.

Disqualified members. But in all proceedings under this Act no person shall be entitled to vote or be counted as a member whose subscription at the time shall have been in arrear for a period exceeding three months.

Governing Body Defined

16. The governing body of the society shall be the governors, council, directors, committee, trustees or other body

to whom by the rules and regulations of the society the management of its affairs is entrusted.

Registration of Societies Formed Before Act

17. Any company or society established for a literary, scientific or charitable purpose, and registered under Act 43 of 1850, or any such society established and constituted previously to the passing of this Act but not registered under the said Act 43 of 1850, may at any time hereafter be registered as a society under this Act.

Assent required. Subject to the proviso that no such company or society shall be registered under this Act unless an assent to its being so registered has been given by three-fifths of the members present personally, or by proxy, at some general meeting convened for that purpose by the governing body.

In the case of a company or society registered under Act 43 of 1850, the directors shall be deemed to be such governing body.

In the case of a society not so registered, if no such body shall have been constituted on the establishment of the society, it shall be competent for the members thereof, upon due notice, to create for itself a governing body to act for the society thenceforth.

Such Societies to File Memorandum, etc., with Register of Joint- Stock Companies

18. In order to any such society as is mentioned in the last preceding section obtaining registry under this Act. It shall be sufficient that the governing body file with the

Registrar of Joint- stock Companies a memorandum showing the name of the society, the objects of the society, and the names, addresses and occupations of the governing body, together with a copy of the rules and regulations of the society certified as provided in section 2, and a copy of the report of the proceedings of the general meeting at which the registration was resolved on.

Inspection of Documents

19. Any person may inspect all documents filed with the Registrar under this Act on Payment of a fee of one rupee for each inspection; and any person may require a copy or extract of any document or any part of any document, to be certified by the Registrar, on Payment of two annas for every hundred words of such copy or extract:

Certified copies. And such certified copy shall be prima facie evidence of the matters therein contained in all legal proceedings whatever.

To What Societies Act Applies

20. The following societies may be registered under this Act :-

Charitable societies, the military orphan funds or societies established at the several presidencies of India, societies established for the promotion of science, literature or the fine arts, for instruction, the diffusion of useful knowledge, the diffusion of political education, the foundation or maintenance of libraries or reading- rooms for general use among the members or open to the public, or public museums and galleries of paintings and other works of art, collections of natural history, mechanical and philosophical inventions, instruments, or designs.

How to Form A Section 25 Company ?

The first step towards registration of a company (under section 25 of the Indian Companies Act) is the application for availability of name to the registrar of Companies, which must be made in the prescribed from no. 1A, together with a fee of Rs 500/-. It is advisable to suggest a choice of three other names by which the company will be called, in case the first name which in proposed is not found acceptable by the registrar.

The office of the registrar of companies in Bombay is situated at Everest, Marine Drive, Bombay 400002.

According to section 25 of the Indian Companies Act, "where it is proved to the satisfaction of the Central Government that an association is to be formed as a Limited Company for promoting Commerce, Art, Science, Religion, Charity or any other useful purpose, and it intends to apply its profits, if any, or other income in promoting its objects and prohibits the payment of any dividend to its members, then the Government may, by a licence, direct that the association be registered as a Company with limited liability without the addition to its name, of the word, "Limited" or the words, "Private Limited".

Once the availability of name is confirmed, an application should be made in writing to the regional director of the company law board. The application should be accompanied by the following documents:

⇒ Three printed or typewritten copies of the memorandum

and articles of association of the proposed company, duly signed by all the promoters with full name, address and occupation.

⇒ A declaration by an advocate or a chartered accountant that the memorandum and articles of association have been drawn up in conformity with the provisions of the Act and that all the requirements of the Act and the rules made thereunder have been duly compiled with, in respect of registration or matters incidental or supplementary thereto.

⇒ Three copies of a list of the names, addresses and occupations of the promoters (and where a firm is a promoter, of each partner in the firm), as well as of the members of the proposed board of directors, together with the names of companies, associations and other institutions in which such promoters, partners and members of the proposed board of directors are directors or hold responsible positions, if any, with description of the positions so held.

⇒ A statement showing in detail the assets (with the estimated values thereof) and the liabilities of the association, as on the date of the application or within seven days of than date.

⇒ An estimate of the future annual income and expenditure of the proposed company, specifying the sources of the income and the objects of the expenditure.

⇒ A statement giving a brief description of the work, if any, already done by the association and of the work proposed to be done by it after registration, in pursuance of section 25.

⇒ A statement specifying briefly the grounds on which the application is made.

⇒ A declaration by each of the persons making the application that he/ she is of sound mind, not an undischarged insolvent, not convicted by a court for any offence and does not stand disqualified under section 203 of the companies Act, 1956, for appointment as a director.

The applicants must also furnish to the registrar of companies (of the state in which the registered office of the proposed company is to be, or is situate) a copy of the application and each of the other documents which had been filed before the regional director of the company law board.

The applicants should also, within a week from the date of making the application to the regional director of the company law board, publish a notice in the prescribed manner at least once in a newspaper in a principal language of the district in which the registered office of the proposed company is to be situate or is situate and circulating in that district, and at least once in an English newspaper circulating in that district.

The regional director shall, after considering the objections, if any, received within 30 days from the date of publication of the notice in the newspaper, and after consulting any authority, department or ministry, as he may, in his discretion, decide, determine whether the licence should or should not be granted.

The regional director may also direct the company to insert in its memorandum, or in its articles, or in both, such conditions of the licence as may be specified by him in this behalf. It generally takes about 8 to 12 weeks after application to receive the licence under section 25 of the Companies Act, 1956.

4

Nature and Character of An Indian NGO

A non- governmental organisation (NGO) is any non-profit, voluntary citizens' group which is organized on a local, national or international level.

Task- oriented and driven by people with a common interest, NGOs perform a variety of service and humanitarian functions, bring citizen concerns to Governments, advocate and monitor policies and encourage political participation through provision of information. Some are organized around specific issues, such as human rights, environment or health.

While most of the NGOs work at the grassroots level with the communities, some provide analysis and expertise, serve as early warning mechanisms and help monitor and implement international agreements.

The World Bank, defines NGOs as "private organisations that pursue activities to relieve suffering, promote the interests of the poor, protect the environment, provide basic social services, or undertake community development". A World Bank Key Document, Working With NGOs, adds, "In wider usage, the term NGO can be applied to any non- profit organisation which is independent from government. NGOs are typically value- based organisations which depend, in whole or in part, on charitable donations and voluntary service. Although the NGO sector has become increasingly professionalized over the last two decades, principles of altruism and voluntarism remain key defining characteristics".

How are NGOs Registered?

⇒ Society

⇒ Trust

⇒ Section 25 Company

NGOs are not for profits. So can they make profits?

Yes. It would be called as surplus and not profit. Like Companies, which can distribute profits in the form of dividends, NGOs can not distribute surplus.

NGOs are referred in many ways

⇒ NPOs or Not for profit

⇒ VOs or Voluntary Organisations

⇒ CSOs or Civil Society Organisations

⇒ CBOs or Community Based Organisations

⇒ Charitable Organisations

⇒ Third Sector Organisations

(The other two sectors are state and the market)

Note : Social Sector professionals define all of them differently. The above similarities are only for lay persons.

Typical Forms of NGOs

⇒ Advocacy

These NGOs basically work on advocacy or campaigning on issues or causes. As a focus, they do not implement programmes. e.g. PETA works on advocating the cause of Ethical Treatment of Animals. It is not an animals shelter, which many expect.

⇒ Consultancy / Research Organisations

These NGOs work on Social and Development Research & Consultancy.

⇒ Training / Capacity Building Organisations

In the NGOs Sector, training is usually called as Capacity Building. Some NGOs only work on Capacity Building of the other NGOs.

⇒ Networking Organisations

These NGOs provide vital network opportunities for NGOs in a specific field e.g. Association of Voluntary Agencies for Rural Development (AVARD) works on networking of NGOs working in the field of Rural Development.

⇒ Mother NGOs

These NGOs are recipients as well as givers e. g. large NGOs like CRY, Concern India receive funds as well as disburse funds. They have a work focus, but instead of implementing projects, they identify projects and monitor, evaluate and build capacities of participating NGOs.

⇒ Grassroot Organisations

These NGOs work directly with the community e.g. Apnalaya works with the underprivileged in the slums of

Govandi directly. Traditionally one can look at all Mahila Mandals fall in this category.

⇒ City Based Organisations

These NGOs restrict their focus to cities e.g. AGNI focusses its work in Mumbai City.

⇒ National Organisations

These NGOs have national presence. In India, very few NGOs are national level. e.g. CRY, Pratham, Concern India.

⇒ International Organisations

These are part of an International NGOs e.g.CARE India is an integral part of CARE's global operations. Like mother NGOs, these NGOs receive and disburse grants.

⇒ Self Help Groups

They are not typically terms as NGOs. These are formed by beneficiary communities, typically women who come together in a groups of 10 plus. India is witnessing a great movement of SHGs presently and these women are transforming the Rural Andhra Pradesh and Rural Tamil Nadu.

Religious NGOs

Large percentage of NGO Funding goes to religious based Organisations. e.g. Siddhivinayak Trust in Mumbai.

How many NGOs are working in India

IndianNGOs. com estimates that there would be around 1.5 million NGOs working in India.

The estimates of different sources vary but largely people agree this figure to be between 1 million to 2 million.

NGOs registered in Mumbai (around 55 000)

NGOs registered in Thane (around 11 000)

If you cant believe the 55000 number of NGOs, remember that temples, churches, mosques, gurudwara's.... are all registered as NGOs. All your neighbourhood sports associations are NGOs and all Ganeshotsav Mandals would also be NGOs. Some of the cities top hospitals are NGOs, so are educational institutions.

Some of the States with high numbers of NGOs

⇒ Gujarat

⇒ Maharashtra

⇒ Tamil Nadu

⇒ West Bengal

What is the size of NGOs ?

PRIA had done an extensive research on the NPO Sector and its publication indicates the following

Paid Staff	% of NGOs
One or less paid staff	73.4%
Between 2 to 5 paid staff	13.3%
Between 6 to 10 paid staff	04.8%
Above 10 paid staff	08.5%

While referring these statistics please quote the source as PRIA

Is it possible to work with one or less staff ?

Yes. Many NGOs are entirely managed with the help of volunteers.

How many people work in the NPO Sector ?

PRIA Research indicates the following:

All India/ State	Number	Volunteers	Paid
All India	19.4 million	85%	15%
West Bengal	1.52 million	90%	10%
Tamil Nadu	1.49 million	72%	28%
Delhi	1.03 million	80%	20%
Maharashtra	0.77 million	89%	11%
Meghalaya	0.12 million	83%	17%

Number of full time equivalent persons working in NPOs in India

All India / State	Number	Volunteers	Paid
All India	60.35 lakhs	56%	44%
West Bengal	3.51 lakhs	62%	38%
Tamil Nadu	6.41 lakhs	42.5%	57.5%
Delhi	3.45 lakhs	50%	50%
Maharashtra	2.43 lakhs	71.3%	28.7%
Meghalaya	0.43 lakhs	55%	45%

Receipt of Foreign Contribution during 2000- 2001

⇒ 22,924 associations stood registered under FCRA as on

31st March 2001. FCRA means Foreign Contribution Regulation Act. Each NGO receiving foreign funds must have FCRA Registration. In order to ensure that foreign funds do not go to terrorist supported organisations or any such elements, the FCRA is given by the Home Ministry and not the Finance Ministry Attention participants: If any of your customer from any foreign country wants to donate funds to an NGO in India, the recipient NGO must have FCRA.

⇒ 638 associations were granted prior permission to receive foreign contribution during 2000- 2001.

⇒ 14,598 associations field returns for 2000- 2001.

⇒ The receipt of foreign contribution during 2000- 2001 amounted to Rs 4535,23 crores. This is 15.56% more than the amount received in the previous year (Rs 3924,63 crores)

Top three recipient States and UTs	**Amount (Rs.)**	**Top three donor Countries**	**(Rs.)**
Delhi	763.05 crores	USA	1492.62 crores
Tamil Nadu	649.45 crores	UK	677.59 crores
Andhra Pradesh	589.52 crores	Germany	664.51 crores

Leading donor agencies	Amount (Rs.)	Largest recipient of foreign contribution	
World Vision Int., USA	80.43 crores	Sri Sathya Sai Central Trust, Andhra Pradesh	88.18 crores
Foster Parents Plan Int. USA	76.37 crores	World Vision of India, Tamil Nadu	85.42 crores
Watch Tower Bible and Tract Society	68.11 crores	Watch Tower Bible and Tract Society	74.88 crores
USA		India, Maharashtra	

⇒ Causes with largest amount received

Rural Development: Rs 547.47 crores

Health Care & Family Welfare: Rs 432.98 crores

Relief for natural calamities: Rs 339.77 crores

Some Basic Information

Receipt of Foreign Contribution

The provisions of the Foreign Contribution (Regulation) Act, 1976 regulate the receipt of foreign contribution in the country. The Foreign Contribution (Regulation) Rules, 1976 contain the various forms prescribed for this purpose.

What is Foreign Contribution ?

Foreign contribution means the donation, delivery or transfer, made by any foreign source of any.

a) article, not given to a person as a gift, for personal use, if the market value, in India, of such article exceeds one thousand rupees;

b) currency, whether Indian or foreign

c) foreign security as defined in clause 2(1) of the Foreign Exchange Regulation Act, 1973

Note: Contributions made by a citizen of India living in another country, from his personal savings, through the normal banking channels, is not treated as foreign contribution. It is advisable to obtain the passport details of the concerned citizen of India before accepting such contributions.

What is a Foreign Source ?

Foreign source means the government of any foreign country or territory or its agency; international agency; a foreign company; citizen of a foreign country. For more details see section 2(1) (e) of the Foreign Contribution (Regulation) Act, 1976.

Who cannot receive Foreign Contribution ?

Foreign contribution cannot be accepted by a candidate for election; correspondent, columnist, cartoonist, editor, owner, printer or publisher of a registered newspaper, judge, government servant or employee of any corporation, member of any legislature; political party or office bearer thereof.

Who can receive Foreign Contribution ?

An association having a definite cultural, economic, educational, religious or social programme, after it obtains the prior permission of the Central Government or gets itself registered with the Central Government can receive foreign contribution.

Are all these NGOs good and credible ?

NGOs are formed by people. So, like every industry, there are good and bad intentions. The NGO Sector is suffering more from the credibility image because they are dependent on donations from others rather than their self generated income. Also, people feel that there could be corruption at corporate or government level but at least the non profit social sector should be free of corruption.

What is the typical of an NGO ?

The size of the NGO depends on its activities and budgets e.g. CRY is more of a funding and monitoring organisation, working with 171 partner organisations across the country. CRY employs around 150 people. For implementing organisations of the same budget, the number of employees will be higher.

Typically most of the NGOs in the country have less than 10 people.

Why the role of NGOs is critical to build empowered society ?

Individual, institutional and even government funding to communities is channelled through NGOs. That is why the role of NGOs is critical to the development of the nation.

5

Strengthening The Role of NGOs:

Partners For Sustainable Development

Basis for action

1. Non-governmental organisations play a vital role in the shaping and implementation of participatory democracy. Their credibility lies in the responsible and constructive role they play in society. Formal and informal organizations, as well as grass-roots movements, should be recognized as partners in the implementation of Agenda 21. The nature of the independent role played by non-governmental organizations within a society calls for real participation; therefore, independence is a major attribute of non-governmental organizations and is the precondition of real participation.

2. One of the major challenges facing the world community as it seeks to replace unsustainable development patterns with environmentally sound and sustainable development is the need to activate a sense of common purpose on behalf of all sectors of society. The chances of forging such a sense of purpose will

depend on the willingness of all sectors to participate in genuine social partnership and dialogue, while recognizing the independent roles, responsibilities and special capacities of each.

3. Non-governmental organizations, including those non-profit organizations representing groups addressed in the present section of Agenda 21, possess well-established and diverse experience, expertise and capacity in fields which will be of particular importance to the implementation and review of environmentally sound and socially responsible sustainable development, as envisaged throughout Agenda 21. The community of non- governmental organizations, therefore, offers a global network that should be tapped, enabled and strengthened in support of efforts to achieve these common goals.

4. To ensure that the full potential contribution of non-governmental organizations is realized, the fullest possible communication and cooperation between international organizations, national and local governments and non-governmental organizations should be promoted in institutions mandated, and programmes designed to carry out Agenda 21. Non-governmental organizations will also need to foster cooperation and communication among themselves to reinforce their effectiveness as actors in the implementation of sustainable development.

Objectives

5. Society, Governments and international bodies should develop mechanisms to allow non-governmental organizations to play their partnership role responsibly

and effectively in the process of environmentally sound and sustainable development.

6. With a view to strengthening the role of non-governmental organization as social partners, the United Nations System and Governments should initiate a process, in consultation with non-governmental organizations, to review formal procedures and mechanisms for the involvement of these organizations at all levels from policy- making and decision- making to implementation.

7. By 1995, a mutually productive dialogue should be established at the national level between all Governments and non- governmental organizations and their self- organized networks to recognize and strengthen their respective roles in implementing environmentally sound and sustainable development.

8. Governments and international bodies should promote and allow the participation of non- governmental organizations in the conception, establishment and evaluation of official mechanisms and formal procedures designed to review the implementation of Agenda 21 at all levels.

Activities

9. The United Nations system, including international finance and development agencies, and all intergovernmental organization and forums should, in consultation with non- governmental organizations, take measures to:

a. Review and report on ways of enhancing existing procedures and mechanisms by which non-governmental organizations contribute to policy design, decision-making, implementation and evaluation at the individual agency level, in inter- agency discussions and in United Nations conferences;

b. On the basis of subparagraph (a) above, enhance existing or, where they do not exist, establish, mechanisms and procedures within each agency to draw on the expertise and views of non- governmental organizations in policy and programme design, implementation and evaluation;

c. Review levels of financial and administrative support for non- governmental organizations and the extent and effectiveness of their involvement in project and programme implementation, with a view to augmenting their role as social partners;

d. Design open and effective means of achieving the participation of non- governmental organizations in the processes established to review and evaluate the implementation of Agenda 21 at all levels;

e. Promote and allow non- governmental organizations and their self- organized networks to contribute to the review and evaluation of policies and programmes designed to implement Agenda 21, including support for developing country non- governmental organizations and their self- organized networks;

f. Take into account the findings of non- governmental review systems and evaluation processes in relevant reports of the Secretary- General to the General Assembly, and of all pertinent United Nations organizations and other intergovernmental organizations and forums concerning implementation of Agenda 21, in accordance with the review process for Agenda 21;

g. Provide access for non- governmental organizations to accurate and timely data and information to promote the effectiveness of their programmes and activities and their roles in support of sustainable development.

10. Governments should take measures to:

a. Establish or enhance an existing dialogue with non-governmental organizations and their self-organized networks representing various sectors, which could serve to: (i) consider the rights and responsibilities of these organizations; (ii) efficiently channel integrated non-governmental inputs to the governmental policy development process; and (iii) facilitate non- governmental coordination in implementing national policies at the programme level;

b. Encourage and enable partnership and dialogue between local non- governmental organizations and local authorities in activities aimed at sustainable development;

c. Involve non- governmental organizations in national mechanisms or procedures established to carry out Agenda 21, making the best use of their particular capacities, especially in the fields of education, poverty alleviation and environmental protection and rehabilitation;

d. Take into account the findings of non- governmental monitoring and review mechanisms in the design and evaluation of policies concerning the implementation of Agenda 21 at all levels;

e. Review government education systems to identify ways to include and expand the involvement of non-governmental organizations in the field of formal and informal education and of public awareness;

f. Make available and accessible to non- governmental organizations the data and information necessary for their effective contribution to research and to the design, implementation and evaluation of programmes.

Means of Implementation

(a) Financing and Cost Evaluation

11. Depending on the outcome of review processes and the evolution of views as to how best to build partnership and dialogue between official organizations and groups of non-governmental organizations, relatively limited but unpredictable, costs will be involved at the international and national levels in enhancing consultative procedures and mechanisms. Non-governmental organizations will also require additional funding in support of their establishment of, improvement of or contributions to Agenda 21 monitoring systems. These costs will be significant but cannot be reliably estimated on the basis of existing information.

(b) Capacity- building

12. The organizations of the United Nations system and other intergovernmental organizations and forums, bilateral programmes and the private sector, as appropriate, will need to provide increased financial and administrative support for non- governmental organizations and their self-organized networks, in particular those based in developing countries, that contribute to the monitoring and evaluation of Agenda 21 programmes, and provide training for non-

governmental organizations (and assist them to develop their own training programmes) at the international and regional levels to enhance their partnership role in programme design and implementation.

13. Governments will need to promulgate or strengthen, subject to country- specific conditions, any legislative measures necessary to enable the establishment by non-governmental organizations of consultative groups, and to ensure the right of non-governmental organizations to protect the public interest through legal action.

6

The Building of An NGO

NGO, is non- profit; non- commercial; non-government; legally registered; and subscribing to universal humanitarian values and practices. However, legal registration may pose problems where the government is hostile; It can, for example, block external funding.

Other international agencies look for additional characteristics. Perhaps the most important are that the NGO has capacity- meaning that it knows how to make a plan and has the resources to carry it out- and that it is ready to be held accountable for its actions.

Agencies may also look for:

⇒ an established headquarters;

⇒ a democratically adopted constitution;

⇒ Separation of policy- makers and executive: this means that there is one group of people who decide on the policy of the NGO (e.g. a Board) and a different group of people doing the work- the employees or the Executive. The third group involved are the people who benefit from the NGO- the beneficiaries -- and the policy-makers should represent these beneficiaries. They should also have some real control over the way the employees approach their job.

⇒ that the NGO has existed for at least two years;

⇒ that it is not politically partisan;

⇒ that it does not use or advocate violence;

⇒ that it is funded mainly by individual members- although in poor countries this is often impossible.

We are not saying that each NGO should do all of the above. An NGO can take different forms. Think about what is really important:

⇒ Many of the factors listed above are about behaving as a formal organisation. Small NGOs may do fine without much formal shape.

⇒ Some countries make legal registration unnecessarily difficult, or attach political strings.

⇒ It is possible to have various interpretations of many of these terms, such as "universal humanitarian values".

So good NGOs may end up looking very different from each other.

The definition we wish to use in this manual is that an NGO should aim to be non- profit, non- commercial and non-government. It should subscribe to universal humanitarian values and practices. It should have capacity, and be ready to be held accountable for its actions.

But the bottom line is this:

⇒ A lot of NGOs do, on the whole, more good than bad.

⇒ A number of others are clearly lining the pockets of the boss or helping one group grind down another- doing more bad than good.

⇒ And a third group has so little capacity, so few staff with any conviction, that they are completely ineffective.

In which group, in ten years time, will you have placed your own NGO ?

The Beginning Stages of An NGO

First Steps

For all of you starting up an NGO, hopping to be successful, you need there things;

⇒ The first is passion

⇒ The second is a group of people who share this passion, and the vision to match

⇒ The third is a good relationship with the people you want to help- the beneficiaries.

In most countries, NGOs start in two ways: one is where there is a group that has no voice but needs to find one. A few people in this group- perhaps the parents of children with disabilities- start to meet, decide to organise themselves in order to get more resources for their children and for their family. This is the classic bottom- up beginning. Another way is that a group of people with education or status decide to adopt a cause, decide that they will help, for example, older people with cancer or village groups who are planting trees.

The difference between these two groups is that, with the parents of disabled children and other bottom- up groups, the prime or original beneficiaries of the NGO are themselves and their families. This ensures that the beneficiaries are treated well. With the second group there is an "Us", the people who are doing good, and the "Them", the people being done good to. Whether this second group of NGOs will build well depends on whether they move the beneficiaries from outside to inside, making them part of the "Us". This has to happen very quickly, otherwise the central relationship sets hard and can be poisonous- Do- Gooders helping Objects of Charity.

There is usually a period of informality, when the group beginning the enterprise treat each other more or less as equals and everyone does everything, from sweeping the floor to deciding on policy. This is the period which you may remember later as the best time, when your passion was strongest, the feeling of working together for a common cause.

Very quickly, though the number of people gets bigger, jobs start to require specialisation. Outside organisations push you towards a proper office, a computer, towards legal registration, the creation of a board. Everyone starts to get a salary.

So now the main actors are: the workers; the beneficiaries; the board; and the individual or small group who keeps it all going. These last may be workers or the boss, may be a board member who was previously a beneficiary. But they are key- the person or people who keeps the engine running, who provides the energy and drive. If you are that person or one of those people, then as the NGO gets bigger and has different jobs within it, one of your big tasks is to make all the workers feel that they belong in the NGO and that the NGO belongs to them. You need to create a sense of ownership, among the beneficiaries and also among the workers.

Why a Board' Not every organisation makes one. A Board becomes important when the workers start to be paid, and perhaps become more concerned with earning a living than with good service. A Board should have members who truly represent the beneficiaries and who listen to the workers, but they make policy away from the people doing the daily tasks. They ideally have no personal interest except the good of the beneficiaries. In practice, checks and balances should make sure they are acting appropriately.

Example: **The Story of how one NGO in West Africa got started** *Jean-Robert Mbane*

> This is the story of our NGO so far, though I will say that it is only recently that we claim to be an NGO. We have been working with older people for about 4 years. Everything came out of the pity we had, seeing older people suffering. We started in our main village by paying regular visits to them, discussion about their concerns, the heyday of their life; after that we brought them the food they liked which could not be found in our village. We brought them cloths against the cold, we brought them medicine and helped them to read the directions for the medicines they got.
>
> We were encouraged in these activities by some other people who came to help by giving food (rice, oil) cloths and other useful things. We were six founder members.

Then we started work with young people who was not able to complete their higher studies and who had settled in the village then, more and more, our action spread to the neighbouring villages. It is only recently that we learned that other organisations around the world had the same interests as us and saw the necessity and the use of legalising our NGO.

Now we face the problem of having different views of what we should be doing. Some among us think we need to build community houses for older people. Others, including myself, think that we should keep older people in their own houses and assist them there.

Exercise:

Is this NGO top- down or bottom- up?

What is its relationship with its beneficiaries?

What are the there most important steps it should take next?

The factors that will help you build an NGO of good quality

1. If you are clear about your goals, values and ethos; if you are clear about the field in which you are building your specialism; if you know what approach you are taking, whether advocacy or implementation, and if you find ways of making a recognisable name profile;
2. If you build a relationship with your beneficiary group which has good will and respect on both sides.
3. If you adopt a single objective, because then it is easier to achieve it;
4. If you live in a country with a strong civil society. This

means that there are enough NGOs and Associations to from a mass big enough to be listened to, a mass existing between government and people. An example of a country with a strong civil society is Senegal;

5. If you build up your professional capacity and build partnerships with other groups.

Here is a formula to fellow:

*** Capacity- Building+ Partnership- Building= Power ***

A good example of where you need to be professional is in your handing of money. If you do the job properly you will also show yourself to be transparent- anyone can see how you are spending the money- and accountable- if money goes missing then it will be noticed and someone will have to take the blame.

6. If your NGO builds structures and ways of acting which are transparent, accountable and democratic.
7. If you develop a clear and sensible policy on gender. If no thought is given, then women will be under-represented in the group which makes decisions, and the needs of both sexes among the beneficiaries will not be thought through.

Getting The Principles Right

Every NGO will do better if the workers have agreed on its vision, strategies, principles etc. It may take a period of discussion, during which each individual and group has a chance to argue and brainstorm. The way in which vision, mission and strategies flow one from the other and then lead to projects is very clear in the following example.

About the words used here...

Please note that different organisations use words a little differently. For example when some NGOs talk about the long- term, most encompassing point to aim at, they call it their "goal", not their "Vision". In addition, words like "goals are used at different points in this whole planning process. But this is not so important. What is vital is that every project has its place in a logical plan that the NGO workers know and have agreed to.

Choosing good strategies and goals

It is very important that your NGO chooses good strategies. Another way of stating a strategy would be to say " The main thrust of our work will be..." so strategies are practical, and you will only be able to manage a few. Here are two examples:

1) "One strategy is to ensure that after five years, in this very poor community, each family will have one member who can earn money.

2) "As an environmental NGO, one of our strategies is to protect the existing trees and soil by building sustainable cooling fuel techniques into the community (e. g. by tree- planting, solar cookers, improved stoves, etc.)".

We all know small NGOs with great commitment, who work hard but whose projects and activities are not part of any sensible strategy and are, in the end, a waste of time.

Example

An NGO in Asia was trying to help families on the

edge of survival. Most of their energy went into providing a school. The children came out of the school able to read, but not equipped to earn an income. The families stayed poor. If the NGO had adopted the strategy "To ensure that one member of each family can earn a living "they might have made better progress.

How to decide on good strategies, goals etc.

This manual talks on a number of occasions about ways to deal with serious issues. We suggest the use of SWOT exercises, (Strengths Weaknesses, Opportunities and Threats), when an organisation sets aside a few days, finds a good workshop leader and works alternatively all together and in smaller groups. Good strategies have to be based on a good understanding of all the actors, potentials, limitations, needs, problems, leadership structure, etc. The SWOT approach is use for identifying strategies, you might want to invite one or two outsiders with good analytical skills and a view of the role of an NGO. Senior people from another, successful NGO might be the right choice.

After brainstorming a number of possibilities, you need to narrow down and prioritise the few that are most important- and also identify the core problem which underlies everything else, perhaps landlessness, displacement, poverty.

Then comes the brainstorm on strategies- what would each achieve? Would they really meet the problem? Which strategies would build on the strengths of the NGO? If people want to concentrate on income generation, do you have people with experience, with an understanding of markets, profit margins, how money works? if the expertise of the

NGO is running creches and none of you can do simple sums, then to concentrate on income generation would be to build on your weaknesses, not your strengths.

How your vision is built on principles

Part of this process of identifying goals, strategies etc. is recognising the principles held within the NGO, which most people subscribe to but do not normally discuss very much. Maybe your workers believe that all people deserve respect and a living wage, or that if you are born better off, you have to give something back. At the level of the NGO there may be a strong principle that its workings should always be transparent. Sometimes this principle is adopted as a strategy, and systematic action is taken to ensure it. Sometimes the principle is put on one side -" We will tackle transparency next year, after we have made progress with other strategies" - but it does not go away. Principles do not go away. Strategies, however, can be replaced when they have served their purpose

Another principle might be friendliness towards the environment.

Another, we would hope, is the principle of inclusivity- that all the people with a say in an NGO, whether bosses, cleaners or those who get help, should feel included and have a way to make their opinion heard. No one should be silenced because of their ethnic group, because they are disabled, too old, too poor or because they are a women. Many NGOs have started to translate this principle into something real by looking at gender.

Including women and men: working out a gender policy

What is gender ? We are born, most of us, as one of the two sexes. But boy babies and girl babies get treated differently from the moment their umbilical cord is cut. We are taught how to be girls/ women, boys/ men. So gender roles are the social and economic roles that our culture gives us. They apply to both main genders. But women tend to be behind men in their situation (often poorer, less well- fed) and in their ability to get to resources. In most countries, for example, they find it much more difficult to get credit even though they have a better record of repayment.

Example: **The Effect of having a gender policy**

In 1998, there was a pause in the fighting in Sierra Leone. The planting season was only six weeks away and the big international agencies had to get seeds and tools to everybody, fast- to settled villages and to the displaced people in and around the villages. They worked through national NGOs who in turn worked through Village Heads. Those NGOs with no gender policy allowed the Village Heads to control who benefited, which meant that the 13% of displaced families headed by women got nothing. The NGOs with a gender policy knew how important it was to reach these families and made sure they were helped.

Here are the reasons why we say that an NGO should work out its own gender policy:

The first reason is that it will help you provide better services to beneficiaries (look at the example above). For a long time, certain groups have been getting less attention in development projects than others. Women have been sold short; so have different ethnic minorities, people with physical disabilities, the elderly. Meanwhile the groups with the highest profile and loudest voice get the most attention. A crude example is the crowd waiting for the bread handouts, a mass of young men elbowing the women to the back. But the women- leaving empty- handed as the bread runs out- look after, on average, five other people. If the distributors knew this, and acted on their knowledge, they would provide a more effective service.

So to some extent a gender policy is about knowing the people you are helping and the groups within the group. It is similar to doing a Vulnerable Group Analysis. It is a planing tool.

The second reason is that it is an issue of Capacity Building Developing a gender policy will force you to look at how your own organisation has developed and whether your staff are representative of the groups you are helping. NGOs that are dominated by a higher class, or by one sex, NGOs where everyone is young and able- bodied, will probably not provide a sympathetic service for anyone different, especially not the other sex, the elderly, the most despised minorities.

Exercise: **It tomorrow your NGO started a project for prostitutes, would everyone treat them as well as they would treat an old friend they went to school with, who is now in trouble? If not, why not? Where does kind- heartedness start and end?**

On a more practical level, most NGOs need women staff for certain tasks, like talking in confidence to female beneficiaries or providing family planing. But if they are only employed to do jobs decided on by male bosses alone, then the NGO is under- using their abilities and treating them with disrespect- and it probably disrespects its beneficiaries as well.

NGOs which want to change can organise staff training, demand a proven record of gender skills for certain posts etc.

A third reason is that many donors and bigger NGOs take the issue very seriously. They have a gender policy and will expect you to have one too. This is not true for all- UNHCR has a gender policy, Medecins sans Frontieres does not. Find out from your donors and partner NGOs where they stand and then look at their work.

A fourth reason is that gender is a matter of principle. If people get what they need then the service is fairer, more ethical. And we cannot know what they need unless we understand their situation. Analysing it from the perspective of gender is one way to understand, and a helpful way.

Example: **How developing gender awareness improved services for the elderly in Africa**

By Amleset Tewodros, Help Age Int.

Help Age Int. works through local NGOs with older women and men, and to do a good job it needs gender awareness- an understanding of the situation of both women and men and how they are affected by social and psychological factors. With good understanding, the rights of both women and men can be equally supported

On average, women in the developing world outlive

men by 3-5 years, and by 2025, the numbers of women aged over 60 will have increased by 150 percent. Longer lives mean that, compared with men, women have more chance of being widowed, of living without a partner. Older widows have few opportunities to marry again and often face loneliness, isolation and dependence on their children- this in societies where status is linked to having a husband. In HAI's experience, many older women continue to work into very old age. In addition to producing food or earning income themselves, they often take on domestic responsibilities to enable other family members to earn money. Care for the 'old old' still falls largely on female family members, often themselves ageing and in falling health; so does supporting the sick and disabled in both the immediate and the extended family.

At the Africa Regional Development Centre of Help Age International, we felt that we needed to do more to make our programmes gender- sensitive. So a consultancy firm was involved to guide our work. They started looking at the current programmes implemented by the organisation and whether they could be more gender- responsive. Various tools useful for mainstreaming gender were developed, for example tools for advocacy, for indicators and for programme monitoring. Then, a three day's workshop was carried out, to share these tools and increase the capacity of the staff to use them.

The workshop was an eye- opener for the staff. They saw the need to change beliefs and practices which marginalise women and the need to be more systematic and alert about ensuring that older women and men benefit more fairly from programmes.

What Best Practice Means

Best Practice for you?

In each field of development, people have been working and gaining experience for centuries. Aspects of Best Practical depend on the situation; in the example given below of working with the physically disabled, the setting is South Africa. The economic situation is varied but more developed than in other countries, so standards are higher. Elsewhere, the only Practice possible may be helping the disabled just to keep alive. But whatever the economic level, helping the beneficiaries build self- respect and gain some power is both important and possible.

If your NGO looks seriously at what is considered Best Practice in its field, and after hard arguing decide that it is not right for your circumstances, then that is fair enough. But if you just ignore the whole body of experience and do what you want to do, you are looking after your own egos, not the well- being of your beneficiaries.

Is building an orphanage Good Practice or Bad?

Traditionally in Africa, orphans were accommodated by the extended family. But in Europe people built orphanages. The characteristics of orphanages for the last two hundred years have been:

⇒ insufficient numbers of staff to meet the physical and psychological needs of the children;

⇒ a failure to teach the children how to relate to adults of both sexes, and in doing so learn how to be a women or a man;

⇒ a failure to teach them how to build relationships of their own;

⇒ lack of planing of the children's work futures. In Europe, girl babies are put into orphanages, grow up without relationships with boys and men, come out at sixteen, get pregnant.... and put their girl baby back into the orphanage.

People seem to love building orphanages. The idea makes a nice mental picture- the saintly founders, surrounded by the loving children who are only alive because of them, all in a building that is a concrete proof of their benevolence. But this picture is about the egos of the builders, not what is best for children.

Today, AIDS has brought a large numbers of orphans. How should they be cared for? The money that can build an orphanage can also be spent on fostering the babies with their grannies and paying an allowance. If there are no grannies, aunties or big sisters, they can be fostered with non- related families. If land tenure is closed to outsiders, then older orphans will do better in towns, where they can be found a Master or Mistress and apprenticed to a trade, and ideally fostered with the Mistress's or Master's family.

Working out Best Principles and Practice

Example: **Working out Best Principles and Practice for Projects with Older People in Africa**

By Amleset Tewodros

We work for Help Age International Africa Regional Development Centre, in Kenya. Our job is to provide support for national and local NGOs working with older people. Through their efforts we try to ensure that a number of best principles and practice are reflected in project work. Here are some of them:

Checking our attitudes and those of other key people

We try to ensure that everyone concerned sees older people as equal partners, not as objects of charity. Getting older is a natural process that affects us all. We should recognise that older women and men are an important part of society. They contribute, and their rights, needs and contributions need to be well understood. It is important to recognise that older men and women have a wealth of experience acquired over time.

"I never believed these poor older people had anything to say. Now I have changed my mind and will always consult them", Government officer, Ethiopia, after attending a needs assessment workshop with older people.

Involving the elderly in NGO structures and in their planning processes

Our partner NGOs are involving the elderly in their structures. Like other NGOs they share powers, rights, and accountability by having strong Boards and older men and women are represented on these Boards. They can use their experiences and capacities in project designing, implementing and monitoring.

Understanding their physical limitations but also their strengths

As people advance in age, they may become weaker

and more susceptible to illness. We have found that it is important to take this into consideration while dealing with older people. We have to see each of them as an individual, to try to encourage participation, independence and dignified living- what we call active ageing. But we must not be overprotective. Older people have great strengths.

You are never too old to learn. For me, it was like stepping from darkness into the light", Mrs. Mchuru, 82 years, a literacy programme participant, Durban, South Africa.

Good Practice in the context of a country with some resources

Example: **Working with physical disability in south Africa** *By Gordon Freer*

MODE is a group of companies that is dedicated to finding socio- economic solutions for persons with disabilities- helping them find paying work. In many cases disabled people are seen as being a drain on families and on society. But paid work is economically empowering and can help reintegrate them into their society.

Previously there was a welfare mindset which ensured that the disabled remained dependent on grants and handouts- in a proverbial sense, people were given fish instead of being taught how to fish. One beneficiary said "What does it help if we can dress ourselves and operate our wheelchairs, but we are unable to find jobs to earn a living? We are a burden to our families and we have no dignity".

Through the MODE methodology, inactive, dependent

people with disabilities are transformed into active, productive citizens who contribute to the economy. MODE is a "best practice" model of teaching people with disability how to fish. Provided with opportunities and support, many people with disabilities have proved that they can start and run their own, viable small businesses.

The person must be highly motivated to improved his or her financial situation, through his or her own effort and not relying on hand- outs. It is also very important that the persons has a reliable support network of friends and family. To achieve our aim, Mode uses a numbers of different tools including:

⇒ Empowerment opportunities to the sector of society who are labelled as "disabled". Motivated individuals with disabilities are promoted to discover their abilities.

⇒ Vocational rehabilitation, which includes pre- vocational skills, work performance skills and problem- solving skills.

⇒ Work placement/ job creation/ business placement in the formal as well as the informal sector.

⇒ Environment- enabling solutions to overcome physical and social obstacles in the work place.

How you find out what is Best Practice in your field:

To find the best practice in your field:

⇒ Find an experienced NGO in your field. Ask if you can visit and look at what they do.

⇒ Read the literature. Pay a visit to the nearest town with a library. Look at the list of addresses, contacts and resources in Annex Six at the end of this manual and find what applies to your specialism. Fellow it up. Try to find some useful sites on the Web.

⇒ Find an experienced worker in your field, perhaps retired, and ask them to join the Board of your NGO.

Getting Legal Status

As part of the process of becoming accepted at international level, you will probably have to become registered, legal by the rules of your country. In each country there is a NGO umbrella organisation to which you will need to sign up. This step give you access to information about other organisations and their activities, about current best practice in your field. It is usually a necessary step in getting funding by most international donors.

Example: **A NGO in India becomes legal**

By Professor Saraswati Swain

Before I retired I was a full- time professor in a Medical College. I was conducting a lot of studies with funding from the Indian Council of Medical Research, WHO, UNICEF etc. After retirement I wanted to continue and the only way financially to do that was to become a NGO. I sat with some of my like-minded friends to deliberate and formed an NGO called National Institute of Applied Human Research and Development (NIAHRD).

In order to legal and get financing, there registrations were necessary:

⇒ A registration und ·r Indian Societies Registration Act.

⇒ A registration with the Home Ministry under Foreign Contribution Regulation Act to receive and utilise grant- in- aids or contributions from outside the country.

⇒ A registration with the Finance Ministry under section 12 A of Income Tax Act to be a non- profit and non-taxed organisation.

Such registration in India take a lot of time and involve filling in many forms After it was launched NIAHRD started to take up projects and studies on behalf of many national and international funding agencies and also successfully completed those projects. We were invited to many workshops and Seminars and became an active member of many networks.

Example: **The South African NGO Sector**

By Khathatso Mokoetle

Background: Non- governmental organisations (NGOs) in South Africa have a unique history. In the apartheid years up until 1994, organisations that were more conservative and mainly run by whites were referred to as private welfare organisations. Most of them were easy to register as they functioned within the law. Most received good subsidies from government and acquired fund-raising numbers.

In those years, the term NGO predominantly referred to charity organisations that addressed the problems of disadvantaged communities. Most of them were run by the progressives, served black communities and depended a lot on membership fees, bequests and overseas philanthropic financial support. The criteria set for registration made it difficult for NGOs to register. They were generally seen as anti- government in their criticism of apartheid laws and service delivery. Members were in and out for what they said or did in defiance of the government of the day. Requirements for registration included, among other things, submission of the organizational constitution, staff names and particulars to the registering office. As registered members, they had to make available whatever documents the state required. This made it easy for police to track down and arrest "trouble makers" Given this context, progressive organisation preferred not to be legally registered. But local fund-raising was illegal if the organisation did not have a fund-raising number.

After the New Democratic Government, Post 1994

With the new government, NGOs experienced survival difficulties. Private welfare organisations, most of which survived in government subsidies, lost benefits from the new government and had to close. Progressive organisations also faced survival difficulties; the overseas assistance received was now diverted to the new democratic government. This drastic change in the financial environment adversely affected lots of organisations, many of which had to close.

Evolution of the NGO Sector

In the new democratic government, some old organisations died for reasons already given. New ones emerged for several reasons, the main reason being the increasing incidence of HIV/ AIDS, with more and more HIV/ AIDS organisations being formed. With historical perceptions equating non- governments anti- government in South

Africa, the term NGO is gradually being replaced by the term NPO (Non- Profit Organisation).

Non- Profit Organisations Act, No. 21 of 1997

The Act was promulgate to make it easier for NGOs/ NPOs to register. The procedures are easier and more user friendly. Under this Act, charity/ non- profit- making organisations are now free to resister either as Charitable Organisations or Section 21 Organisations. The private welfare organisations are also now registered under the two options.

7

Mechanisms For NGO Accountability

In recent years, accountability has emerged as one of the key approaches in the search for new modes of democratic governance beyond the nation-state. The call for more accountability in global governance is now common in political debates, but it is noteworthy that the understanding of the term is more limited than its use. If the debate is to have meaning as well as useful practical relevance, the conceptual foundations of the term accountability need to be clarified: including the potential and limits of accountability in facilitating democracy, and how accountability of actors and processes of global governance can be improved.

Accountability in Global Governance

"Exploring and Analyzing the Role of Accountability in Global Governance" is to take a first step towards developing a "pluralistic system of accountability" both conceptually and operationally. It seeks to contribute to a better understanding of the role and significance of accountability in global governance, and the various ways in which it is put in practice.

Today, global public policy is the product of negotiations between states, business and civil society actors, or NGOs. As the role of NGOs in policy formulation, implementation and enforcement has risen, so have questions concerning their effectiveness, reliability and legitimacy as actors in the governance process. Lisa Jordan discusses the costs and benefits of ensuring NGO accountability, particularly with regards to the current practice that emphasizes 'upward' and 'external' accountability to donors. She proposes that NGOs and the academic community develop mechanisms that ensure NGO accountability to multiple stakeholders. These tools and processes must not only assure accountability to donors but also to NGO staff ('internal' accountability) as well as to the general public and the beneficiaries of NGO services ('downward' accountability').

Introduction

NGO Accountability is one of the hottest topics to accompany the rise of civil society. The discussions and debates around accountability suggest that NGOs have 'arrived' as an accepted form of civic expression. This paper seeks to lay out the basic parameters of the NGO accountability discussion in three sections. The first section places the question of accountability into a political landscape. It outlines the questions that are being asked, who is asking them and postulated as to why they are being asked now. The second section reviews the responses, the mechanisms that NGOs use to legitimize their work, evaluate and improve their work and respond to attacks on their credibility. The third section analyses the mechanisms and discusses ways to strengthen NGO accountability.

Who's Asking And Way Now?

In May of 2003 the American Enterprise Institute, a non-governmental organization (NGO) based in Washington DC. with overt ties to the Bush Administration co- sponsored a conference in NGO Accountability. The title of the conference was: "We're not from the government but we're here to help you. The growing power of an unelected few". The main issue of debate was whether or not civic associations had the right to participate in international political debates, global public policy or even operate internationally. The target of debate was international non- governmental organisations (NGOs) and the accusation stemming from the conference was that NGOs undermine national sovereignty and democracy. The conference papers constituted a political attack and the effort was ultimately received by the mainstream press as an attempt to discredit NGOs whose views American Enterprise Institute tends to disagree with. Nevertheless, the conference demonstrated two things: one, that NGOs are a potent political force and two, that there are some serious issues confronting civil society that need to be addressed.

One of those serious issues is a changing political landscape. Today, global public policy is formed through a negotiated process between states, civil society- the organizational associations between the state and the family- and the profit- seeking sector. NGOs have become a de-facto partner in the establishment of global norms and standards, negotiating, influencing and proposing policy solutions to social public problems like the spread of communicable diseases, poverty, housing and education crises, shrinking wages, ecosystem fragility and human rights violations. At the national level, many social services that traditionally were in the purview of government are today delivered by the private sector or through NGOs. Governance is practised through a negotiated process between political parties, the state, civil society and the profit seeking sector. There is a public perception or fear in many emerging democratic countries that the nascent civil society is developing in a vacuum or is somehow, undermining political society. In both global and national arenas NGOs are often demanding democratic practice in governance, yet they themselves are not democratic or are not clearly recognized as an important part of democratic practice.

Part of the changing governance reality is a need for new social contracts as our existing contracts are no longer adequate for the challenges that we face either locally or globally. New social contracts are needed especially to address problems that extend beyond national borders like the spread of communicable diseases, the changing climate, the scarcity of fresh water, etc. To fulfil those needs we have generated new social actors, of which one is NGOs, who increasingly play a part in identifying and resolving these major global social dilemmas but do not have clearly defined rights or responsibilities. NGOs are often acting in public-private partnership where they are appointed to deliver social services or monitor environmental health. They are also developing partnerships with the private sector to address a social need or monitor private sector practices. There are myriad accountability questions embedded in these partnerships and new roles.

The second realization and related to the rise of new social actors, is that civil society has replaced some functions traditionally carried out by the state. In this and other ways, NGOs have grown to a size and scale to rival the very government or intergovernmental agencies with which they interact. Solidarity in Literacy, a Brazillian NGO for example services 4 million illiterate individuals. Conservation International is currently an 84 million dollar operation and is active in 42 countries while its sister, The Nature Conservancy is a $ 3 billion dollar operation active in 30 countries. World Vision rivals the World Food Program in both financial size and geographic impact. No matter the humanitarian nature of these operations, the power represented within multimillion and billion dollar operations is substantial.

A third issue is scandals in the sector. The public, vis-a- vis journalists, has begun to ask some pointed questions. In the Netherlands, journalists made an issue of the salary of a senior NGO official who commanded more money than the Prime Minister. In the U.S., a series of reports regarding an environmental NGO noted that it was running mining operations in environmentally sensitive areas. And a third example came from Africa when the press exposed a practice of trading relief supplies for sexual favour. Self- dealing, conflicts of interest, complicated business deals, a lack of transparency, and fund-raising schemes that leave less than ten cents on the dollar for ultimate beneficiaries have all been reported in the press as problem in the non- profit sector.

Lastly, the American Enterprise Institute bases its attacks on NGO upon exceptions to the advocacy role undertaken when setting national and global policy. These latter political attacks are inevitable as NGOs move out of the fringes of political debate and influence decisions, either by sheer size or through concerted action.

The rise of questions of accountability is not in doubt. In part, it is a natural extension of the shifting role between the state and the private sector (of which NGOs are a part). As governments shrink and responsibility for delivering public goods and services is shouldered by NGOs the issue of responsibility to the public naturally stems from the roles NGOs have undertaken on behalf of, or instead of, the state.

However, there is more to it than that. NGOs are negotiating global public policy and often play an enforcement role once those policies are in place. For example *Traffic,* an international NGO, enforces the CITES treaty. Their power vis-a-vis sovereign governments comes into question especially when they make a decision that separates a nation-state from a potential source of revenue, or challenge the right of states to act in the 'national' interest. NGOs can make states and market players quite uncomfortable in reminding these powerful actors of a broader societal interest and the impact that decisions can have on a broad public. For example, debates raised by NGOs about which states have the moral authority or credibility to sit on the UN Human Rights Council call into question the value states place on conventions and treaties they pledged to enforce.

Types of Accountability Questions

Today, NGOs are asked to address three types of accountability questions by a wide variety of actors effectiveness questions, questions of organizational reliability and legitimacy questions.

The first type of question is embedded in the title of the American Enterprise Institute conference (we are not from the government, But we're here to help you). This query questions the effectiveness of NGOs as a social service delivery agent arising from the prominent role that many NGOs play in delivering social services. Effectiveness questions usually have to do with the quality and the quantity of services offered like distribution of medicines, food, textbooks or other educational services etc. Quantity and quality of service delivery is under query here. Sometimes this type of question is accompanied by a question regarding the responsiveness of the NGO to the beneficiaries, but that is rare.

Donors most often ask these questions. Governments which would have once had responsibility for delivering the respective services, but whose role has changed to oversight might also ask these questions. In rarer instances they might be asked by the beneficiaries but it is not the most common source of query. These questions are currently very popular due to a shift in resources over the past decade from governments to NGOs for the purpose of delivering social services. There is an entire battery of administrative processes often designed by donors that NGOs employ in order to answer these questions. In almost all instances these administrative processes help to account for how money is spent. In large part, effectiveness questions embody a response to another agency which holds authoritative power over the NGO and thus can be seen as often generating accountability towards an external overseer or 'upward'.

A second type of question is oriented toward the independence and reliability of the organizational structures of NGOs. For example, NGOs are frequently asked about the role and composition of the board, financial accounting, management structures, compensation policies, hiring and firing practices, etc. These kinds of questions are similar to questions that drove the 'capacity building' phase of NGO development in the nineties. However, they are clearly articulated today as accountability questions. Donor and aid agencies often ask these questions along with sector wide associations that are established by NGOs to strengthen the sector. These questions emanate from the rapid growth in the sector worldwide and help those who wish to strengthen the sector to suggest ways in which to improve NGOs. These questions help to define the sector (often called 'third' sector or 'independent' sector) and generate trust and accountability to the sector as a whole. Thus they stimulate some horizontal accountability toward other organisations of the same caliber. However, they may also be used to generate accountability towards a higher authority like effectiveness questions often do.

A third question surrounds the legitimacy of NGOs. These questions are oriented toward ties to the pubic, transparency and adherence to the mission of an NGO, representative status (who do you represent?), relationship to community served, the value base of NGO, the relationship between NGOs and democracy or value to society as a whole. These questions are raised by both friends and foes to the NGO. Political opponents or those who disagree with a given mission expressed through an NGO action are likely to ask this type of question. A recent spate of claims that charities have been used to funnel money to terrorists falls into this category. The legitimacy of the entire sector has been questioned by raising the possibility that there may be links to terrorists. However, potential partners of an NGO who may wish to join the NGO in a coalition, network or campaign may also ask legitimacy questions. The press, when exposing a bad apple in the bunch could question the legitimacy of an NGO. And peers who are concerned about corruption within the sector are also likely to raise legitimacy questions. Legitimacy questions can stimulate upward, horizontal or broader societal 'downward' accountability.

What kind of question?	Effectiveness	Reliability	Legitimacy
Who is asking	Donors	Donors	Political Opponents
	Governments	Sector Associations	Advocacy Partners
		Partners	Academics

Legitimacy questions often arise in political arenas where NGOs are plying advocacy roles or in arenas where NGOs have grown to become multimillion dollar operations. They are particularly prevalent in the nascent global political arena where NGOs are involved in global public policy discussions and in newly emerging democratic nation- states, like Indonesia or Mexico. As multiple forms of democracy are debated or jockey alongside each other, these questions are increasingly raised to challenge the right of NGOs to a voice in policy debates.

Who is not asking ?

Public perception of NGOs varies widely across the world, thus it is difficult to make statements regarding the intensity of the debate. In one country NGOs may not be well- known while in other countries they can regularly be front page news. The treatment of NGOs as a sector by national media also varies. It is rare to find news articles, radio programs, etc. that address NGOs as a sector in some countries like the U.S. where the term is not widely used. In Uganda, Bangladesh and Indonesia NGOs are widely reported on as a sector. In order of frequency, one could postulate that donors ask the most questions of NGOs, other NGOs ask the second most, and governments ask the third most. The private sector asks periodically and when they do it, is usually through associated organizations like European Policy Forum or the United Nations Global Compact. Academics are beginning to review these issues. Beneficiaries of NGO services, members, and the general public seem to ask the least often.

Regardless of the variations at national level, some organizations have attempted to conduct global polling that included questions about trust in NGOs. The results would suggest that NGOs as a sector enjoy high levels of public trust, at least higher than corporations, churches and governments (Environics International and Edelman). A British based business, sustainability, recently conducted an overview of the field and found that NGOs are held in high esteem with the public (Sustainability 2003). Nevertheless, amongst some circles accountability questions are on the rise.

Accountability Mechanisms

This section attempts to answer what accountability mechanisms are most pervasive. Are there differences in the use of accountability mechanisms across various type of NGOs?

There are reams of materials available on NGO accountability. Most of it starts with mechanisms that preface operational capacity, management structure, performance measurements, and accounting practices with an emphasis on legal obligations (Ball and Dunn 1995). Outcome tracking software has been developed to measure how many clients have been served by an individual caseworker (The Non-profit Quarterly 2001). Proposals have been made to increase and improve accounting as a measure of accountability (International Journal of Civil Society Law, 2003). The tools used in the development industry are riddled with accountability mechanisms like exit strategies, participatory assessments, etc. In India, commercial ratings and certification systems have arisen in droves and they are beginning to be created at a global scale as well.

Alnoor Ebrahim notes that NGOs respond to issues of accountability with both tools and processes (Ebrahim 2003). Tools are often oriented towards external stakeholders that have considerable leverage over an NGO like a donor or a government regulator. Tools are often created by these stakeholders for purpose intrinsic to donor or regulator needs. Familiar tools are annual reports, financial accounts, performance assessments, quarterly reports, independent evaluations, audits, metrics, logical framework analysis, etc. They make available to oversight bodies and the general public (if released) data pertaining to the governance and performance of an NGO (Ebrahim 2003).

These accountability tools are most often employed by NGOs in the business of social service delivery. They are an integral part of the principle-agent contracting relationships which exist between many NGOs and donor agencies. They span across the North South global divide. They result in clarity as regards the relationship and well defined performance benchmarks.

However, they are not without defects. What they do not allow for is a negotiated process of what is to be measured. For example, an NGO engaged in health education may be most interested in measuring behavioural changes while the donors that provided funds for health equipment or medicines may want to measure how many units of medicine were delivered. The needs of the donor to be able to account for medicines, bed nets, needles, condoms, etc. often prevail over the desire of the NGO to measure or evaluate its programs results or structural behavioural changes. Reports are time- consuming and expensive. One type of reporting often precludes the possibility of undertaking other types of reporting. A lack of flexibility within donor agencies and the need to keep the resources flowing results in the NGO prioritizing donor needs over its own. Even further down the chain is the community, which may want entirely different types of health services or may be most interested in holding the NGO to account for how many illnesses are cured.

However, when applied with finesse these types of tools can strengthen the infrastructure of an NGO and serve multiple purpose for both internal and external stakeholders. For example, Solidarity in Literacy spent three years developing a software program that allows stakeholders that have rights to financial resources or have provided financial resource to the organization to trace the money flow throughout the transaction. Teachers and students can at any time see where their money is in the system and can hold administrators or municipal officials to account when the money owed to them is 'stuck'. Donors can trace how, when and where their donations are allocated or spent. A hotline has been established to help stakeholders access resources. The introduction of this transparency mechanism has helped Solidarity in Literacy demonstrate their responsibility both to donor and to beneficiary with a single tool. Furthermore, when all the information gathered is made public through a website, it tends to strengthen the NGOs considerably, as it suggests that the organization in question has nothing to hide.

Tools are beginning to be consolidated through a process of accountability accreditation in many countries. Perhaps the best known is the Philippines NGO Certification Council which certifies NGOs by measuring or examining the information provided by the tools above and includes a review of the governance structure of an NGO. Once certified, the NGO is able to receive donations that are tax- exempt.

Similarly, some members of Interaction, the development industry association, are about to undergo a social audit that would verify whether they adhere to the accountability standards developed to guide member's actions. However, the costs to certification/ accreditation can be prohibitive for smaller NGOs. Very few of the more than 8000 NGOs in the Philippines have actually received accreditation as of yet, which in some circles, is seen as proof that the process is too complex and costly for many non-profits to undergo. Similarly, NGOs that are based on child- sponsorship have recently agreed to act as guinea- pigs in a social audit in the United States undertaken through Interaction and SAI will spend tens of thousands of dollars on the process (Interaction 2004).

Other tools that have recently been employed by NGOs comprise an array of management practices that strengthen the focus of an organization on its mission. These include: strong oversight boards that are independent from management and include key stakeholders affected by the organization's operation; complaints procedures oriented toward internal and external stakeholders; conflict-of-interest policies; officers to make sure the organization pursues only those opportunities that speak directly to the core values or mission of an institution; whistleblower protection policies; and ombuds functionaries who can respond to concerns from external stakeholders.

Accountability is more of a process, however, than a set of tools. Two primary stakeholders that accountability tools need to respond to are those that are internal to the organisation or network and those that are external yet impacted by the actions of an NGO. The accountability process often undertaken by NGOs beings with developing a clear mission statement, then undertaking a broad stakeholder assessment, i.e. determining who is important to the ability of the organization to carry out its mission, a focused effort to solicit the views of those stakeholders, a learning process that would include real time independent evaluations or social audits, review of concerns or issues that may arise or have arisen in the operations of the organization or network, oversight mechanisms like sector wide self regulation; a communications process with all critical stakeholders and a corrective procedure to help maintain flexibility (mid- course corrections) when actions fail to achieve desired results, or problems arise.

Different types of NGOs rely on different types of mechanisms. Ebrahim has conveniently separated out three types of NGOs that rely on differing mechanisms. (Ebrahim 2003). Membership organizations for example are principally accountable to their members and they use franchise, reform and dues as accountability mechanisms, Consumers International and Women's League of Voters are both primarily responsible to the General Assembly, a meeting of their members which occurs every year or every other year. Sierra Club members vote not only on the topics to be undertaken by the club but also on the positions to be advocated. Friends of the Earth International also has elaborate voting procedures among its federal global structure that govern its actions. Not all members enjoy the same rights. Some member based organization do not offer accountability mechanisms to the membership. Greenpeace, for example, in which one can become a member by sending in a donation but membership does not entail an active say in the operations of the organization.

Service organizations usually are principally accountable to their donors and they use performance assessment, evaluation, reporting requirements, laws and self- regulation as principle accountability mechanisms.

Ebrahim notes that networks of NGOs are principally accountable to the organization member, but I would argue that they are generally not accountable to each other but often feel a responsibility to the shared mission, values or goals of the network. Examples of accountability mechanisms in networks, or in even more tenuous relationships like coalitions, are difficult to find. When network members are accountable to one another mechanism that are employed between network members can span five areas: clarity in who is the primary actor or voice in any given political arena; clarity in agenda setting and strategy building; robust, frequent, useful and transparent information flows; transparency in resource distribution; and agreement on how to characterize the relationship among network actors (Jordan and Van Tuijl 2000). Accountability in networks, federations, coalitions and partnerships is the most muddled of areas, but perhaps the most critical as these relationships are very modern and have arisen in response to complex global crises that cannot be solved through command and control hierarchical relationships. Questions of accountability in partnerships become even more complex when one realizes that these partnerships are often formed to deliver a social service in lieu of state or local government action. Beneficiaries, who relied upon their representative democratic process to hold actors to account, no longer have those options, when delivery of services is carried out through a partnership of an array of global private actors.

Are There Costs Associated with Accountability?

This section queries what do accountability mechanisms "cost"? Are there any trade-offs in addressing accountability, e.g. with program implementation effectiveness? Are such trade- offs pervasive, and how do NGOs try to address them? What are the built in biases and towards whom are they biased?

Accountability (the obligation to report on one's activities to a set of legitimate authorities) is the basic principle of responsible practice for any institution, public, private or NGO (Edwards, 2002). And it matters who is asking the NGO to be accountable. Almost all mechanisms now employed at the organizational level and sector have arisen predominantly from queries from government or other donor sources and have led to a series of accountability mechanisms that include log- frames, certification systems, complex reporting requirements, reams of forms, rating systems, infrastructure and management capacity building tools and codes of conduct.

These types of accountability mechanisms can be helpful in creating a standard in particular fields (like the child sponsorship field), clearly defining expectations in a contractual relationship, clarifying the role of an NGO and allowing the public or the donor to evaluate the NGO on terms set by the donor.

The downside to these mechanisms is that they prioritize the needs and desires of donors and governments over those of other stakeholders within and surrounding NGOs. They do not always address the immediate knowledge needs of the NGOs, they rarely reflect the value-base of NGO activities, they can be quite expensive and when they become the standard for the industry they can lock out smaller NGOs. They can often seem to NGOs to be quite divorced from the mission of the organization. Accountability mechanisms as they now exist rarely address the rights of NGOs to operate (For example the right to associate freely) nor the responsibilities of NGOs to a wide array of stakeholders. They can fail to recognize the context within which NGOs operate, especially when developed in one context but than utilized in another national or local setting. Lastly, the complex web of relationships that mark the role of NGOs is not reflected in many accountability mechanisms. In part the inadequacies of these mechanisms reflect the source from which they have arisen. More worrisome, however, is that they suggest a lack of serious discourse amongst NGOs themselves.

As noted by Alnoor Ebrahim 'accountability in practice has emphasized 'upward' and 'external' accountability to donors while 'downward' and 'internal' mechanisms remain comparatively underdeveloped. NGOs and donors have focused primarily on short- term 'functional' accountability responses at the expense of longer- term 'strategic' processes (Ebrahim 2003). NGO typically have relationships with at least six identifiable stakeholders of which donor and governments are two. The others are its own staff, the general public, other NGOs, social movements, beneficiaries of services, global organisations and the private sector. Not every NGO has a relationship with each of these societal sectors, but one or more come into play with almost every

NGO. Accountability mechanisms as they now exist often do not prioritize these other relationships.

The needs of donor are driving an 'accountability industry'. Global market solutions to the NGO accountability question are on the rise and are divorced from context and the values base of much NGO practice. Certification standards are being proposed by the private sector to 'certify' NGOs. Societe Generale de Surveillance markets the 'SGS solution', based upon the so- called 'NGO 2000 Standard', to governments and donors (SGS 2000). It appears that SGS hopes to create a market demand for ratings and certification systems amongst donors so as to force NGOs to undergo scrutiny. SGS suggests that all stakeholders have the same interests; that there is a baseline from which to measure acceptable practice; that efficiency is a key goal in NGO work; and essentially that an NGO is no different from a profit driven business (and uses market terms like 'suppliers' for donors and 'customers' for beneficiaries). The 'SGS Solution' is based upon a private- sector model of independent verification that has been widely discredited over the past few years in the wake of corporate scandals. It would do very little to address the legitimacy type of questions outlined in section one and may do more harm than good to the sector by cementing the idea that NGOs are just like big business.

Beyond the reputation costs, accountability, when narrowly defined as external oversight, can also result in stringent directives imposed by donors stifling experimentation, innovation and flexibility to respond to the needs of a constituency that an NGO serves. A second costs lies in 'goal deflection' whereby the donor agency frame of the problem prevails over the needs of the constituency (Ebrahim 2003). These costs must be taken into account by donors and others who have the power to regulate or coerce changes in NGOs.

The focus on accountability mechanisms divorced from questions like 'accountability to whom' and 'for what purpose' has engendered negative responses from NGOs. Many do not see the purpose in taking up the issues of accountability. Jan Aart Scholte, a researcher at the University of Warwick has undertaken surveys of over 600 NGOs worldwide. He and his global team found that most NGOs had given almost no thought to the issue of their own accountability (Scholte, 2003). Arguments range from efficiency arguments (It's too expensive) to questions about the behavior of other actors in a political arena (the real accountability problem is with the government/ private sector) to questioning the purpose (how is this related to our mission). Most accountability mechanisms are viewed with suspicion as controlling elements imposed by actors more powerful than the NGOs.

Sadly, there is no conclusive evidence that developing codes of conduct and certification schemes actually helps to broaden or protect the political space in which NGOs operate. NGOs attacked by AEI all have proper and recognizable independent boards and good management infrastructure. They all report to donors in a timely fashion and many have independent audits. There legitimacy to advocate for policy change was called into question and the exiting accountability mechanisms have not helped them cope with the broad based question of representation or the accusation that they undermine state sovereignty. Thus, one of the most prominent reasons for NGOs to undertake accountability issues is called into question. Some people argue that the certification scheme in the Phillippines did help stave off a change in the tax code that would have been unfavorable to NGOs. The relationship between political space and self-regulatory systems is an under- explored area, ripe for academic review.

Implications of the Debate

Why should NGOs undertake the issue of accountability? A rising polarization of political debate which tends to demand that society organize itself into neatly formed sectors with clear roles- into enemies or friends- has led to increased questioning of the third sector, which is not easily boxed or categorized and thus is considered with suspicion by those who, for lack of a better way to phrase it, would like human beings to live a little more tidily. Rising polarization is something that can be seen in political society in the United States and in the rise of fundamentalism elsewhere. It is hard to say clearly whether this is a global trends. But I believe that its implications for the density of associational life are negative.

It could weed out creative solutions and creative associational responses to the need for new social contracts and could have a negative impact on the creation of new partnerships and NGOs. Furthermore, if questions on NGO accountability are not addressed credibly by NGOs the ability of NGOs to negotiate peace arrangements, to reach the very poor, to call states to account for violations of international human rights and other treaties will be undermined. Without strong NGOs human society would be left facing hugely complex problems with a vastly diminished tool box. Finding credible and creative ways to respond to effectiveness, reliability and especially legitimacy questions can help to overcome rising polarization by demonstrating the useful, necessary and valuable roles NGOs play.

In the grand scheme of societal relations, NGOs ultimately have very little power. They do not have coercive power, financial power, or even the authority and power that derives from representation. What they do have is flexibility, innovation, ideas, the ability to persuade and the power of a voice. These are all soft powers that can be and often are overridden by the power of money and guns. Already, many powerful actors are unhappy with the perceived power of NGOs to threaten nationalistic interests, corporate interests and the traditional roles of government. There is a concerted campaign amongst nationalists of all types to undermine the universalistic behaviour, ideals and actions of many NGOs. Corporations and intergovernmental institutions have begun to fund think tanks like the Caux Roundtable and the European Policy Institute to question the accountability of NGOs and to propose 'solutions' that, in general, work for the private sector and nation- states to the detriment of democracy and a greater public good. It is critical for NGOs to seriously answer accountability concerns for themselves before other more powerful actors define the parameters of the debate.

Fortunately, some efforts are now underway. The Hauser Centre at Harvard University in alliance with Civicus has begun to gather an elite set of NGO executives on an annual basis to grapple in part with this question. Codes of Conduct are popping up nationally and internationally to help define standard in the field. Account Ability has an Access Initiative which is meant to work on a global scale and help to steer local resources to local NGOs that have proven track records. The important point of these efforts is that they are driven by and for NGOs. While they vary in scope they are all attempting to define common standards within sectors, amongst memberships of associations, within geographical boundaries, etc. It is a trickly task to define acceptable standards of behaviour for non- profits whose only common characteristic is that they are not governments and not pursuing profits.

Strengthening NGO Accountability

NGOs have many reasons to embrace the issue of accountability. The first one is to stave off systems that are costly, and do not speak to the organizational or network learning needs. The second is to respond to stakeholders impacted by decisions made by NGOs. The third is to improve outcomes. The fourth is to strengthen the role of NGOs within civil society (where NGOs are just one form of association). NGOs whose actions speak to a strong values base will need to publicly define the goals that they are oriented toward in order to bring more supporters into their universe and fend off political attacks. These reasons speak to a need for different types of accountability processes than those often proposed by donors.

Scattered throughout this paper I have made reference to interesting approaches to accountability that while time consuming and sometimes even expensive, can serve the needs of multiple stakeholders. These include Action Aid's Applied Learning Program, Solidarity in Literacy's transparency mechanism for its resources allocation, and the Humanitarian Accountability Project based in Geneva which applies a rights- based approach to emergency relief services. There are others. All have taken a common approach to the issue. The differences between donor- driven approaches and those embraced below are: developing a clearly defined mission statement; a 360 degree process of identifying internal and external stakeholders; defining accountability to whom and ranking stakeholders; reviewing existing processes; identifying gaps and then developing new mechanisms that respond to the needs of multiple stakeholders.

NGO accountability can be strengthened by understanding first that accountability is a socially derived concept that varies from one culture to the next. The rights and responsibilities that define societal norms within that context are important to consider when addressing the responsibilities and rights of active NGOs.

Many donor organizations fund assessment and evaluation. For the most part, assessment and evaluation are good forms of accountability mechanisms because when undertaken with care, they can lead to organizational learning. However, if a donor is too stringent in defining acceptable forms of evaluation and assessment, it may squander an NGOs opportunity to learn. NGOs should be pro-active in seeking funds for assessment and evaluation so that they have the possibility of defining their own process.

And, while donors could serve the sector by providing resources for NGOs to develop evaluative processes without prescribing approaches, donors are also accountable to others, like regulators, legislators and their own boards. Thus, the ensuing accountability mechanisms should contain the information that donors need to be accountable themselves. Most donors need similar types of information or to ensure that funds are spent as agreed in the proposal. Donors could work as a sector to coordinate their own reporting requirements so that NGOs with multiple donors are able to provide one report to multiple agencies. Some donors are beginning to explore this issue. Flexibility in the donors community could help to ensure that accountability mechanisms developed for the donor also serve as learning mechanisms for the NGO. Lastly, donors could develop incentives for risk- taking and experimentation by sharing lessons that they learn from evaluating lines of programming. Donors can help others to learn from the incredibly rich experiences that are now often held internally in donor agencies. This would include both successes and failures. Failure, after all, is a profound learning opportunity.

An important accountability mechanism often neglected by all actors in the accountability field is a good communications strategy that helps NGOs reach the public and the stakeholders they prioritize. Transparency is a part of that process. It is often, but not always, an important goodwill ambassador. Clarifying the mission statement, repeating it often and providing basic information about the organization, campaign, etc. can go a long way to solidifying accountability, protecting the NGO and clarifying to whom and for what and NGO is responsible. While not everyone will agree, I also believe that it is important for NGOs to reflect the changes that it wishes to see in the world. This would allow an NGO to stake out the moral high ground.

One yardstick that could be applied is whether an accountability mechanism can serve more than one stakeholder. As mentioned earlier, Solidarity in Literacy has developed one that serves many of its stakeholders simultaneously. Action Aid's very complex and comprehensive Applied Learning Program and the Humanitarian Accountability Project undertaken by One World Trust stand out as exemplary models in which the missions of the NGOs involved informed the accountability mechanisms (called democratic accountability). These examples prioritize the communities served by the NGOs over donors and governments. Nevertheless, these examples are not popular as they are not simple, direct or easily implemented. They are systems that ultimately, however, will make the NGOs that adhere to them more secure operations that are able to publicly articulate their value and values in a way that will protect them from politically motivated attacks. Furthermore, they will also allow the NGOs to evolve and learn from their operations, something that cannot be claimed by all accountability mechanism. Most NGOs are keen to measure their impact, demonstrate their effectiveness and account for their actions. Donor organizations should encourage accountability processes that serve multiple stakeholders including the internal organizational need of the NGO itself to learn.

It is uncomfortable for an organization, donor or NGO to explore its failures. Thus, there is a role for the academic community to assess large programs with social change goals that are desired by both donors and NGOs. The real symbiotic relationship between donor and NGO is best reviewed by an independent evaluator. The academic community can assess whether accountability mechanisms serve the larger desirable goals (Poverty alleviation, conservation, women's empowerment, etc.) and the impact of these mechanisms on the relationship amongst a broad array of stakeholders. The academic community has already begun to help sort out useful tools and processes that can help assess outcomes verse outputs. There is a particular need to better assess the responsibility and rights of advocacy NGOs operating in the global political arena, where public policy is increasingly democratic checks and balances pervasive at the national level.

Researchers could also help answer what kind of accountability mechanisms and processes actually can address the greater societal questions of democratic accountability in an era of globalization. They can continually remind others that accountability is not just a question to be addressed in respect of NGOs, but within governments, the private sector, and other civic associations like standard setting bodies, social movements, think tanks, and non-profits that sometimes get lumped into an 'NGO' category and sometimes are not. Furthermore, if researchers could help sort out the relationship between accountability and democracy, including illuminating issues surrounding representation in non - democratic spheres of policy debate like the global sphere, it would help all actors find new frameworks that are necessary to define our responsibilities and rights in shifting contexts.

8

Tax Transactions of NGOs

This chapter gives an overview of the fiscal incentives that are granted to NGOs and their donors around the world it discusses a set of principles of best practice for such fiscal incentives and tax transactions.

It is clear that there are several different taxes from which NGOs may be exempt: income and profits taxes, property taxes, transfer taxes (on gift and death transfers), excise taxes, value added taxes, sales taxes, etc. NGOs are typically not exempted from employment taxes, but frequently are exempted from income, property, and transfer taxes. Some countries may, for example, make certain transactions of NGOs subject to VAT, while others will include them but give them a low or zero rating.

The fiscal laws also frequently allow tax preferences such as deductions or tax credits or rebates for contributions by individuals or commercial corporations or other commercial entities to a defined class of NGOs (e.g. public benefit organisations). Individuals may be allowed similar deductions from or credits against transfer (estate and gift) taxes for similar contributions. The class of NGOs to which such gift may be made is sometimes smaller than the class of tax exempt entities. For example, deductions might be allowed for union or trade association dues, but not social club membership dues, even thought all three groups of NGOs are themselves exempt from the income tax. There also may be numerical or percentage limits on creditable contributions.

The tax laws also tend to state the extent to which NGO will be taxed on their income from economic activities. It is important to permit NGO to conduct such activities for their support, particularly in countries where there is little private wealth. As will be seen in the discussion below, countries differ on whether profits from activities not directly related to a NGOs principal purpose should be taxed.

Legal systems governing NGO frequently make a distinction between mutual benefit organisations (MBOs) and public benefit organisations (PBOs), which is of great importance in the area of taxation. By definition, a PBO benefits the public or some defined segment of it. Accordingly, PBOs are generally regarded as entitled to greater benefits from the state than are MBOs, which primarily serve the interests of their members. Tax preferences are one of the principal benefits extended to NGOs, and in most legal system they are extended preferentially or even exclusively to PBOs.

Most legal systems do not use the terms MBO and PBO as such. These reflect an attempt to generalize and put on a sounder theoretical footing the actual, more fragmented practices that exist in various legal systems. Most tax laws focus on the functions or purposes of an organisation in determining whether it is entitled to tax preferences. For example, the tax laws of a particular country might extend the privilege of receiving tax deductible contributions or property tax exemption only to organisations formed for the primary purpose of advancing education, health, science, culture, or the relief of poverty. Over the years other purpose may be added to the list, such as the protection of the interests of minority groups or the environment.

As a legal system matures it is often the case that the law writers realize that a common theme runs through the list of purpose or activities they have crafted over the years and that no more listing can capture all of the possible kinds of organisations that deserve preference and support from the state. It is common, then, to find, tracked on to the end of such a list, a final, catch- all category such as "or any other organisation formed primarily for the benefit of the public." In such a catch-all the unifying principle emerges and, in a sense, informs the entire list. It is education, health, and scientific organisations *that serve the public interest* that are entitled to a tax preference. The officials in charge of determining eligibility for tax preferences can now test each organisation seeking a tax preference by the more expansive criterion of whether it is formed primarily to serve the public interest. In other words, is it a PBO? It should also be emphasizes that the selection of the agency to make the determination of whether an NGO is a PBO or not is crucially important.

In the actual state of development of the tax laws of any country, lists of purposes or activities rather than principles predominate. And the lists vary. The kinds of organisations that qualify for a sales tax exemption may be different from the kinds of organisations that qualify for customs duty preferences. This is the natural result of the ad hoc way in which tax and other legal rules develop. It is useful, through, to look at the entire collection of tax rules affecting NGOs and determine whether a more consistent set of rules founded in principle could be carried consistently across the entire landscape of laws. The strong suggestion here is that the distinction between mutual benefit and public benefit organisations and activities has enormous analytic power and can be used to rationalize and round off what otherwise might be a rather jumbled and inconsistent set of rules.

The focus of the sections that follow is on the special tax preferences that should or might be extended to NGOs, or at least to PBOs. Something that deserves special mention is that, virtually without exception, tax preferences are voluntary and are extended only to organisations that want and seek them. A special application must be field in virtually every system in order to establish entitlement to one more tax preferences. This means that any organisation that prefers to operate without out the higher level of oversight and scrutiny that accompanies tax preferences, can choose not to subject itself to the process. Since tax laws, like other laws, can be used improperly to harass unpopular NGOs, this option to either seek or avoid tax preferences is of fundamental importance.

Another point also deserves special emphasis. Aside from the possible imposition of penalty taxes as a sanction for the kinds of special problems that occur in the non governmental sector, these should not be special taxes or tax rates imposed on NGOs. Most NGOs add something of benefit to society, and society benefits enormously from the existence of a strong, vibrant, and independent nongovernmental sector. The interests of society in having a strong nongovernmental sector would be undermined and frustated by the imposition of special taxes or tax rates on NGOs. In fact, as societies mature they generally embrace indirect methods of macro- managing the institutions of society, and fiscal preferences have proven to be a powerful tool for encouraging the constructive development of the NGO sector while avoiding discrimination, excessive governmental bureaucracy, and market distortion that results from excessive direct intervention by the government.

Best Practices

1. ***Income Taxation Exemption of NGOs:*** *Every nongovermental organisation, whether organized for mutual benefit or for public benefit, and whether a membership or nonmembership organisation, should be exempt from income taxation on money or other items of value received from donors or governmental agencies (by grant or contract), membership dues, if any, and any interest, dividends, rents, royalties or capital gains earned on assets or the sale of assets.*

Discussion: Since NGOs as defined here preclude the possibility of personal benefit or the distribution of profits, there is a powerful argument that they are not proper objects of an income tax in any system. Income taxes are imposed on the "profits" of legal entities because they are surrogates for the individuals who own them or who can receive a distribution of profits from them. In countries, such as New Zealand, which have fully integrated their corporate and individual income taxes, there is no need to impose separate income taxes on corporations. There is a single income tax and it is imposed on corporate profits once, at the shareholder level and at shareholder level and at shareholder rates. Profits at the corporate level are subject to a tax, but all dividends are "franked"- that is, the shareholder receiving franked dividends is entitled to take a credit against his or her own taxes for the taxes paid at the corporate level.

NGOs as defined here, stand on an entirely different footing. They are not "owned" by anyone and cannot distribute profits as such. Whatever profits they may earn from economic activities are reinvested or spent on appropriate nonprofit activities. They are not surrogates for the shareholders who own them, and thus it can be strongly argued that they should not be subject to income taxation at all. Unfortunately, most countries around the world assume that NGOs, like for- profit entities, are natural subjects of taxation, and that not applying tax to them is a matter of grace and exemption.

The typical sources of revenue for NGO are donations, membership dues, and interest and dividends on investments. There is general agreement that these items should not be taxed. There are, however, two different ways of arriving at this result. One approach assures that NGO are not taxable on these ordinary sources of revenue by defining those sources as not constituting "income" for tax purpose. The other approach recognizes these receipt as income but confers exempt status on NGOs.

Generally accepted tax theory defines income as any receipt during period of time that is either expended or that increases net worth. Under this approach and in common understanding, it is clear that dividends and interest are generally considered income for tax purposes. Accordingly, the approach taken here is to recognize all receipts of a NGO-donations, membership fees, interest, dividends, and capital gains-as income, but to advocate tax exempt status for all NGO for these items. This approach leaves several open questions-- should those who make donations receive a tax preference? Should trade or business income of an NGO be exempt ? And how should NGO be dealt with under other tax laws ? These questions are dealt with in the succeeding sections.

One specialized issue deserves mention here. Should a donation received by one NGO but earmarked for another be treated as a donation to, and the revenue of, the first NGO? For the donor this can be an important question, for the item might be deductible if a donation to the first entity but not if it is given to the second. For example, a donation to a foreign organisation might not be deductible, but a donation to a domestic organisation, might be, even if it passes the donation along to the foreign organisation. Some countries, such as the United States, have complex rules for distinguishing between contributions that have been permissibly earmarked and passed along from those that fail certain very technical tests.

On the side of the recipient NGO, there is a question of whether an earmarked or "passthrough" donation should properly be reflected as its income, and whether it is improperly being used as a more conduit, perhaps obscuring from regulations or the public the real purpose of the donation. Again, these issues become very technical very quickly, but it is important to note their existence and hence the need to take account of them in any fully developed set of laws.

2. Income Tax Deductions or Credits for Donations: *Within reasonably generous limits, individuals and business entities should be entitled to an income tax deduction or credit with respect to donations made to PBOs (but not MBOs). As a matter of tax policy, credit are preferable to deductions for individuals under a progressive income tax system, though deductions may attract more and larger gifts from wealthy donors.*

Discussion: Under the rule recommended in the previous section, no NGO would be taxed on donations it receives. If in addition, the giver is entitled to a tax credit or deduction against his or her personal or business income tax, the same donation receives double tax preference, once to the giver and again to the recipient. As a best practice, this generous tax treatment is deemed justified when the activities of the NGO in question are for the public benefit--when, in other words, it is a PBO rather than an MBO. If this distinction is drawn in the tax laws of a country--permitting a tax preference to those who make contributions-then there will be great pressure on the supervising authority (presumably the tax authority) to classify NGOs as PBOs. As discussed above, this distinction is often difficult to draw.

In actual experience the tax authorities tend to proceed on a case- by- case basis.

A separate and different question is raised by whether a contributor to a PBO should get a tax credit or a tax deduction. The distinction is of great importance in a tax system with a progressive rate structure. A tax credit reduces the amount of tax owed, often unit- for- unit. Whereas a deduction only reduces the amount of income that is subject to tax. Where rates are progressive deductions tend to favor higher income tax payers, who are paying a higher rate of tax on income. Tax credits give each taxpayer the same tax preference for a contribution of the same amount, and hence represent greater equity as a matter of tax policy. Most countries with progressive rate structures, however , allow deductions rather than credits. This may be justified by data which show that lower income individuals tend to make charitable contributions without regard to their tax impact, and, indeed, other tax rules may preclude them from getting any tax preference at all from a charitable contribution. On the other hand, there are substantial empirical data showing that high income taxpayers are quite sensitive to tax rates and that allowing deductions rather than credits tends to attract more and larger gifts from wealthy donors.

Another question that must be dealt with in any scheme of taxation are the limits, if any, put on the amount of tax preferences that can be achieved. For example, in Russia individuals can claim deductions only up to 3% of their income, and business entities are limited to 1%. In the United States, by contrast, individuals can claim deductions for up to 50% of their income, and in Australia there is no limit at all. Empirical studies show that few business entities contribute more than 1-2% of their income, so it is an essentially empty debate whether deduction limits should be higher than that.

The same is not true of individuals, however, and where there is no limit on allowable charitable deductions wealthy individuals can avoid paying any taxes by contributing to charity an amount equal to their taxable income each year. In a democracy it is appropriate that each citizen who is financially able to should bear a fair share of the costs of government, and it is therefore not a best practice to allow unlimited deductions. At the same time, if deductions are limited to contributions to PBO-- i.e., organisations contributing to the public good and often relieving the burdens of government-- generous deduction limits are appropriate. The laws of most countries need to be reconsidered in light of these considerations.

3. Taxation of Economic Activities: *NGOs should be allowed to engage in economic activities so long as those activities do not constitute the principal purpose or activity of the organisation. Any net profit earned by an NGO from the active conduct of a trade or business could be---*

(a) exempted from income taxation,

(b) subjected to income taxation,

(c) subjected to income taxation only if the trade or business is not related to and in furtherance of the non-for- profit purpose of the organisation, or

(d) *subjected to a mechanical test that allows a modest amount of profits from economic activities to escape taxation, but imposes tax on amounts in excess of the limit.*

Discussion: The tests involved in selecting among these possible tax rules are complex and technical. Under a "destination of income" test, alternative (a) would apply to a properly formed NGO. Thus, all income from economic activities would be exempt from tax as long as all of the profits earned from the active conduct of a trade or business were committed for and actually used to carry out the principal purpose for which the NGO was formed. Thus, an organisation that spent 99% of its time and money making profit from a purely commercial activity, such as manufacturing noodles, would be treated as a tax exempt NGO if each year it gave all of its profits to charitable causes. Whether such an outcome would actually exist in practice would depend on whether the proper authorities would accept that such an organisation was or was not properly registered as a NGO. They might, for example, require it to register as a business entity, depending on the circumstances.

In a country with a developing market economy, it may be appropriate to strike the balance in favor of tax exemption for all profits destined for use by a NGO to carry out its statutory activities. Countries in which the market economy is developing are generally also countries where the civic sector is just beginning to flourish. NGOs in such countries are often desperate for money simply to survive, and the profits from economic activities may make the difference between their continued existence and termination. In such countries it is also possible to argue that there is such a strong need to develop economic activities independent of the state that all entities, whether NGOs or business entities, ought to be encouraged to engage in them.

On the other hand, the problem of unfair competition can become a serious issue, particularly when the scale and number of economic activities by NGOs begins to pose a threat to private enterprises. Obviously, if a large and wealthy NGO can engage in a particular activity (e.g. book publishing) without paying taxes, it has an economic advantage over its for- profit competitors. When this issues becomes significant for the fiscal policy of a country, the obvious solution is to tax such profits, at least if they are unrelated to the purposes of the organisation.

Exempting the profits from "related" activities makes a great deal of theoretical sense. Often the most effective way for a NGO to achieve its purpose is to pursue it through economic means. For example, the most effective way to disseminate information about a particular kind of art or culture that a NGO wants to promote may be to publish and sell a high-quality magazine devoted to that topic. If the primary purpose of the organisation is to promote the particular kind of art or culture, it is not primarily seeking to make a profit, and no profits are distributed, then publication of the magazine is simply the method that has been chosen to pursue the civic purpose. Publishing a magazine is a means for achieving the end of promotion of the art or culture. Exempting income from such related activities makes good theoretical sense.

Unfortunately, it is extremely difficult to distinguish "related" economic activities from "unrelated" activities, and hence this rule is very difficult to administer. For example, if a museum sets up a shop on its premises to sell copies of the outstanding works in its collection, or perhaps books that picture them or postcards that replicate them, this can easily be argued to be "related" to the museum's activities. What should happen if the museum opens a chain of retail stores that sell books related to art and culture, most of which have no connection with its collection? Is it engaging in an "unrelated" activity, or has it simply broadened its purposes and chosen to pursue the broader purpose using economic means? The fact that a distinction between related and unrelated economic activities is very difficult to apply is demonstrated by the fact that very little revenue is raised by a tax that is imposed only on "unrelated" activities.

If the principal purpose test is adopted, it is then necessary to determine how economic activities undertaken in furtherance of the purpose of a NGO.. "related" economic activities as that term is being used here --- are to be counted in determining whether the principal purpose of an organisation is to engage in economic activities or to pursue civic ends. To the extent that economic activities (e.g., publication of a magazine or of books) is simply a chosen means by which most effectively to pursue a given end (e.g., promotion of a particular art or culture), there is a strong argument that they should not be counted as economic activities that would disqualify the entity for status as a NGO if they constituted the principal activity of the organisation. One must be careful, however, for if "related" economic activities constituted the only activities of a NGO, one would in effect have come back to the "destination of income" test, under which economic activities can constitute the entire active work of a NGO as long as all profits go to a civic purpose. Designing administrable rules that adequately repond to these considerations is not easy.

A mechanical test for determining the difference between economic activities that are taxed and those that are not is a far simpler system of taxing NGOs. It might be possible, for example, to tax income from all economic activities if it exceeds a certain figure or percentage of all income. Another possible remedy has been chosen by Hungary, where NGOs are exempt on the net profit from economic activities if the annual unrelated business income does not exceed the lesser of 10 million forint or 10% of total revenue. This works fine as a tax rule, for the only consequence of exceeding the minimum in any year is that taxes must be paid. But in the Hungarian case taxes are levied on all business income if the threshold is exceeded, whether the activities are related or not, presumably on the theory that if the organisation has a lot of business income it is more like a business than a NGO. The principal purpose test takes a similar approach for determining eligibility for classification as a NGO. Thus, if more than 50 percent of the activities and expenditures of a NGO constitute economic activities for a significant period of time (e.g., 3 years), the organisation is reclassified as a business entity. As long as "related" economic activities are not disregarded, this mechanical test will generally be adequate to permit significant economic activities while not creating the risk that the entire sector will develop a bad reputation (as does the destination of income test).

As an alternative to stating an absolute preference for any of these test, It is sufficient to state that each of the above rules has been adopted and implemented, and that the NGO sector has been able to flourish under any of the rules. The considerations in choosing among these rules often are determined by considerations unrelated to the NGO sector itself (e.g., a desire to avoid unfair competition with for- profit entities), issues of general tax policy, or considerations of practicability and administrability.

4. VAT and Customs Duties

(a) PBOs should be given preferential treatment under a value added tax (VAT).

Discussion. If an organisation is excluded from a VAT system, it pays VAT on goods and services it buys from other, for the tax is built into the price it must pay (input VAT). However, since it is not in the system, it cannot apply for a refund. Although exclusion from the VAT system is not desirable from a tax point of view, small NGOs might rationally prefer it in order to be relieved of compliance burdens.

The best situation for an NGO is to be included in the VAT system but to zero- rated. This means that, though the NGO pays VAT on the goods and services it buys, it does not have to pay output VAT, and it gets back as a rebate the input VAT paid plus the amount of any imputed VAT on goods and services it sells to others. This approach is not adopted in many countries. The more general approach is to give PBOs a favorable VAT rate, but not a zero rate. For example, if the general rate of VAT is 20%, the special rate for PBOs might be 6- 10%.

(b) PBOs should be given preferential treatment under or exemption from customs duties on imported goods or services that are used to further their public benefit purposes.

Discussion. Customs duties are among the most contentious and difficult of issues faced by NGO in practice. If the law of a particular country provided for exemption for NGOs, customs officials often disregard the law, and NGOs must spend a disproportionate amount of time getting more senior officers to actually get the benefit of the exemption. At the same time, laws allowing customs exemptions for NGOs tempt charlatans and crooks into the NGO sector with the prime motive of establishing an NGO to get customs exemption.

If customs duties are imposed on legitimate NGOs, however, they can dramatically increase the costs of operations. This problem faces both foreign and domestic NGOs. The problem can be particularly severe for humanitarian relief organisations that typically must import all of their goods and services in order to meet emergency relief needs. It is a problem, though, for even the smallest NGO, which might want to import a fax machine or computer to make its work more productive.

The best practice in this area is to provide customs duty exemptions to PBOs, to have a fair but thorough process for assuring that only genuine PBOs qualify for the process, but then to have a certification, licensing, or similar process that insure that a PBO's exemption from customs duties will be honored at the border. To protect against the improper use of the exemption, it is appropriate to provide that imports will be exempt only if they are going to be used by the NGO in its operations. Any item sold by an NGO (e.g., a truck or automobile) within a short period (e.g., 2-3 years) would be subject to customs duties at the time of sale.

5. Other Taxes

(a) Depending upon the extent to which a government wishes to encourage NGOs, exemption from or preferential treatment under other tax laws (e.g., taxes on real or personal property, sales taxes, estate or inheritance taxes) should be considered.

Discussion. Practices vary widely around the globe. As one example, Indonesia, Thailand, and The Philippines exempt religious organisations from land taxes, while Australia provides not income tax preferences for religious organisations.

(b) No NGO should be exempted or given preferential treatment under applicable employment or payroll taxes.

Discussion. Despite the fact that NGO employees typically expect and receive a lower level of compensation than that which is paid for comparable work in the for- profit sector, there is no justification for exempting them from the usual social security and related employment taxes that are exacted from workers in the governmental or for- profit sector.

Social security and similar taxes are exacted on basis of actuarial estimates of what is required in order to meet the state's obligations to retired workers over the long term. Those who are employed in the not - for - profit sector should not be excluded from the benefits of state - provided benefits, nor should they be exempted from the benefits that are provided for those who participate in these state schemes.

In short, although it is a valuable tax preference to exempt NGOs for many forms of regular taxation, it would prefer such organisations over the long- term interests of their employees to exempt them from the employment taxes usually imposed on employers with respect to employees. Employees of NGOs should not suffer the double disability of working for a lower wage and being excluded from basic employee benefit programs imposed on other employees in that society.

Notes

1. Brazil is a notable exception to this rule because it permits a very limited group of NGOs to be exempt from employment taxes. This is however, not a good practice because employees of such organisations are no different than employees of business of business entities or government organisations and need access to social taxes for retirement savings.
2. Being excluded from VAT is worse than full inclusion, because the civic organisation then pays VAT on all goods and services received but gets no credit for those it provides. Zero rating is the best status.
3. In Cameroon, however, no NGOs receive any tax benefits. South Africa represents a more typical approach, for tax

exemptions are limited to institutions and funds that are ecclesiastical, charitable, or educational in nature, and of a public character.

4. Although not desirable, there may be a list or purposes or activities. It is clearly not a best practice, however, to list by name or specific description the organisation that are entitled to receive tax benefits. Such lists nearly always derive from special or political preferences rather than from any consistent set of principles.

5. In a bizarre development, NGOs in Israel are subject to certain employment taxes to which business companies are not subject. The genesis of this rule was the need to encourage employment for recent immigrants to Israel, but there can be no question that the result makes little sense.

6. Sri Lanka illustrates that there can be positions in between treating NGOs as full taxpayers and exempting them. In that country tax on charitable institution is levied at a concessional rate of 10 percent on income in excess of Rs. 42,000 per annum, and this tax can be waived for charities providing institutional care. The theory behind this rule is that better accountability will be assured if sizable charities are required to file tax returns, even though the tax rate is quite low. In Uganda, although income tax exemptions were previously available, there are reports that the exemptions will be repealed for the next fiscal year.

7. A typical example of how difficult it is for NGOs to obtain tax exemption is provided by Thailand: In that country NGOs registered as foundations or associations may seek tax exemption of there purpose is charitable, which means that it is related to religion, education, health, or social

welfare. No NGO can qualify for exemption until it has operated for three years, though this rule may be waived by Ministry of Finance. During the prior three years, the NGO must have spent 60% of its income or 75% of its total expenditures on charitable purposes. The result of these, rules if that only about 200 NGOs have tax exempt status in Thailand. ESCAP, Fiscal Incentives.

8. For example, the income of any ecclesiastical, charitable, or educational institution of a public character is exempted from the corporate income tax so long as the income is not derived from the conduct of a trade or business.

9. Sec R.M. Haig, "The Concept of Income, The Federal Income Tax 1, 27 (1921); Henry Simons, Personal Income Taxation 50 (1938).

10. In Romania, however, interest is deemed to be "without economic character" and therefore not subject to the profits tax. See Ministry of Finance Methodological Rules No.5910 of 1991. Obviously, if interest income is not generally taxed, as in the case of Romania, NGOs should not be taxed on their interest income.

11. "It is particularly important that NGOs carrying out "watchdog" functions through policy research, lobbying and public awareness- raising be financially independent of both their own governments and foreign donors. To encourage such independence, divided income on NGOs' financial endowments could be made tax- free. NGOs providing services to other NGOs (e.g., as, "umbrella" organisations, as federations, as subcontractors) or those playing a catalyst role on behalf of the NGO community could also be given that concession on income from all funds held in trust. "ESCAP, Fiscal Incentives, p. 48 (1994). In Ireland the tax on interest income is the one from which

charitable organisations most frequently seek exemption. See Joe Ryan, Reliefs from Tax on the Income and Property of Charities (1995).

12. There is no limit to the ingenious tax rules that can be devised, and often tax rules can be used to attempt to achieve very targeted goals. For example, in China enterprises in which disabled persons constitute a minimum of 10 percent of the work force receive a 50 percent tax concession, while those whose workforce comprises 35 percent disabled employees receive complete exemption from economic taxation. Some countries place very strict limits on charitable deductions. In Indonesia, Botswana, and Bangladesh, no deductions are allowed for contributions to NGOs. In Thailand companies are limited to 1 percent of net profits for contributions to public charities and a further 2 percent for education and sports, though individual contributions of up to 10 percent of gross income are tax deductible. A 100 percent tax deductions is allowed to individuals for donations made to accredited NGOs for disaster relief in areas approved by the President. In South Africa the limit is 2%, and in Egypt it is 3%. By contrast, in the Philippines the limit on contributions for organisations that promote social welfare or serve religious, charitable, scientific, athletic, or cultural purposes is 6% for individuals and 3% for corporations. In the United States individuals can deduct amounts up to 50% of their income for contributions to an even wider group of charities. In Australia the limit is 100%, but the category of eligible recipient organisations ("public benevolent institutions"), organisations set up for the direct relief of poverty, misfortune, destitution, or helplessness, is quite narrow. In Japan rather strict monetary, not percentage, limits are imposed. In many

developing countries policy makers generally resist the notion that tax preferences ought to be extended to NGOs, for they are not regarded as contributors to economic development. The structural adjustment policies being pursued by many countries, often with strong support from the World Bank and the International Monetary Fund, emphasize deficit control and fiscal austerity. However, it may be appropriate for policy makers to reconsider the importance of extending tax preferences to NGOs as part of an overall strategy of promoting sound development.

13. Some countries may, for example, make certain transactions of NGOs subject to VAT, while others will include them but give them a low or zero rating.

14. India provides an example of a relatively generous tax deduction scheme. India, cash donations to charitable organisations are 50% tax deductible up to 10% of gross income. A recent study concluded that in India, "The scheme of deductions for charitable contributions increased the quantum of such contributions substantially. In the absence of incentive provisions, the contributions of companies would have been lower by about 64 percent of the actual contributions. "ESCAP, Fiscal Incentives, pp. 23-24 (1994). Through an inexplicable lapse, the polish Parliament allowed individuals to take tax deductions during 1996 for contribution to other individuals. Thus, a brother might claim a tax deduction for a donation to his sister to enable her to get her teeth fixed, and she might get a similar deduction for giving him money to provide special education to his children. This law will be repealed for 1997 and subsequent years; deductions will be limited to donations to legally constituted charities, demonstrating again the great value of formal registration. Under the

Law of the Leningrad Region on Charities adopted on April 21, 1995, charitable activities may be conducted either with or without establishing a legal entity, but donors receive tax preferences (deductions of up to 3% of net profits) only if the state certifies that the activities were charitable. This requirement for certification saves the Leningrad Region, law from the defect of the Polish law, which imposed no similar requirement.

15. Canada has allowed a credit for individuals rather than a deduction since 1998. The switch does not seem to have affected giving patterns. See Carl Juneau, Charity and Taxes in Canada,1996).

16. In the United States, for example, taxpayers must choose between claiming the "standard deduction" or itemizing all deductible expenses. For lower bracket taxpayers the standard deduction tends to be more valuable, but by choosing it a taxpayer is precluded from listing, and hence from deducting, actual gifts made to charity. In other countries salaried individuals to not file tax returns because taxes are simply subtracted from their wages. In such situations it is difficult to claim a refund if a charitable contribution is made.

17. See, e.g., Charles Clotfelter, Tax Incentives and Charitable Giving: Evidence from a Panel of Taxpayers in 30 Journal of Public Economics, 319 (1980): Richard Steinberg, Taxes and Giving, 1 Voluntas 61 (1990); Kevin S. Berrett, Anya M Mc Guirk and Richard Steinberg, Further Evidence of the Dynamic Impact of Taxes on Charitable Giving (1996).

18. *Id.*

19. Another possibility may be to use a scheme similar to that currently in use in the U K, where the tax benefit is not actually given to the donor but rather is passed on to

the charity itself as a cash receipt from the Treasury in addition to the cash receipt from the donor.

20. If the active trade or business is carried out indirectly, though a subsidiary, the legal system might regard the subsidiary as a for- profit business entity, but simply exempt it from income taxation. The result is the same: the activity is permitted and the profits are not taxed. Although the substance of the rule is the same for both associations and foundations in Poland, associations get the rule only if they engage in economic activities through a wholly owned subsidiary, whereas foundations are exempt on activities that they carry on directly.

21. For an analysis of the issues related to taxation of profits from economic activities, see Industry Commission. Charitable Organisations in Australia, 311-312 and Appendix J (1995).

22. See Henry B. Hansmann, Unfair Competition and the Unrelated Business Income Tax, 75 Va. L. Rev. 605 (1989).

23. In Bangladesh, Indonesia, The Philippines, and Thailand, NGOs receive no exemption from the VAT, but in some cases they benefit from lower rates levied on primary, unprocessed agricultural products. In most Western European countries there are certain VAT preferences, although these vary considerably from country to country. See Derek Allen, VAT in the European Community.

24. For a fuller discussion of VAT issues, see Ole Gejms-Onstad, VAT, 1996.

25. In Rwanda the only tax benefits for NGOs are exemption from customs duties and exemption for expatriate NGO employees from the entrance fee.

26. Often the problem is not the absence of an exemption for NGOs, but the red tape involved in claiming it. In India NGOs wishing to obtain concession from duties imposed on equipment imports donated by foreigners have to apply for Central Government approval six months in advance, and strict rules and procedures are invoked. In Sri Lanka and The Philippines exemption from, customs duties and the VAT on donation from foreign sources can be obtained only if the donations are consigned to the relevant government agency. This procedure generally involves numerous bureaucratic obstacles and conditionally provisions.

27. "It may be useful to remove the distinction between NGOs that provide direct relief, social protection or opportunities for self- improvement and those that play representational, catalytic or advocacy roles. Rather, it may be advisable to introduce concessions on the basis of voluntarism, so that those NGOs which are run entirely by volunteers and which provide free services and labour would be entirely exempt from taxes on income from all sources as well as being permitted duty- free imports to build up their organisations. That could provide an especially significant boost to development- oriented community and grass- roots NGOs. "ESCAP, Fiscal Incentives, p. 46 (1994).

28. In Australia, however, NGOs involved in social welfare work pay reduced sales taxes and, if their payroll is over A $ 10,000 a month, a reduced payroll tax well, depending on which State they are in.

9

NGOs and Civil Society

The purpose here is to explore ways of moving beyond the limitations of the many particular ways of discussing "civil society". It endeavours to identify broader issues of relevance to public policy formulation in response to the challenge of "civil society" to governance.

One of the difficulties is that "civil society" itself is discussed through a variety of terms whose partial equivalence has not been effectively explored. These include: NGOs, voluntary associations, nonprofit sector, not- for-profit sector, charitable organisations, benevolent societies and third sector. Depending on who uses these terms, they may, or may not, include bodies such as labour unions, trade associations, professional societies, or legally unrecognized (can even illegal) bodies such as cartels and crime rings. In many cases it is not what a particular approach includes that is as significant as what is effectively excluded and why.?

Many modern protagonists fail to recognize that the debate about the nature of "NGOs" has been in progress since the beginning of the century. Many of the points concerning the relationship between governmental and nongovernmental organisations have been made many times over---- some of them over a period of decades.

There is therefore merit in reflecting on the collective ability to process these questions in new and fruitful ways. There is a sense in which it is in the interests of many to avoid clarity and conclusion and simply to perpetuate the discussion. And there is the continuing interest of others to arrive at simplistic solutions if possible. The debate is complicated by a degree of unwillingness to recognize some weaknesses in the present arrangements.

Times have changed in that the credibility of all international institutions and programmes is questioned to a greater degree, notably in the case of the United Nations. There is increasing scope for organisations to act independently, especially when any form of collaboration with other bodies, and especially the United Nations, is fraught with unproductive dynamics that constitute an unreasonable drain on resources.

The purpose here is to attempt briefly to indicate the range of contexts within which the debate on "NGOs" takes place and which give it different emphases and flavours. It is too readily assumed that the truths emerging from one such context are applicable or relevant to others. "NGO" continues to escape simplistic definitions.

A. Approaches to Civil Society

1. Possibilities of the Legal Approach

It might be assumed that the most straightforward

approach to "civil society" is through the legal provisions made for civil action and especially in relation to freedom of association. The challenge for Russia would then be seen as one of adjusting in some way to the criteria defined in this way, But even "freedom of association" tends to be understood in international law primarily in terms of the right of workers to assemble and form labour unions as defined by an ILO Convention.

This approach would involve a review of national legislation relevant to associations and collective civil action. This is no easy task. The most useful collection, covering the European Union countries plus Switzerland, is that of Elie Alfandari (1990). A second part comments on developments in European Community law in relation to associations. A comparative study of national legislation regarding non-profit organisations in European countries has been made by Carl Hemstrom (1990). A useful brief review of the differences appears in a report by N Fontaine (1986) in relation to the European Parliament's initiative towards a resolution on such bodies. This has been superseded by the work of the Commission of the European Communities (1992) towards the definition of a "European Association". This currently takes the form of a proposal for a programme of work "to assist cooperatives, mutual societies, associations and foundations" (1994).

These efforts are the culmination of a long history of some ten initiatives, dating from 1912, to clarify the legal status of international associations. These are summarized, with texts, in a study by the Union of International Associations (1988) which has been involved in several of them. Of these initiatives, only the Council of Europe's *European Convention on the Recognition of the Legal Personality of International NGOs* has as yet come into force (in 1991, currently with seven signatures).

Clearly the efforts to define or recognize a European or international association call for the clarification of criteria which may be considered to largely define the nature of civil society, independently of its purely civil and human rights aspects. It may be assumed that in the absence of any systematic comparative review of national legislation in this regard, that the points raised in the international texts are effectively efforts to summarize and harmonize whatever shared understanding there is.

From this perspective there is therefore merit in a systematic comparison of the different initiatives towards international legal recognition of what effectively amounts to a "Western" attempt to define such civil activity in its associative dimension. An issue- by- issues comparison of these initiatives forms part of the study for the Union of International Associations (1988). Included in this comparison is the ILO Convention Concerning Freedom of Association and Protection (in force July 1950), and the proposed statute for European Commercial Companies.

A similar approach could be taken by identifying relevant articles in the various human rights treaties. As an experiment, in order to broaden the basis for discussion, it is even possible to use the Universal Declaration of Human Rights as a template to construct a set of articles relevant to human organisations.

Such efforts are undoubtedly necessary and will be a principal focus of other papers at this seminar. But, as Guthrie and Ghils have shown, it is questionable whether they are sufficient to clarify the nature of "civil society", especially where there are concerns about the effective functioning of society. There is always a danger of relying on legislation which emerges from unfortunate compromises or whose implementation is inadequate or lends itself to distorting misinterpretations--- as has proven to be the case with regard to approaches to legal recognition of international NGOs. Nina Belyaeva (1994) makes the point that it is not any single law which can meet the challenge in Russia, but rather there is need for a "whole package of laws, each designed to solve its concrete problem. "But to that requirement she adds the additional conditions:

⇒ Adequate quality of laws designed to meet concrete needs of society in its different forms.

⇒ Close correspondence of laws, not only as to their meaning, but also to the accuracy of legal wording.

There are however dangers in relying too much on legal initiatives especially when democratic pressure for such legal structures must emerge from widespread understanding based on quite different perspectives. Legislation can contributed to the reinforcement of that understanding, but it cannot evoke it.

2. Effective Functioning of Society

In his exploration of Civic, civil or servile?, Robin Guthrie (1994) defines Civil Society as:

It is what citizens do together in their own right at the

bidding of no higher authority, for the common good, and apart, generally speaking, from direct party political affiliation or alignment. The civil society is not concerned primarily with power, although it way be ranged against the excessive concentration or abuse of power in any quarter.

Beyond the purely legal criteria, Daniel Siegel and Jenny Yancey (1992, p.15) comment on the potential for creating a deeply rooted network of organisations and institutions that mediate between the citizen and the State: the connective tissue of a democratic culture. Such organisations are seen as serving several essential functions:

⇒ Providing a means for expressing and actively addressing the varied and complex needs of society

⇒ Motivating individuals to act as citizens in all aspects of society rather than bowing to or depending on state power and beneficence

⇒ Promoting pluralism and diversity in society, such as protecting and strengthening cultural, ethnic, religious, linguistic and other identities

⇒ Creating an alternative to centralized state agencies for providing services with greater independence and flexibility

⇒ Establishing the mechanisms by which governments and the market can be held accountable by the public

They recognize as a major challenge the need to create legal and fiscal structures to regulate and support what is increasingly being referred to as the "third sector". It can however be argued that the legislation in many Western countries, and especially in developing countries, is not especially supportive of such organisations (Judge, 1976). This derives from a continuing debate over the relevance of the third sector to particular social and other issues and to government initiatives in relation to those issues. This ambiguity, often between (and even within) government ministries, is also reflected at the international level, notably amongst United Nations agencies and their departments.

It is clear that associations are often effectively used as partners by some government agencies. It is also clear that the nature of this relationship, and those it benefits, is continually challenged by both sides. Perhaps the most valuable recent evaluations from the United Nations side are the Report of the Secretary- General (1994) and of the Joint Inspection Unit (1993)-- both of which can usefully interpreted for insights on the challenge at the national level, despite the best of intentions. Issues include (Judge, 1976):

⇒ Fiscal support or handicaps, of associations and their personnel;

⇒ Politicization, by government co-optation (or as front organisations), or in opposition to government initiatives;

⇒ Conflicting interpretations of civil rights;

⇒ Fraudulent practices both by associations and by government agencies supporting them (including collusive practices);

⇒ The nature of unacceptable association objectives and practices (including the challenge of sects);

⇒ Conflicting perceptions of the role of nonprofit bodies, notably perception of them as propaganda vehicles for government campaigns;

⇒ Development of patterns of privilege and collusion between certain associations and agencies;

⇒ Human rights issues raised by associations with restrictive membership (whether by religion, gender, age, education, ethnic origin, or other criteria);

⇒ The nature of membership and other relationships to international associations (headquartered elsewhere), especially with regard to programmes defined elsewhere;

⇒ The ability to provide secretariat facilities for international associations with members in other countries, receiving funds from them, and distributing funds to them;

⇒ The nature of any partnership between associations and government agencies.

It is also clear that a multitude of associations are created and develop quite independent of any reference to government initiatives and support--- and often despite subtle efforts to undermine or handicap them. They provide a vehicle for individual expression, as exemplified by sporting and recreational bodies. Despite opposition from certain Western perspectives, Guthrie quotes Ralf Dahrendorf's, view that in a certain sense civil society sustains itself and does not seem to need the state.

It can be argued that the ongoing debates on these issues are in fact themselves a crucial feature of the nature of civil society. Its nature is them as much defined by the questions that are continually being raised as by the particular answer that are sought and found at any one time, in any particular country, or in relationship to any particular issue or government department.

3. Efficiency and Effectiveness Approach

Following from the above, and irrespective of the approaches outlined below, there has emerged a tendency to explore the significance of associations in terms of their efficiency or effectiveness. This approach is naturally favoured by government agencies which have some responsibility for the allocation of subsidies to associations. The argument is that unless an association is efficient or effective according to government- established criteria, then it is irrelevant to government action. A particularly tough review of charities in the UK was completed from this perspective in 1994.

Whilst this approach has its place in the allocation of scarce funds, its limitations are apparent when the significance of an association is not captured by simplistic management criteria. From the perspective of their members, and even for those they may serve, many associations operate quite "satisfactorily" at a high level of "inefficiency". Especially when such bodies make extensive use of voluntary personnel and borrowed facilities, they are able to accomplish a great deal. It is often the case that obsession with criteria of efficiency and effectiveness is specifically rejected by voluntary associations sensitive to other features of civil society.

4. Economic Approach

Efforts to establish the relevance of nonprofit associations have long been marked by a purely economic perspective. Early thinking amongst intergovernmental development agencies, notably the World Bank, UNDP and

OECD, discounted NGOs as of marginal significance to national development. This reinforced national government biases.

With the recognition by UNICEF of the inhuman consequences of "structural adjustment", the role of NGOs in alleviating such "anti- social" effects has been increasingly recognized, especially at the grass- roots level. Recent humanitarian crises in a number of countries, have dramatized the role of NGOs prepared to act under circumstances which forced United Nations agencies, including military forces, to withdraw. Less dramatic examples have been documented in industrialized countries.

The approach of the European Union is still heavily, if not exclusively, marked by the economic perspective. The above- mentioned proposal in the Community for a multi- annual programme of work for cooperatives, mutual societies, associations and foundations (described therein as "enterprises") is justified solely by economic arguments:

⇒ "Whereas cooperatives, mutuals and associations occupy a significant place in economic activity in general and in the development of regions...."

⇒ "Whereas the development of Community policy for cooperatives, mutuals and associations, based on effective competition, is of major importance in terms of boosting the competitiveness of the European economy, job growth, economic and social cohesion in the Community, the further enlargement of the market after 1993, and the development of cooperation with certain non- member countries";

Decisions at the national level with regard to support for

nonprofit associations of any kind are almost solely based on economic criteria--- with their contributions to social welfare being treated in this light as well.

Thinking within United Nations agencies continues to be heavily influenced by the potential relevance of NGOs for development--- itself narrowly defined. Repeated efforts are made to seek proof of this, despite continuing evidence of a remarkable growth in the number of associations, both locally, nationally, regionally, and internationally. Individuals and associations have not been influenced by government efforts to question their relevance to broader and changing understandings of development (as documented, for example, in the UIA's Encyclopedia of World Problems and Human Potential).

Ironically, It is the travel and tourism sector that has least difficulty in recognizing the economic importance of associations and is most interested in promoting their activity. When a large international association holds its meeting in a particular city, bringing together thousands of members from many countries, the economic impact in terms of hotel, travel and tourism is unquestioned--- leading to vigorous efforts to construct Congress centres to profit from this opportunity. The Olympic Games is perhaps the most extreme example. However in 1993 there were some 10,921 international meeting (as registered in the *International Congress Calendar* published by the Union of International Associations) of which 9,227 were not organized by intergovernmental organisations (and of these 6,547 were organized by international NGOs). The number of meetings at the national level is many times greater.

5. Political Approach

The role and relevance of nongovernmental associations has long been questioned from a political perspective, even prior to the stress on their economic role. International recognition of this role was first formally recognized through Article 71 of the United Nations Charter although some recognition of their importance had been accorded by the League of Nations. The political impact of organisations such as Amnesty International and Greenpeace requires no comment. The role of bodies like the Club of Rome (Dror, 1995) in helping to frame the challenges of governance at all levels of society is also unquestioned.

Political Science as a discipline is concerned with the acquisition and use of power, notably in relationship to the governance of society. The associated discipline of international relations is concerned with equivalent phenomena at the international level, especially with regard to foreign relations. NGO have traditionally been of marginal interest from these perspectives because they are considered inherently less powerful than the governments with which these disciplines have been obsessed. International organisations when studied at all are considered an extension of the interest in national foreign policy, leading naturally to a focus on intergovernmental organisations. International NGOs, when studied at all, tend to be viewed through a very limited number of fashionable case studies, notably those on the Red Cross. They have been obliged to take account of transnational corporations once it was demonstrated that their effective power far exceeds that of many nation states. Liberation movements and terrorist groups have also necessitated new thinking.

Despite their recognition of the political power of "lobbies" at the national and international level, practitioners of these disciplines consider NGOs to be essentially irrelevant as serious actors in the fields which they study (Judge, 1977). Many of the lobbies are however institutionalized as associations and NGOs. Ironically political scientists, like lawyers, have themselves created national and international NGOs to represent the international interests of political science and international studies--- but apparently without any concern for the relevance or significance of such organisations according to their own criteria.

Through their obsession with power and influence, and a simplistic approach to the complex ecosystem of NGO, political scientists have reinforced the inability of the international community to appreciate how influence is systematically articulated on global issues. Whether at the national or the international level, there is a misguided attempt to demonstrate that NGOs follow the guidance of governmental organisations. On most, if not all, issues it can however be shown that NGOs functioned as look- out institution warning of problems which governments then reluctantly considered, after as much delay as possible. It is indeed correct that NGOs may then follow the guidance of government organisations, and indeed some may only be capable of following such guidance. But governmental organisations have proven quick to drop issues that can be treated as too controversial or of lower priority. NGOs again then serve to maintain a focus on such issues until those institutions are again prepared to consider them.

Political scientists have also been naive in their

treatment of democratic systems as any assessment of the number and quality of studies on corruption in its many forms will show. Prior to the Italian "clean hands" campaign, there were almost no published studies of corruption in democratic societies-- in comparison with a plethora of studies on other topics which can now be seen to be irrelevant by comparison. As suggested elsewhere (Judge, 1994), even criminal networks can be usefully treated as "NGO". Their influence internationally, notably with respect to the illegal drug and arms trade, should have triggered interest on the part of that discipline. Instead it has reinforced a "candy-floss" (Pre-Watergate) image of the civil society and its democratic processes-- with a naivety which the current evolution of democratic processes-- with a naivety which the current evolution of democracy in Eastern European countries has admirably highlighted. Beyond that one might ask what studies have been undertaken on the power of elitist clubs and secret societies to influence the course of events.

The theoretical interests of political scientists, and the attention accorded to them within the international community, have served to obscure the significance of the continuing proliferation of NGO which have no desire to seek power. Their concern is to articulate their members interests in many fields of human activity, whether it be recreation, science, the arts, religion, or the like. All this political science has served to disparage at a time when international community building and the articulation of values is increasingly perceived as a major issue. The late interest of the discipline in transnational social movements merely serves as a reminder that this discipline's strengths lie in offering explanations about the past not in guiding the evolution of the future and the institutional arrangements required for it.

6. Social Approach

The social sciences concerned with other features of associative activity have been remarkably slow in developing interest in this centuries-old phenomenon (of Dominique Colas, 1992). But the dramatic increase in the numbers of such bodies (Guthrie cites 54,000 associations created in France in 1987, and 4,000 charities each year in the U.K.). At the international level the number of NGOs, in which such bodies may be represented, continues to increase as documented in the Yearbook of International Organisation edited by the Union of International Associations. The number of country-to-international NGO links increased from 24,136 in 1960 to 126,655 in 1994.

At the national and local level, associations have come to be seen as part of the community building process, whether it involves social welfare, philanthropic, recreational or other interests. So many associations have been created in response to concrete social needs that since the end of the 1970s social scientists have been obliged to focus on them, or themselves be found to be irrelevant in their understanding of contemporary society. This has lead to the emergence of an academic specialization termed "third sector research".

Such voluntary associations are of course "NGOs". Many may be referred to as "NGOs" in other settings. However as voluntary associations they tend not to include other bodies known under the NGOs label. Thus it is questionable whether professional, labour, trade, academic or special interest groups would be included as voluntary associations in any "third sector" focus on "NGOs". Third sector research is noteworthy for its total lack of interest in the international NGOs (of which those they study are often members), whatever that might mean within that research framework. However there is much interest in cross-national comparisons of voluntary associations emerging in different countries. The key question is always what is excluded under any label such as "nonprofit" or "NGO".

With rare exceptions, the social sciences, as reinforced by UNESCO (which has a mandate in this area), have never been able to treat NGOs as a phenomenon in their own right. Consequently there is no sense of the variety of organisations falling under this label or of the complex social (eco) system which they constitute. Ironically most of the social sciences are admirably represented through a whole range of international NGOs reflecting their various disciplinary concerns. Such bodies have never considered the social function or setting of what they are.

Such attitudes have prevented the emergence of any understanding of what this rich pattern of thousands of organisations represents for the future of the global system. This is especially tragic when there is concern in many countries at the challenge of community building and the construction of a civil society. Their failure is to be seen notably in their inability to respond effectively to the emerging conditions in Eastern Europe--- and to the appeals for assistance and insights from those regions and the developing world.

7. Psycho-Cultural Approach

The above approaches favoured by government institutions and mainstream academic tend to obscure what might usefully be called a psycho- cultural approach. At best the social sciences, even in their applied form, tend to be concerned with "community building" as an aspect of social welfare, or with the provision of basic needs, and social safety nets. Consequently there is little concern for what would be perceived as the subjective importance of associative activity.

It is clear that the ability of individuals to form associations is a valued human right--- however obscure the concern of the association. It is a form of expression that is vital in an increasingly alienating and atomized society. Membership of associations provides people with opportunities to participate in larger communities, whether or not their are any political implications. It can be vital to the development of an individual sense of identity.

It is ironic that associations of the disabled, of music lovers, of those with particular religious or philosophical beliefs, of obscure scientific specialities, of those concerned with unrecognized values or poorly recognized sports, and the like, should be required to demonstrate their political or economic value in order to justify their existence. The value of such bodies has recently been demonstrated in the case of associations in support of minority ethnic groups in different countries. At the international level this has been most obvious in the case of indigenous peoples. In many of these cases the issue is more cultural identity and its expression-- and the manner in which they are threatened by a variety of social forces-- rather than more conventional social and economic issues.

B. Contrasting Forms of "NGO"

1. Consultative Relationships

Well known to some within the international community is the recognition of certain NGOs by various United Nations bodies for "consultative" purposes. ECOSOC and a number of Specialized Agencies of the UN have such systems of relationships, each governed by different sets of regulations and procedures. As a consequence, "NGO" for one such institution is not the same as "NGO" for another--- notably for any statistical purposes. In practical terms this means that an NGO in consultative relationship with one institution may literally not exist for another. This strange phenomenon is due to the legalistic perspective applied to any form of "consultative" relationship. In this sense a nongovernmental organisation only acquires existence, for a particular part of the UN system, through being recognized through the procedures of the consultative relationship. The consultative status procedure has been replicated in various forms with intergovernmental systems other than the United Nations.

The regulations governing admission to different levels of consultative status are in principal designed to privilege those NGOs of greatest relevance to the programmes of the intergovernmental institution in question. In practice, and increasingly, such relevance is determined on purely political grounds as part of the wider trade-off between factions amongst the number states. Some very curious bodies thus manage to acquire consultative relationship, whilst other quite genuine bodies fail to do so. Ironically, some intergovernmental bodies unable to relate effectively to major intergovernmental institutions through other channels, actually choose to define themselves as NGO in order to achieve such a relationship-- and are accepted in that capacity.

2. Consultancy Relationships

The rigorous approach to consultative relationship is in total contrast to the pragmatism governing any form of "consultancy" practised by intergovernmental institutions (whether or not it has a system of consultative relationship). Thus when in need the secretariats of such institutions are usually free to involve, through a system of subcontracting, any nongovernmental body they choose (whether or not it "exists" in the above sense, or is appropriately representative). Thus nongovernmental bodies may work under formal contract, in a "consultative" capacity, whether or not they have any "consultative relationship". This is one reason that many NGOs find it unnecessary to seek recognition through a system of consultative arrangements. It is also a reason why many other intergovernmental bodies find it unnecessary to develop a system of consultative arrangements. It is equally true that many bodies recognized through such arrangements are never called upon to do contract work, whether or not they are "consulted" as provided by such arrangements. Ironically, form a legal point of view, any such formal contract should only be entered into by the intergovernmental organisations with a legally recognized entity (whether or not its existence is recognized by the institution as indicated above)-- but this constraint is not necessarily respected in practice.

3. Public Information Programmes

Intergovernmental institutions, such as that of the United Nations, devote a considerable proportion of their resources to some form of public relations. In the relevant departments of the institution the role of NGOs in disseminating the message to wider publics has long been recognized-- often to the point of considering it their only role. Such departments therefore enter into semi-formal relationship ("Associate" in the case of the UN Department of Public Information) with organisations--- without any reference to whether the organisations have "consultative relationship". In fact it is not clear whether it is necessary for them to prove that they "exist" in any way. Such bodies may be brought together for regular briefing sessions and may even be better and more rapidly informed than those in consultative relationship. Given the budgetary priorities, it is likely that more institutional resources are devoted per organisation to such associates than to those in consultative relationship

4. Conference Participation

Intergovernmental institutions frequently invite representatives of "NGOs" to their conferences, whether as experts, full participants or observers. Given the level of expertise of some NGOs, such invitations may be necessary to give substantive legitimacy to the intergovernmental conference. Such invitations may be limited to representatives of those bodies in consultative relationship, although they may be extended to those associated with its public relations programme, or they may include or be limited to other bodies considered relevant to the theme or purpose of the event (even to the point of excluding those in consultative relationship). Participation may be arranged with all expenses paid, or even under some consultancy contract. The broad approach to accrediting "NGOs" for the Earth Summit (Rio de Janeiro, 1992) has been experienced as extremely challenging to the formal consultative status procedure, because of the precedent it set in opening participation to organisations not previously considered to be "NGOs" by such intergovernmental organisations.

5. Transnational Corporations

The United Nations has devoted considerable resources to documenting the questionable activities of "transnational corporations"-- which it distinguishes, in contrast to common practice, from "multinational corporations" (a termed reserved by the UN for intergovernmental for profit corporations). Transnational corporations are NGOs, although they may have governmental stockholders. They are of course not "non profit" NGOs, except when they are ineffective in achieving their objectives. However there is considerable debate about how many "NGOs" are actually "non profit-making", especially when they sell publications or services to fund their other activities or are effectively fronts for commercial interests. Transnational corporations have long been viewed negatively by intergovernmental institutions which, on the surface, have few formal relations with them. There are however significant exceptions, notably in the banking world with which the World Bank group is necessarily intimately linked. Given the selective ability to recognize NGOs as "existing", it might be asked how the UN was able to study transnational corporations, which do not have any more international legal existence than NGOs.

Despite their questionable existence, some transnational corporations, like other NGOs, are capable of supplying goods and services. International institutions have a need for such goods and services and consequently have found ways to enter into long- and short -term contracts with transnational corporations (or their local subsidiaries) for their supply. Often the transnational corporations most criticized by the UN have been those on which intergovernmental institutions have been most dependent for office and other supplies and services. Ironically member governments are often major stockholders in transnational corporations and consequently are far from being disinterested parties when institutions put out any call for tender (as their acquisitions of computer equipment have always illustrated). International institutions often have very cosy long-term arrangement with travel agencies, banks and catering services as a visit to any secretariat will reveal.

Ironically, so skilled are transnational corporations in their use of the law and their cultivation of political influence, that they can take the form (in some countries) of "nonprofit" organisations-- known variously as "coordination centres" or "distribution centres". This is notably the case where they can arrange for their regional headquarters (for Europe, say) to receive funds from elsewhere "for administrative purposes", whether or not they are disbursed to other countries. The salaries of hundreds of people coordinating the activities of the corporation may be funded in this way because in such a country the corporation manufactures nothing and makes no profits. In this sense they are "nongovernmental, non profit organisations". In Belgium there is even a Federation of Coordination Centres benefitting from such facilities and assisting other corporations to acquire such nonprofit status. The criteria of a "coordination centres" are specified by royal decree and even make it possible for administrative units within a profit-making corporation office to acquire such status--- provided that the unit (such as a finance department) does not itself make a profit.

6. Press and Media

As part of their public information programme, international institutions necessarily cultivate most assiduously the press, media and wire services. In many cases the media are effectively "NGOs", often as divisions of transnational corporations (see above). They may also be divisions of "NGOs", or NGOs in their own right---whether national or international. There is also the delicate sociological question (see Internet organisations below) of how it is useful to distinguish functionally between an organisation (with its membership) and a media service (with its subscribers and audience). From this perspective, how "nongovernmental" is an international press or media service, whether government owned or not ?

7. Consultative Status NGO Conferences

Some of the NGOs in consultative relationship with a particular institution (as in the case of ECOSOC or UNESCO) may meet together occasionally at a conference and elect some form of committee to represent them in their dealings with that institution (although, despite their function, such bodies are not recognized through any consultative relationship). The conference may have its own semi-permanent task forces and working groups. Each such conference necessarily has a particular understanding of the nature of an "NGO" as defined by the particular rules governing relationship with the accrediting institution--whether or not some of the members of one such conference are also members of another. There has been relatively little coordination between such conferences over the years, whether or not this might have been considered fruitful. Given that such conferences only attract a proportion of the potential membership of those in consultative relationship with the accrediting institution, it might be asked whether the non-participating members reflect some alternative understanding of the nature of an "NGO".

8. "Fundamentalist" NGOs: Citizens Movements

Amongst NGO with some contact with the intergovernmental organisations and their conference there has arisen a tendency to distinguish between "elitist" bodies and those which are genuinely "democratic", "peoples organisations" and "citizens movements". From this perspective only the latter are considered "NGOs" worthy of the name. The many conventional bodies serving a variety of other purposes are considered by them to be of little relevance, being more a part of the problem than of the solution.

9. Humanitarian NGOs

The dramatic problems of disasters, wars and underdevelopment have encouraged a specific kind of "NGO" to respond with various forms of aid and relief. These NGOs have, especially with Somalia, Bosnia and Rwanda, acquired a great deal of prominence in the media.

Consequently for many sectors of the public, the media, as well as public institutions, these are the only kind of "NGO" known. Some of these relief and aid bodies are only too happy to reinforce this view by considering no other NGOs as relevant--- especially to the emergencies with which they deal on an hourly basis. This view is encouraged by the fact that many of these relief bodies are national in origin, with little if any claim to being international in their membership or source of funds. They therefore have little reason to associate themselves with other kinds of NGO, such as those typical of the consultative relationship. They often seek to provide aid quite independently of the intergovernmental system, often prior to any willingness of intergovernmental institutions to acknowledge any need for that relief. Somalia highlighted situations in which such NGOs were acting before the UN was aware of the problem, in areas where UN military subsequently did not dare to go, and continued to act after UN forces had been withdrawn because of the level of danger. Bosnia highlighted situations in which the UN refused to provide military protection to nongovernmental relief convoys for fear of endangering the UN military.

10. Field- Level NGOs

There was a time when the UN- inspired terminology of "NGO" was only applied to those international bodies in some form of direct relationship with intergovernmental institutions. With the recognition of vital role played by NGOs at grass- roots level, came the recognition of the role of national and local NGOs, especially in developing countries. This had long been argued by international NGOs, since many of these local bodies were represented internationally through them as members. National suspicion towards NGOs sending aid workers from industrialized countries reinforced the tendency within intergovernmental institutions, notably UNDP, to bypass international NGOs and enter into direct relationship with local bodies. International NGOs were perceived as inappropriate partners in many forms of development aid--- despite the crisis in development aid. UNDP Resident Representatives, never enthusiastic about international NGOs (or any NGOs for that matter), were instructed to establish relationships with grass roots organisations within their operating territory. For many intergovernmental development programmes, the nation of "NGOs" was thus extended to grass- roots organisations-- despite the legal problems of recognizing the existence of bodies that were not in consultative status.

11. Semi-Autonomous Organisations

A significant number of NGOs are not created in a way that leaves them totally independent. Some international "NGOs" are deliberately set up on government initiative (as was the case in the Communist bloc). Unknown to many of their members, some may be "front" organisations set up by governments or commercial interests for political or other purposes-- even at the international level. Whether or not they are created in this way, they may be provided with offices and subsidies by government throughout their existence, so that although they may have an international board of some kind, they are bound to the country of their origin. A number of intergovernmental institutes exist on the same basis. Intergovernmental organisations may themselves catalyze the creation of an international "NGOs". This may be followed by provision of office and other facilities (even within the intergovernmental secretariat) together with some form of financial support even on a long-term basis.

12. Staff Associations in Intergovernmental Institutions

It is seldom recognized that the staff of large intergovernmental institutions form associations ranging from staff labour unions, through sporting, dramatic and other interest groups, to some which may have a humanitarian purpose. These bodies are of course "NGOs", although few would name them as such, and they themselves would reject the label. They are certainly not intergovernmental organisations by any definition of the term, although in the case of the unions they may acquire a special form of recognition and may be the subject of resolutions and agreements with the intergovernmental body. They are not however part of any consultative relationship arrangement. Extensive facilities may be provided for them. Only as federations of civil servants (from a variety of institutions) do they acquire a status resembling that of more conventional NGOs.

13. Voluntary Associations: The Third Sectors

At the neighbourhood, urban, regional and national level, there is a burgeoning of associative activity. Much of this is seen as part of the community building process, whether it involves social welfare, philanthropic, recreational or other interests. Such voluntary associations have become of considerable interest to social scientists leading to the emergence of an academic specialization termed "third sector research". Such voluntary associations are of course "NGO". Many may be referred to as "NGOs" in other settings. However as voluntary associations they tend not to include other bodies known under the NGO label. Thus it is questionable whether professional, labour, trade, academic or special interest groups would be included as voluntary associations in any "third sector" focus on "NGOs". The emphasis on "voluntary" precludes the inclusion of many kinds of body and fails to address the issue of the ways in which even intergovernmental bodies may be considered "voluntary". Third sector research is noteworthy for its total lack of interest in the international NGOs (of which those they study are often members), whatever that might mean within that research framework. However there is much interest in cross-national comparisons of voluntary associations emerging in different countries.

14. Cooperatives and Mutual Aid Societies

The cooperatives sector involves millions of people as members of some form of cooperative. Such cooperatives are "NGOs" as are mutual aid societies (and "tontines" in Africa). They are also "nonprofit-making" according to some definitions of the term. However, tainted as they are by a commercial interest in satisfying their basic needs, cooperatives are rarely if ever recognized as NGOs, although this is not the case of groupings of cooperatives into federations or associations.

15. Philanthropic Foundations

Foundations allocating funds to worthy causes are in most cases "NGOs" and are seldom set up to be "profit-making". They are not however commonly recognized as NGOs, although some may even be closely associated with development and relief activity. Few of them are international in their source of funds and decision-making, although many are international in the distribution of their funds. Few are recognized within any consultative status or other arrangement by intergovernmental institutions, although a number of them have been a source of funds for the programmes and meetings of such institutions which may assiduously cultivate them for that purpose. UNESCO has special provisions for relating to "foundation and similar institutions", although in attempting carefully to distinguish them from NGOs creates problems in relation to the understanding in other parts of the UN systems.

16. Trade Associations and Cartels

Trade associations are groupings of manufacturers and trading groups seeking to protect and further the interest of their economic sector. They are certainly "NGOs" and may be considered "nonprofit-making" in that they do not seek to make or distribute a profit to their members. But like labour unions and other professional bodies, they exist in order to further the economic interests of their members--- effectively to ensure that their members reap some kind of financial benefit as a consequence of their membership. It is for this reason that, at least in the case of the trade associations, they are viewed as not being "genuine" NGOs by other bodies in the "NGO community" who do not have this indirect pecuniary interest--- however much such NGOs may otherwise be preoccupied by fund-raising and the compromises it may entail. And whilst trade associations may take the legal form of a nonprofit organisation, semi-formal cartels and price-fixing arrangements, may not be institutionalized in any conventional way. However it is often difficult to distinguish functionally between a trade association and a cartel--- since many are deliberately set up to "regulate" their industry, to ensure a "higher quality" of service, which is frequently the justification for the exclusion of potential members perceived as threatening their interests. This tendency can often be seen in professional organisations--- even those purporting to have scientific and similar commitments. As part of the interest of the United Nations in transnational corporations, international cartels and price-fixing arrangements have been the focus of considerable attention even though such arrangements do not "exist" in any legal sense.

17. Lobbies

The secretariats and conferences of intergovernmental institutions are the subject of considerable attention from special interest lobbies, as is the case at the national level. This phenomenon has acquired major proportions in the case of the European Union, especially in Brussels, where they have become one of the major vehicles for "consulting" wider society--- no lobby, no consultation! These lobbies may in fact be set up by trade associations and may be the sole reason for their existence. Lobbies may however be loose coalitions of special interest groups (including more conventional NGOs), whether or not they are economically based or have some non-economic, social or other interest. Lobbies may of course be coalitions of government representatives, or be heavily supported by particular governments. Although questionable in the latter case, all lobbies may be considered "NGOs"-- although what of cases where intergovernmental alliances act as lobbies and/or voting blocs ?

18. Political Parties

A political party is a "NGO" even when its representatives are elected to government, whether in power or in opposition. Of course it would not be referred to as an "NGO". Political parties of similar tendencies in different countries may combine together internationally, as in the case of the socialists or liberals, to form a body which takes the form of a conventional international NGO. Looser coalitions may take the form of a lobby, or voting bloc, as in the case of the European Parliament. It is questionable how "nongovernmental" these can be considered, even though they are certainly not "intergovernmental."

19. Elitist, Secretive Clubs

There is a tendency for the key figures of major international and other bodies to form semi-formal international clubs. This is notably the case when such people retire, or lose their formal positions. These clubs are definitely "NGOs", although the representative of one endeavoured to label it as a "NGO". Some of them may include key figures in transnational corporations-- or they may even be restricted to such people. Such organisations have absolutely no need to seek any form of consultative or other status. Indeed they are wont to boast of their ability to gain (immediate) access to key-decision makers, whether from within international institutions or in their member states. These decision makers may even be members (in their private capacity) of elitist clubs, and consider themselves privileged to be so.

20. Secret Societies

The existence of many secret societies has been documented, both prior to recognition of "NGOs" and up to the present day. Best known and documented in the West is perhaps freemasonry in its various forms and branches -- involving those at the highest level of society. Related forms are the Muslim brotherhoods, although many of these may resemble religious orders. Such bodies must certainly be considered "NGOs" whether or not they accept the label or are accepted as part of the "NGO community", especially when "illegal" (as in the case of Chinese triads and tongs). As with trade associations, whether all of these bodies are "nonprofit- making" is also open to question-- especially when membership is seen as a guarantee of competitive and career advantages.

21. Religious orders and cults

These bodies, and above all those within the framework of the Catholic Church, may be considered as the historical precursors of many NGOs. Some date back to the early centuries of the Christian era. Some were responsible for articulating many of the voting and other practices now widespread within the international community. As missionary orders many initiated the first crude forms of "development aid", however questionable this may now be seen to have been. Some, such as Opus Dei, resemble secret societies. They are certainly "NGOs", although few would seek to be considered as "NGOs" or would seek institutional recognition by intergovernmental Organisations. The early military and hospitaller orders of knights have acquired considerable prestige, to the point that some are even accorded diplomatic status in certain countries. Ironically the relationship of many of them to the Vatican is functionally very similar to the consultative relationship other NGOs have with intergovernmental institutions. Very similar to such orders, but lacking their legitimacy, are the many international groupings of individuals which are frequently labelled as cults and sects--- although some would be considered religious groups and churches. They resemble the religious orders in that they may have a strong hierarchical structure and well-defined practices and rituals. Often they owe their origin to some charismatic individual.

22. International Crime Rings

Also neccessarily secretive by nature are the increasingly international criminal groups of which the mafia (and its other Mediterranean variants), and their East Asian analogues, have been well-publicized. Although they themselves may not be illegal, since they have no "existence" anyway, their activities are very much so, at least in certain jurisdictions. They may like transnational corporations be considered "NGOs", even "voluntary associations", although like the corporations any pecuniary interest excludes them from the nonprofit cluster of organisations. However it should be recognized that not all crime rings have strictly pecuniary interests, as is the case of the paedophile networks and terrorist groups-- which could be seen from some perspectives as legitimate interests that have been driven underground. Their "illegality" is of course a matter of question and degree, especially when compared to the many de facto NGOs which decline to register themselves within the national jurisdictions where they operate.

23. Terrorist Groups and Liberation Movements

Terrorist groups should definitely be considered "NGOs" and may well operate internationally with international membership, funding and support. Like many "NGOs" they may receive special support from particular governments and IGOs. As noted above, their "illegality" may be a matter of interpretation, depending on the jurisdiction where the question is raised. Their relationship to political parties, and even intergovernmental organisations, may raise many questions. There is of course a confusion between "liberation movements" and "terrorists groups" depending on perspective. Few liberation movements have avoided the lable of "terrorist" group at some stage in their existence. Ironically some "liberation movements" have been funded by more conventional "NGOs" and IGOs, leading to action interpreted as "terrorist" in the countries where they were perpetrated. Intergovernmental organisations have at times adopted exceptionally supportive policies to liberation movements (such as the PLO)---whether or not they were experienced by others as terrorist groups, and whether or not they could be said to have any legal existence within the terms of the intergovernmental organisation.

24. Legally Established International NGOs

The initiatives to provide international legal status to NGOs date back to the beginning of the century (although religious orders may be said to have had legal status for centuries within the framework of canon law). Most recently these have resulted in a Convention of the Council of Europe which has been ratified by a handful of countries. The European Union has also taken major steps to provide legal status in other member countries for any nongovernmental established in one of its member countries. This has yet to take any tangible form-- and when it does it may apply only to European organisations and not to those with membership in other regions. For all intents and purposes so-called "international nongovernmental organisations" are not legally recognized international entities. They do not exist in any legal sense at the international level. The pretence is cultivated that such bodies having acquired national legal status, for administrative purposes in one country, can be considered as legal entities in other countries. In a few countries the situation is slightly more creative in that special provision may be made for "national" organisations with foreigners on the board. The major exception is Belgium where a specific law allows for the establishment of "international nongovernmental organisations". Like transnational corporations, NGOs cannot yet exist as international legal entities, although they can exist as distinct legal entities in more than one country.

25. Informal Organisations and Networks

There are many associations of individuals and groups which have been deliberately set up internationally so as not to take the form of a structured organisation in any conventional sense. The lable "network" is often favoured when such groupings choose to lable themselves at all. Although organized according to many interpretations of the term, such groupings are often quite vigorous in claiming that they are not an "organisation", although they may well function with greater energy, effectiveness and continuity than many organisations. But clearly, according to a looser definition, they are definitely "NGOs". Lacking statutes, however, they are seldom drawn into any form of relationship with intergovernmental organisations. However, within the intergovernmental community, many informal networks of officials and government representatives may be created in order to bypass perceived bureaucratic and procedural inefficiencies. Whether these too are to be considered "ngos" is a matter of debate, although they would undoubtedly resist the label. Informal organisations are often most fruitful when membership is not restricted by conventional categories. In this way they may acquire some of the character of hybrid organisations.

26. Electronic Organisations: Internet

Since the late 1970s electronic mail and computer conferencing systems have developed from their purely inter-university and military origins in the USA, to the point of including an estimated 35 million subscribers worldwide on various systems loosely grouped within a framework described as Internet. This is essentially a computer communication protocol allowing many computer systems to link their communication facilities. Within this highly complex system of networks there are literally thousands of "conferences" and discussion groups which functionally differ little from a conventional membership organisations-- except that communications are much more rapid and the need for formal structures may be much reduced. Very formal structures may however be provided by software protocols.

Many of these electronic organisations or networks have international participants. Many focus on the same issues as more conventional voluntary organisations. Some of then are highly involved in coordinating response to disasters, whether within countries or around the world, and in the preparation for major United Nations Conferences (to the point that much preparatory documentation for such conferences is now circulated, consulted and commented upon through such electronic organisations). Some users are so imbued by the advantages of this form of communication that they consider more conventional organisations as completely obsolete.

Although some of these networks are "governmental", notably those set up by the military, most can be usefully perceived as "ngos" for which legal status is clearly not an issue. For an increasing number of conventional nongovernmental bodies, one immediate strategic issue is to work out ways of transferring some (if not all) of their traditional communication procedures and administration into an electronic environment--- bearing in mind the level of electronic surveillance that such communications have been designed to permit. There is therefore a sense of international organisations moving into some form of electronic "orbit" around the "global village". There is also the attendant danger that, whilst very real to themselves, their reality and value to those without such facilities may continue to be quite questionable.

It is possible that many of the more problematic issues concerning the relationship between State and Society will be bypassed within this new communication environment. In fact it could be argued that the mode of operation of the Internet is an extremely good illustration of many of the dimensions of the civil society. References by many authors to the "global village" are an indication of this.

27. Transnational Social Movements

There is increasing recognition that, irrespective of the existence of particular organisations, there are a number of transnational movements which transcend any conventional organisational focus. These include the women's movement, the peace movement, the environmental movement, the civil rights movement, the youth movement, and the like. Internet may itself be seen as such a movement. Many organisations may be associated with each such movement, but the movement is not identified with any particular organisation. This is especially important since many such organisations tend to emerge and disappear with some frequency as a result of individual enthusiasms, funding opportunities, personalities and factional squabbles. The unresolved question is the extent to which any such movement can, in its own right, be usefully described as a "ngo".

28. International Communities

Great attention is increasingly given in the media to the views and action of the "international community" which appears to imply some clustering of intergovernmental organisations and powerful member states. The "diplomatic community" (as a collectivity) is something that has long been recognized in a loose form with some legal recognition, notably in the facilities accorded to diplomats individually. Within major capital cities there is often an "international community" of people involved in the diplomatic community, international organisations (governmental and nongovernmental; profit-making and nonprofit-making), international cultural activities, and the like. This could be seen as an informal organisation--- but necessarily of the nongovernmental variety. But international communities may also acquire a more physical form when people from different countries choose (or are obliged) to live in the same area, as tends to be the case with some diplomatic ghettos or "foreign quarters", which may even be enclosed, as with the campus of an international university. But of much more interest here are those efforts to consciously set up international experimental communities to explore various alternative modes of living, spiritual practice or artistic pursuit. These are often perceived as extremely threatening to the national or local cultures where they are physically based, as has been vividly demonstrated by communities such as Findhorn (Scotland), Rajneesh (Poona and Antelope), and Auroville (India). These too are "NGO".

29. Hybrid (or mixed) Organisations

Efforts to define "NGO" often naively assume that organisations must necessarily exist in some pure form. In fact there have been many organisation, like ICSU and IUCN, which combine several seemingly incompatible characteristics, notably the governmental and nongovernmental dimensions. Thus some organisations, which are not recognized as intergovernmental, have both national government bodies and national nongovernmental bodies as members. This may occur where a particular function is articulated through a government body in one member country, but through a nongovernmental body in another country. Organisations may have a whole range of combinations of profit-making and nonprofit-making activities. They may combine informal and formal structures, permanent and periodic structures. Clearly some may combine legal and quasi-legal activities, notably in the case of "front" organisations.

30. "Self-Defined" Organisations

For those who make frequent use of the term "NGO" it is easy to forget that many bodies define their organizational realities with other terms. This is typically the case with many professional, technical and scientific bodies. It is also true of labour unions, trade associations and many religious bodies. Although they are "ngos" they tend to refer to themselves as unions, federations, committees or by some special term. They do not identify with the "nongovernmental" dimension, or with "NGO", possibly in some cases because they may have quite close relations to government (as in the case of the hybrid organisations above). Some international scientific bodies are far more concerned with their recognition by the International Council of Scientific Unions than by any intergovernmental consultative status. In this way ICSU functions rather like the Vatican for religious orders--leaving many scientific bodies as unrecognized, whether they seek such recognition or not. This is also true of sporting federations which acquire wider significance, if they seek it, only when they are recognized by the International Olympic Committee and the General Association of International Sports Federations, not through any relation to the intergovernmental system. Indeed, as the periodic Olympic events demonstrate, it is governments who are hypersensitive to the needs of such nongovernmental bodies. But for self-defined organisations, such wider recognition, whether governmental or nongovernmental, may be largely a matter of indifference provided they can further their particular interests.

C. Implications

1. Desperate Oversimplification: Butterfly Catching

It should be clear from the above that no coherent typology of organisations is likely to emerge in the near future. Those with skills in organisation studies pursue particular examples of "NGOs" in a desperate effort to impose a simplistic label on them and to "fix" them--- rather in the same way as butterfly catchers. The ngo phenomenon, in all its variety and richness, continues to evolve and escape such methodologies. The social sciences succeed only in capturing partial understandings, and often only those typical of the past. There is no ability to articulate understandings relevant to the future, especially to the design of new and more appropriate forms of organization.

Any definition of "NGO" should therefore not be evaluated on the basis of what it includes, but rather should be tested against what it explicitly or implicitly excludes. The reasons for such exclusion should be highlighted, together with their political implications.

2. The Mythical Ideal "NGO"

The review of organisational forms above has in many cases highlighted the fact that creators of organisations are effectively under pressure to produce what amounts to an "ideal" or simplistic form. So ideal, that it is useful to ask whether this is not deliberately done in order to guarantee that it would be impossible to achieve.

In focusing on "nongovernmental", it became clear that other dimensions were implicit in any understanding of "NGO". In the case of the intergovernmental system, there is much ambiguity about whether and how an organisation should be "international".

An associated issue, is the considerable pressure to ensure that organisations are "representative"--- unless of course they are a source of funding for the intergovernmental organisation or its programmes. The criteria of representativity can be pushed to the degree of requiring membership from every country of the world. This requirement may ignore questions as to whether particular intergovernmental organisations themselves respect this principle (as with the case of UNESCO and the absence of countries such as USA and the UK from its membership). There are many specialized intergovernmental organisations without universal membership (it would be ridiculous to expect a landlocked country to be a member of a deep-sea fishing organisation).

Then there is the implicit requirement of permanence and continuity. Can an organisations exist when it really only takes any form on the occasion of some periodic meeting?

But it is not correct that many such meeting series operate functionally, and more effectively, than some organisations?

Another implicit requirement is transparency. To acquire consultative status, organisations are usually required to present their financial report. Unless an organisation is transparent, it cannot be included in the implicit definition of NGO.

Also implicitly important is the openness of an organisation to membership. There is some question as to whether a "closed" organisation should be considered acceptable to the intergovernmental system. This of course raises such questions as male membership in women's organisations, and vice versa, or non-Christian membership of Christian bodies.

Despite the absurdities of the legal system, there is an implicit requirement that the international organisation should have some acceptable form of legal status--- even when the legal status defines the organisation as being "national". Related to this is of course the expectation that the organisation should not be involved in any form of illegal activity, even though promoting some forms of change may itself be defined as illegal under some regimes.

There is also an implicit requirement that an organisation should not only be nonprofit-making but also that it should acquire its funds from a representative range of countries--- even when exchange control regulations make this quite problematic for certain member countries. The fact that an organisation endeavours to raise funds to survive, by selling publications and services at a profit, is also viewed as suspect.

Combining these criteria makes it virtually impossible to create an NGO that cannot be attacked as tainted or blemished in some way-- as is of course true for must intergovernmental organisations.

Should an international NGO therefore endeavour to obtain consultative status ? Perhaps the best answer is that of the 436 organisations represented on all continents, 34% consider that they do not need to seek or acquire any form of consultative status.

3. Multiple Legal Forms

In creating new organisations there need be little sympathy for the niceties of legal status under particular regimes. Nonprofit organisations need to learn from their commercial brethren, the "transnational corporations" who are also international "outlaws".

Such corporations have learnt to distinguish between their legal form in a particular country and the operational form which transcends national frontiers. Nonprofit organisations have given excessive attention to providing themselves with a single legal form, carefully choosing the country in which to do so, and accepting whatever structural compromises this forced upon them.

If organisations can distinguish between their existence as social realities and their existence as legal realities then they can follow, and improve upon, the approach taken by transnational corporations. In some countries it is possible to have de facto organisations which are not legally registered in any way. In this sense the organisation's members must depend upon themselves, rather than any legal regulations, to be self-regulating.

The crucial step is to operate from this social reality, creating legal realities of whatever form, wherever it is appropriate. Since in most cases the social reality does not exist for the law, it is only through some legal "mask" that the organisation becomes visible in whatever legal system the organisations chooses to operate.

In practice this means that the organisation can constitute itself legally in different ways, in different countries, for different purposes. As noted above, transnational corporations can take the form of "nonprofit" organisations in certain countries if this meets their needs. There is no reason way nonprofit organisations should not take a profit-making form where it suits them. In fact some organisations, even within a single country, choose to adopt a triple form of: nonprofit membership organisation; foundation; and profit-making corporation. The only bond between them is a cross-linking directorship that guarantees the coherence of the underlying social reality.

The possibility is in fact analogous to that of multiple passport holders who choose which passport to present when they have to deal with any legal system. Since the legal system can only recognize the piece of paper, this creates no problems. Organisations should consider becoming, in effect, "multiple passport holders". If a particular country does not have adequate provision for nonprofit organisations, then set up the organisation there as a profit-making corporation. If it requires that only nationals of the country should be on the board, then arrange matters in that way for that country.

Note also that on each occasion that an intergovernmental organization accords recognition to an international NGO, the NGO is in effect being given a separate "passport" and identity. For such recognition is currently the only mechanism through which international NGOs acquire some very weak form of identity within the framework of international law. Governed as they are by seperate treaties, the recognition by one intergovernmental body is legally distinct form that by another. Multiple "passport holding" is therefore already a reality for some NGOs with multiple consultative status.

It may be argued that provision of national legal status, where it is supportive rather than deliberately obstructive, provides many guarantees, notably in the event of any abuse of power or funds. Whilst this may be of significance within a particular country, it is quite impractical for an organizations operating in a number of countries, whose secretariat and accounts may not even be in the country where it is legally registered. In fact, unless the organisation is self-regulating, so that abuse is avoided or internally controlled, it is unlikely that recourse to any national legal system would be worth the effort. And there are few documented cases of successful legal pursuit of abuse within international NGOs.

Of course some countries have taken advantage of the absurdities of the international legal system by setting themselves up as "off-shore havens". Transnational corporations have been very skilled in using the opportunities that these create. Is it not possible that some countries could similarly set themselves up as "havens" for international nonprofit organisations? It could offer a lucrative opportunity for an island economy with no other resources--provided telecommunication links were good. Note that this is primarily a question of financial transfers, not necessarily a question of having a secretariat there. And even then, as Liechtenstein has so admirably demonstrated, even grocery shops are willing to put up a brass-plate indicating that they are the "headquarters" of some corporation. Why not of an international NGO ?

Then there is the question of the name of the organisation. Again provided the internal social reality is well- articulated, the organisation can even adopt different names in different contexts without creating any threat to its identity.

Faced with an unsympathetic international legal system, international nonprofit organisations should be encouraged to explore these possibilities with the aid of sympathetic lawyers. In fact it might be asked why lawyers (and especially international associations of lawyers with a strong social commitment) have not taken the lead in articulating these possibilities. For make no mistake, these techniques are already used by some nonprofit organisations, notably those with something to hide. But an innovative approach to legal status can be taken without engaging in any procedures that might be considered unethical.

4. Organisational Apartheid

The manner in which different types of organisation continue to disparage each other is a tragedy. Each kind of organisation trends to think of itself as the only really useful organisation form. Other forms are considered as unfortunate obstacles or completely irrelevant. There is a definite sense in which a system of organisational aparheid has developed. To intergovernmental organisations, NGOs are the "coloured" organisation of the world. The mind set which governed colonial disparagement of coloured peoples has not gone away-- it is embedded in the attitude of intergovernmental organisations to NGOs. There are even parallels in the various forms of condescension practised when NGOs are involved in the activities of intergovernmental organisations.

There is and irony in the dismissive remark of a members of the European parliament that NGOs all seem to be very "worthy" bodies and therefore inappropriate partners in any intergovernmental initiative. Has the situation reached the point that intergovernmental bodies can only effectively relate to "unworthy" bodies ?

Even more tragic is the degree to which, even amongst NGOs, one type of organisation considers the other irrelevant or inappropriate--- a phenomenon analogous to ethnic tensions and conflicts. With the emergence of NGO fundamentalism of various flavours--- the possibility of "ethnic cleansing" should not be excluded.

5. What's In a Name ?

The term "nongovernmental" has been resented by many organisations. It is indeed a manifestation of organisational apartheid--- reminiscent of the "nonwhite" label so frequent in racist societies.

In considering this label, established and reinforced

by the UN, it is interesting to recall the way in which "multinational" corporations became defined as "transnational" corporations within the UN system. No multinational corporation considers itself to be a transnational corporation-- but they are largely indifferent to the UN anyway. And perhaps it was a useful ploy to have all the negative assessments about such corporations attached to the label "transnational" rather than to the name with which the multinationals identify amongst themselves and to the non-intergovernmental community. The power of name calling is considerably undermined if the person does not identify with the name anyway.

So if "NGO" is the result of a UN manipulation of reality analogous to "transnational", the challenge is to discover the name (like "multinational") with which such bodies can identify. The problem may be insoluble, given the level of organisational apartheid practised between organisations-- even between NGOs.

But if it is impossible to abandon the initials "NGO", perhaps it is possible the reframe their significance in a more positive light. One candidate might be "Necessary Governance Organisations" (in French "Organisations Necessaires a la Governance" (ONGs)). The corresponding reframing of "IGO" might then be "Insufficient Governance Organisations" (which again is better in French as "Organisation insuffisantes pour la gouvernance"). Such reframing borrows from the logic of science where factual evidence may be necessary, but not sufficient, for a complete proof.

10

NGOs in A Global Future

NGOs in the new millennium share in the same mixture of feelings that permeates the wider field of politics, ideas and social activism. There is plenty of excitement about new possibilities, tempered by widespread anxiety about the future. In the NGO world, this feeling of excitement stems from the opportunities for civic action that global trends are creating, on a scale never witnessed before. The anxiety arises because more critical questions are being asked about the role development NGOs will play in occupying these spaces, especially aid-dependent intermediaries that lack any democratic means of governance and accountability.

Our purpose here is not to provide a comprehensive review of the literature or of experience, but to suggest a framework to help you think the issues through and make connections between your own contributions, and the wider picture. The first part looks at the changing context for NGOs in international development, and identifies some of the challenges this context throws up. There key trends are explored, corresponding to the themes that will run throughout the conference proceedings:

⇒ globalisation, which re-shapes patterns of global poverty, accentuates inequalities, and promotes new levels of insecurity in the world.

⇒ the reform of international co-operation to deal with these developments, moving away from foreign aid to embrace a broader focus on rules, standards and interventions to protect the most vulnerable.

⇒ "complex political emergencies", which are characteristic of the post-Cold War disorder as state authority erodes and people take refuge in ethnicity and religion.

Underlying these three, inter-related trends is the need for new forms of solidarity- or new "social contracts"-between citizens of different polities and new structures of authority at different levels of the world system. It is these new relationships- expressed through partnerships, alliances and other forms of collaboration- that provide the frameworks for NGO innovations in economics, politics and social policy. However, responding effectively to these challenges requires NGOs to develop different roles, relationship and capacities, and these organisational implications are explored in the second part of the paper.

One might question the wisdom of launching such a wide-ranging, futuristic discussion at a time when so much remains outstanding from the agenda of the first two Manchester Conferences how to achieve and measure impact, work with donors and governments without co-optation, and remain accountable to different constituencies

- yet progress on these issues is taking place, albeit in piecemeal fashion. What is lacking is a broader framework that relates changes inside the NGO community to the great economic and political questions of our times. Our hope is that the conference papers and debates will generate more of this framework than we currently have, so helping us to respond more effectively to global trends to the benefit of those we seek to serve. Ultimately, it is these broader questions that will determine whether development NGOs are major players on the world stage in the 21st Century, for if they are not part of a truly "global future", then the future of NGOs - at least in their present disguise - may be bleak.

The Changing Global Context

Globalisation

What is Globalisation ? Technology and Culture?

In the late- 1990s, no conference is complete without a panel on globalisation. There is much disagreement on the meaning and extent of this phenomenon, but there is surely a basic reality at work which cannot be ignored. This reality is globalisation as technology-driven fact: electronic communication, declining transport costs, more flexible forms of economic organisation, and the growing importance of mobile assets (like finance and knowledge) establish an increasingly uniform horizon of production possibilities across national borders, integrating markets around the world and internationalising decisions about jobs and investment. The consequences of this process in a world of unequal producers and consumers are well-known-spectacular rewards for those well- endowed with the conditions required to take advantage of these opportunities; increasing pressures on those less well-endowed to sell their labour, family life or environment cheaply in order to make a living; and rising inequality between these two groups, both within and between countries. In 1998, the combined income of three billion people in the Third World was less than the collective assets of 358 multi-billionaires; Bill Gates' fortune (prior to the late - summer stock market crash) was worth more than that of the poorest 40 per cent of the US population put together. (UNDP 1998). Rather than solid and stable blocs of 'North and South', NGOs in the 21st Century will confront a rapidly changing patchwork quilt of poverty and exclusion that requires new and genuinely - international responses - notwithstanding the continued presence of a hard core of absolutely-poor people in South Asia and Sub-Saharan Africa. As recent events have demonstrated, the "new rich" (like those in East and Southeast Asia), and those previously well-provided for in social protection (like the former-Soviet Union) can become the "new poor" on an epic scale within a matter of a year. Inequality, exclusion and the insecurity they breed look set to drive global politics for the next generation and beyond.

Underlying these trends is a more controversial process of "globalisation as culture": the homogenising of values and aspirations to Western norms of individualism and consumerism what Hobsbawm (1994) sees as the real "cultural revolution" of our century. The media-recently transformed into a truly global institution controlled by a small number of multinational corporations-now plays a key role in these cultural processes. Some commentators dismiss such conclusions as superficial-capitalism has always adapted to the local context; others see culture as pivotal in the coming "clash of civilisation" as those who see themselves threatened or disempowered by cultural re-colonisation take refuge in ethnic or religious identity, often violently expressed. The conflicts that this process generates are considered in Section 3. Despite these divergent interpretations, all agree that there is considerable room for manoeuvre in retaining the potential benefits of globalisation-as-fact, while addressing the potential costs of globalisation-as-culture. The real debate is not whether globalisation exists and will continue (it does and it will), but about how its costs and benefits are distributed, and on that question there is little that is pre-ordained by technology or impervious to politics. The issue for our conference is clear: what role do NGOs have in reshaping the processes of an evolving global capitalism so that all can enjoy the fruits of economic progress without losing what gives equal meaning to their lives ?

On this issue there is no consensus. Some NGOs advocate de-linking from the world economy in order to promote self-reliance and protect local cultures; others think this unrealistic and opt for various forms of constructive engagement; while the most optimistic embrace globalisation as a progressive social revolution in the making. 3 We hope the conference will explore these positions and look at what NGOs are doing to advance each of them in practice. There are unlikely to be any universal answers here, especially since so much received wisdom has been abandoned in the post Cold-War retreat from grand theory and simplistic 'either/

or' strategic choices. We are all experimenting, and learning as we go. This has important implications for the future of NGO advocacy which are taken up in Section Three.

Responses To Globalisation: The Role Of Civil Society

Despite the diversity that characterises these debates, there remains a common thread that runs through all NGO positions: civil society can act as a countervailing force to the expanding influence of markets and the declining authority of status. Although workers have less power in integrated markets, consumers have more; and while the erosion of national sovereignty does leave some groups more vulnerable to the abuse of unaccountable power, it also opens up more possibilities for civic organisations to link with each-other across national boundaries in new structures of governance, especially as information technology makes it easier to move from traditional hierarchies to more flexible networks and alliances. The potential globalisation of governance and decision-making is explored in Section 2, though it is worth remembering that access to IT is also skewed toward those with more power and resources.

The true extent and potential of civil society is a controversial subject, especially at the global level. Some perceive a fundamental "power shift" as state-based authority recedes, while others questions the ability of non-state groups to fill the resulting political vacuum. These doubts apply especially to development NGOs because of their dependence on foreign aid and their non-representative character. Nevertheless, an increasing number of NGOs are diversifying their funding sources and generating high levels of their own income from a mixture of commercial ventures, cost-recovery and local fund-raising, especially in South Asia and Latin America. In the process , they are sinking roots into their own societies and assuming more of the characteristics of a genuine civic actor, rather than a service delivery contractor. The rise of civil society in the South is uneven and in many areas slow, but it is happening, and this obviously has important implications for NGOs in the North and for the broader global civic alliances that are taking shape around the world. The Johns Hopkins Comparative Study of the "Third- Sector" found more than one million such organisations in India and 210,000 in Brazil (Salamon and Anheier 1997). These are exceptional cases, but even where the number and range of civil society organisations is smaller, individual agencies are developing a research and policy-lobbying capacity to rival those in the North, alongside their activities in service-delivery.

Whatever else globalisation may be doing, it has not changed the fundamental reality of poverty of assets- the maldistribution of productive resources, skills and capacities that lies at the root of the problem. Integrated markets increase the importance of some of these assets (like knowledge and organisational strength), and decrease the significance of others (the fixed factors of production), but the imperative of re-distribution remains. NGOs have a vital role in advocating for it, especially where fuzzy-minded "Third-Way" thinking makes all talk of redistribution unpopular. Underlying these inequalities are the power structures that discriminate against certain groups of people. There is a danger that civil society will be seen as a new "magic bullet", now that politicians are disenchanted with both state planning and "free" markets, ignoring the fact that exclusion results from the interlocking structures of social, economic and political power in which civic associations are also implicated. Most NGOs believe that human rights standards and other social values can be mainstreamed through these power structures in order to spread their benefits and reduce their costs- whether in markets, politics or social discrimination. In that sense, the over-arching role of NGOs is to "help revision the world as an ever-growing web of non-exploitative relationships" (Fowler 1997). Translating these principles into practice at different levels of the world economy is difficult and complex, but the case for doing so is clear. Despite the disagreements and probable future fragmentation of NGOs in both North and South, all agree that there are increasing opportunities to work together across institutional boundaries in order to influence the forces that underpin poverty and discrimination, finding partnerships and synergies where few existed before, and moulding not just a strong civil society but a society that is just and civil in all that it does.

Civil Society Responses At The Local Level

Confronting globalisation begins and ends at the grassroots level, where NGOs are already developing a number of strategies to help poor people address the realities of their position in global markets and play a creative role in re-shaping economic forces. First, by improving the endowments of the poor so that they can complete more effectively and achieve a basic level of security, voice and equality of rights, without which economic "alternatives" are impossible. This continues the traditional NGO role of developing skills, confidence, capacities and forms of associations, and improving access to credit, services and economic opportunities- but underpinned by a more systematic attempt to link different levels and sectors of the economy. Second, NGOs can turn market forces to the advantage of poorer groups by reducing the benefits normally siphoned off by intermediaries-using, for example, joint marketing associations like those supported by NGOs in Latin America (Bebbington 1996) or attempts by NGOs in South Africa to work with community associations to help them negotiable better contracts with commercial hunting and tourism concerns.

Third, civic groups are exploring alternative modes of production and exchange which are less costly in social and environmental terms, build more "social capital" for use in market settings (qualities such as trust, co-operation, and honesty), support men and women to combine their market and non-market roles to better effect, and distribute profits with a social purpose. These deeper changes are crucial in addressing the Achilles heel of most empowerment strategies: a failure to think through what happens when people with less power obtain more of it -a fairer society in which people distribute the costs and benefits of social and economic change more equitably, or more competition against the background of existing gender and other inequalities ? This challenge- the regulation of all exclusionary systems of power- is one that most NGOs have tended to ignore, but it is the key to an agenda for transforming capitalism rather than "humanising" it. Small- scale innovations may be viable at a larger scale it they can be shown to generate material advances sufficient to eradicate absolute poverty, thus building the long-term public and political support that more radical alternatives currently lack. We hope that the conference will explore this issue in detail. At the opposite extreme, NGOs continue their role as carers of last resort, operating safety-nets, and providing welfare to the casualties of globalisation, especially in countries where the transition from protected markets has been far too rapid (as in the Former Soviet Union).

From The Local To The Global

At the national level, grassroots innovations need support from pro-poor macro-economic and social policies. Although globalisation does erode state authority, the re-distributive and protective functions of states remain paramount. There is a tendency among some NGOs to focus on global advocacy to the exclusion of the national-level processes of state-society relations that underpin the ability of any country to pursue progressive goals in an integrated economy- the task of rebuilding government capacity to negotiate, monitor and regulate global regimes; the importance of pro-poor alignments in civil society and between civil society, business and government; and the role of domestic civic groups in combating corruption, pressing for institutional accountability, and preserving a social consensus in favour of economic reform. Few NGOs have given enough thought to their roles in these areas, partly because of a lingering suspicion of states in any form, and partly because of the temptation to "leap-frog" the national arena and go direct to Washington or Brussels. In sustainable development terms, this is a serious mistake.

At the global level, successful strategies must be connected to supportive actions in other parts of the international system. Globalisation means, not only that NGOs must engage more strategically with market forces on a much bigger scale than before, but do so in ways which link micro- to macro-forces together in a coherent way. Examples include: linking alternative production systems to international fair trade networks that gives them some security in open markets; holding corporations to account against minimum social and environmental standards negotiated locally but monitored across global supply chains; and altering patterns of consumption in the "Global North" in ways which do not disadvantage producers in the "global South". With their international presence and connections, NGOs have a natural strength in this field, and in some areas a good start has been made, especially in helping to build a movement for more ethical consumption, investment and trading. NGOs have been key players in attempts to reform corporate accountability, test out multinational codes of conduct, re-shape consumer demand, and alter patterns of global trade. Inevitably, enthusiasm tends to run ahead of actual achievements-there are limits to the extent to which market economies can be reformed- but the principles involved have now been identified, and much is already known about how to operationalise then in practice. The conference provides an opportunity to take stock of what is happening with a greater degree of rigor.

In the same vein, NGOs are becoming more strategic in their lobbying of the International Financial Institutions, the monitoring of international commitments (like Social Watch), and the democratization of global economic and other regimes (like the World Trade Organisation and the proposed Multilateral Agreement on Investment). Although there has been little concrete progress in opening these regimes to civil society participation, they are likely to be the centrepiece of the global system in the 21st century and demand a concerted response. The beginning of such a response are sketched out below. The inadequacy of the IFIs has become an issue on which there is an unusual global consensus. Their focus on ensuring that public sector finances are not overextended has led them to neglect the regulation of private financial transactions. The consequences- financial panic and massive overexposure- are fuelling a global recession that has already cost the world 10 million formal sector jobs. 4 Talk by the G7 leaders about' a new global financial architecture' has not hidden the fact that they have little idea what this might look like, or even how new solutions might be negotiated to more democratic (sustainable) consensus. Are NGOs any better prepared ? Critiques of the World Bank and the IMF have been an easy game; redesigning the international system will require more complex analysis and more subtle proposals than the sweeping campaigns of the past.

The Reform of International Co-operation

From Foreign Aid To New Form Of Governance

In addition to these very broad shifts in global

economics, development NGOs face another set of changes much closer to home. The decline of foreign aid (bar one or two exceptions such as the recent small increase in the UK aid budget) is now well- entrenched the world over. This is the consequence of persistent intellectual and communication failings in the case for aid, continued political disinterest and/ or disillusion, and the emergence of new forms of international co-operation better-suited to the realities of a global economy where private flows of capital predominate (outside Sub-Saharan Africa) and economic integration is perceived as the best motor for change- the emergence of an international system based around rules and standards rather than subsidised resource transfers. This might appear to pose a clear threat to aid-funded NGOs, but there is a positive side to these changes: even if NGOs are unsure or divided about the degree of intervention they advocate in the global economy, they can all be committed to a more democratic process of setting the "rules of the game"- what the philosopher Brian Barry calls "justice as impartiality". Already, municipalities in Latin America and elsewhere are experimenting with "dialogic politics", where civil society and business representatives share with local government in decisions- making. If these experiments can be connected to more democratic structures at higher levels of the world system, the results could be revolutionary- embedding local agreements on labour standards, environmental pollution and human rights in a nested system of authorities that balance necessary room-to-manoeuvre with a core of universal principles.

Currently, these linkages operate through networks of

interest groups (including NGOs), rather than formal representative structures. This raises important questions about NGOs as organisations, especially their weak governance and accountability mechanisms, but the role of civil society is certain to grow as global governance becomes more pluralistic and less confined to state-based systems. We hope the conference will provide concrete examples of how this is happening in different parts of the world, and around different issues and institutions. The issue raised by this radical change in conceptions of governance is clear: how can NGOs help to ensure that the regimes of the future work to the benefit of poor people and deliver concrete benefits on the ground ? This is a deeply-political question: who decides the relative importance of economic growth, political equality, and social benefit, within and between societies ? That question take NGOs into territory way beyond their traditional roles as implementers of projects, providers of funds, and advocates on the margins of world affairs. For the first time in history, they have the opportunity to become vehicles for international co- operation in the mainstream of politics and economics- but only if they put their own house in order and size the opportunities that will surely come their way.

Even if this optimistic scenario does come to pass, it is unlikely that foreign aid will disappear, especially in the world's poorest countries. Rather, it looks set to play a supporting role in future global regimes- used more selectively to help countries meet their obligations under international agreements or smooth out the costs of structural change, for example, in addition to its traditional role in financing development expenditure for a time. The rhetoric of international agencies now converges on the need to change the way aid is provided, moving from a "supply to a demand-led" framework in which consolidated resources are placed at the disposal of local institutions who decide on and "own" the uses to which they are put-ideally through cross-society dialogues between government, business and civil society. The reality of donor practice is somewhat different, but as they gather momentum these trends will have important implications for NGOs, especially those based in the North. It may not be long before Southern NGOs can apply to their local branch of a World Development Fund and buy in technical assistance as they see fit- whether from Oxfam, UNDP or a local consultancy company.

In reality, the current pattern of aid-funding to and through NGOs is confused, an assessment that is no helped by poor statistics which make it impossible to say how much of the World Bank's resources (for example) are channelled in this direction. The evidence we do have suggests a consolidation of trends already visible three years ago: high levels of funding through NGOs despite declining aid budgets, with a slowly-rising proportion sent direct to NGOs in the South, and both a levelling-out and a small re-distribution of resources among different NGOs in the North. There are winners and losers in this process, including "new competitors" for NGOs from business, non-profit consultancy companies, and elements of states that can demonstrate their competence in the marketplace. As multilateral and bilateral agencies decentralise their operations, one might expect Northern NGOs to lose out in this process, but thus far there is little evidence of a major break with the patterns of the past. In part, this is because donor agencies value a reliable delivery or advisory system for their funds above all else, and are prepared to see Northern organisations continue in this role so long as their Southern counterparts are seen to be weak; few small NGOs can afford the overheads necessary to deal with large-scale donor contracts. It is also a consequence of decentralisation among Northern NGOs themselves, and the development of their own capacity to raise official funding in Southern "markets"- a strange form of capacity-building but one which has a clear logic as the supply of foreign aid becomes more competitive. Third, there are few Southern NGOs with the capacity to deliver large-scale humanitarian relief. Therefore, although the financial forecast for Northern NGOs may appear pessimistic in the long run, there is little sense of a crisis in the here and now. Indeed, the absence of such a crisis is one of the reasons why change is so slow in coming.

Changing Roles: Capacity-Building

These trends pose a number of challenges for NGOs in both North and South. First, they imply a gradual shift in roles, away from the direct implementation or delivery of aid-funded projects and services, and towards capacity-building, "learning-for-leverage" and other measures designed to support local institutions to engage in discussions over development priorities, take part in global regimes, and operate successfully as motors for change in economic systems, governance and social policy (Fowler 1997). Traditional NGO roles do not disappear in this scenario, but like foreign aid in general they play a smaller part in a broader menu of options, administered in a different framework of power dynamics and South-North relationships. If there is a problem with village food security. It would be odd to lobby Western supermarket chains to the exclusion of grassroots work, "developmental" funding for Southern intermediaries (with fewer strings attached than official aid), technical support, and other forms of "added value" that Northern NGOs- in theory at last- can provide. All these things are important in addressing problems of poverty and opposition, and they must be provided in a coherent way by different institutions according to their lengths and skills. What is becoming clear is that Northern NGOs are losing their supposed comparative advantage in most areas of their traditional work as Southern NGO sectors matures in their research and policy capacity as well as project-implementation and support. A smaller process may be starting in the south as other groups in civil society and business take on the rules traditionally ascribed to intermediary NGOs.

A loss response to this situation is for NGOs to re-focus their energies on capacity-building and institutional development- activities which are very much the mantra of the moment. Though fashionable, the record of capacity-building in practice is not impressive-though to be it is difficult to make an accurate assessment one way or the other given the paucity of gorous evaluation material that exists. Concerns about quality were one of the reasons behind the formation of the International Forum on Southern NGO Capacity- Building in 1998, an international network which aims to share experience of "good practice" and foster innovation on the ground. The record of Northern agencies is particularly poor in the area of financial sustainability, despite the fact that this is probably the most important form of capacity in all civic organisations (it being difficult to be independent, enter into global partnerships, take risks or innovate while your hand is in "another person's pocket"). Micro-credit is seen as a panacea for sustainability rather than one among many possibilities; project planning procedures tend to be emphasised to the detriment of research and media skills; internal organisational issues take precedence over external linkages and bridging, mediation and partnering; and the ability of Southern NGOs to participate as equals in trans-national alliances is handicapped by the exclusive focus of most donors on their domestic role. Yet these areas are crucial to the future role of civil society in building coalitions for development, forming cross-society dialogues, and extending public participation in development planning. There have been some successes in strengthening the "enabling environment" for civic action (not just non-profit law and less intrusive state regulation, but improved fiscal regimes and a better climate for philanthropy), but in general capacity-building is still in its infancy.

Changing Roles: Constituency-Building

The second challenge concerns the role of NGOs in building constituencies for international co-operation as a pre-requisite for the success of global regimes, new forms of governance, and the sacrifices required to alter global patterns of consumption and trade (especially in the North).

Codes of conduct to govern multi-national corporations, for example, are of little use unless they are backed by large-scale consumer pressure to enforce them and viable alternatives on the ground. NGOs have always talked of the need to build consitituencies, but have focused on problems in the Third World instead of lifestyle change at home, playing on the line that "your five pounds will make the difference." It rarely does of course- and what would make a difference (like mass- based public protest against Western indifference to genocide)- is never given sufficient attention in NGO strategy. It is too expensive or too "political", and wins few plaudits or contracts for foreign aid. Most Northern NGOs are actually dis- investing in development education, claiming that past efforts have been disappointing, which indeed they have, and for reasons which are entirely predictable. NGOs have been telling the wrong story for forty years, and the result is a donor base without a constituency for action, stagnant public support (except for child sponsorship agencies), and a widespread decline in volunteering, especially among the young.

It is unlikely that this situation will be reversed with current NGO communications strategies, since they fail to engage the public beyond and emotional outpouring of concern when starvation hits the headlines. "Development" has proved too abstract a concept and aid is both dull and complex. At root, people want security and stability in a world that seems ever-more uncertain, and they must therefore be convinced that what they want can only be achieved through new- more co-operative- structures of production, exchange, and international relations. That requires a massive investment of imagination and resources to help people connect complex global trends with simple individual responsibilities, bringing home the fact that uncooperative actions at the international level will infringe our own rights, and the rights of our children. It is here that ethical consumption and alliances with the environmental and other movements could provide a vital link for development NGOs, but there are others that deliver the necessary message, like UNDP's "global housekeeping" imagery. A clearer massage and a more sophisticated communications strategy will support the process of "coming to public judgement" which underlies mass- based action far more effectively than NGO shock tactics or the hard sell of charity advertising. Constituency-building means creating an agenda for concern using diffuse channels over the long term, not just narrow policy lobbying within the international aid system. The globalisation of the media provides an opportunity for NGOs to achieve an international outreach for their massages if they can find the right mechanisms to win attention.

Changing Relationships: Trans-National Civic Organising

The gradual replacement of foreign aid by a wider agenda of international co-operation makes it easier for NGOs and other civil society organisations to work together, without the distorting effects of contracts, conditions and unequal access to funding. The most interesting and potentially powerful cases of trans-national civic organising are those where funding is a secondary consideration, leaving participants to focus on exchanging complementary roles and resources that are equally- valued in support of board but common goals. A number of examples of this kind of network will be presented at the conference. The case of the world-wide campaign against land-mines is a useful one, albeit difficult to replicate in areas where there is less consensus and more of a conflict of interest between poor people in different parts of the world (like global trade and labour markets). In a world of "complex multilateralism" these alliances are certain to grow: over 15,000 trans-national civic networks are already active on the global stage, 90 per cent of which have been formed during the last thirty years (O'Brien etal 1998). One should not romanticise these experiences, since they continue to raise difficult questions of:

⇒ *legitimacy*: who speaks for whom, and how are differences of opinion resolved where individual participants very in strength and resources ?

⇒ *accountability*: who enjoys the benefits and suffers the costs of what the alliance achieves, especially at the grassroots level ?

⇒ *structure*: how to deal with the challenges of genuinely international governance, decision making and communication ?

⇒ *strategy*: the need to develop more rigorous arguments and more credible alternatives as a contribution to policy debates.

However, as the conference papers will show, all these problems can be managed, given courage and imagination.

Humanitarian Assistance, Conflict and Peace-Building

Post- Cold War Disorder

In the world of long- term development, there is always some room-to-manoeuvre. In areas of conflict and complex political emergencies choices are harder and the dilemmas of the NGO world are drawn more starkly, yet such situations are characteristic of the post Cold-War disorder and the high levels of insecurity that global processes continue to generate. The shape, scale and parameters of NGO involvement in efforts to provide humanitarian assistance and resolve violent conflict has changed profoundly over the 1990s, as our understanding of the dynamics of insecurity has evolved. Initial optimism at the end of the Cold War and the prospect of a "peace dividend" soon foundered as pre- existing "small wars" began to spread and ethno-nationalist conflicts re-appeared, often fuelled by interests bent on exploiting the political legacy of sectarian history and the financial benefits of a war economy (Keen 1994).

Contemporary conflicts are fundamentally different to those that dominated the first 75 years of this century (Goodhand and Hulme 1998a). These "post-nation state wars" are largely internal struggles in which clear interest are difficult to disentangle (Duffield, 1999); death and disablement are concentrated on civilians rather than combatants; and population movements take place within as well as across national borders. In 1995, around 14 million people were refugees and some 23 million were internally displaced (forced to relocate within their own country; ODI 1998:2). It is one of the great paradoxes of modern times that globalisation has been associated with increased inter-state tensions. Far from the 'end of history' predicted by liberal commentators after the collapse of communism, 'history' (or at least historical forces) has returned with a vengeance across Europe, Asia and Africa as ethnic, nationalist, religious, and cultural groups have proclaimed their identities in often-aggressive and exclusive forms. While it has become fashionable to equate virtue with civil society, these events serve to remind us that civil society (like states and businesses) has a dark side too.

When the Cold War ended, the initial response of the international humanitarian system was to increase the use of direct military action to end civil wars, and co-ordinate relief efforts more effectively (ODI:1). However, the debacle of UNITAF in Somalia in 1993 and the 'retreat' of US forces from the country led to a rapid reversal in policies of military intervention. This change in policy had disastrous consequences in Rwanda where the UN peacekeeping force was progressively run down in early 1994 despite, clear warning that the likelihood of genocide was high. Only 470 UNAMIR troops were stationed in Rwanda when the violence that killed 800,000 people in a few weeks erupted. The international community (especially the UN) looked foolish and inept, while European nations kept quiet about the role of the French government in the events leading up to the genocide.

NGOs And Humanitarian Action: Tensions and Dilemmas

These shifts in policy have presented NGOs with a

range of complex dilemmas that have given rise to an unprecedented bout of soul-searching. Caught between the scale of human suffering on the ground and the international community's unwillingness to tackle the politics of humanitarian intervention, NGOs have been sucked, ill-prepared, into a vortex of conflicting needs and demands- all the more disturbing because the years 1990 to 1994 were bumper years for NGO relief operations (Duffield 1994). Relief budgets expanded rapidly and humanitarian efforts accounted for a steadily increasing share of development aid. The numbers NGOs involved in emergency activities rose (there were more than 200 in the Great Lakes area by late 1994) and Northern NGOs 'prospered' as the number of Southern NGOs able to deliver relief on a large-scale remained small. Despite the self-evident need that "something had to be done', many NGO staff returned to their homes after overseas missions in the Great Lakes, the Horn of Africa, West Africa, Angola, Central Asia, Sri Lanka and Cambodia harbouring grave doubts about the effectiveness of humanitarian assistance. Did their efforts provide additional resources for "conflict entrepreneurs" to prosecute 'small wars'? Is relief activity merely a function of Western strategic interests- a 'band-aid' that allows the international system to pretend that it is taking action when in truth it has disengaged (Prendergast 1997) ? How should NGOs react when the principal of voluntary repatriation is over-ridden on a vast scale and when their own governments are increasingly trying to discourage legitimate asylum seekers (ODI 1982:2)? Just as NGOs have had to develop relationships with new actors in the private sector, relief agencies now deal routinely with both local militia groups and foreign military personnel, raising difficult questions about mandates, competencies and co-ordination that are still being worked through.

Not surprisingly, the mid- 1990s have been a period of intense questioning for Northern NGOs involved in humanitarian activities. The picture with regard to NGOs in the South is less clear, in large part because they have few forums to reflect on their experiences and articulate an independent voice. Inevitably, the questions that confront NGOs vary with context and circumstance, but some common issues can be discerned. First, the importance of being clear about each agency's strategic orientation. A traditional relief focus (on which many NGOs were founded) is increasingly rare, apart from the International Committee of the Red Cross (ICRC) and their focus on neutrality and the impartial provision of relief services to anyone suffering in a conflict. From the late 1980s, researchers and donors have encouraged NGOs to think beyond relief and to conceptualise their interventions along a relief- development continuum so that relief activities contribute to development programmes as peace returns. This represents a second strategic option: providing a mix of relief and development activities that provide for immediate basic needs while creating the physical, human or social capital that will raise the likelihood of economic and social development in the future.

Third, there has been a rapid expansion in NGO attempts to engage directly in the processes of peace-building and conflict resolution. They take many forms- an additional component of a relief and development initiative, or a sole focus (as with Quaker Peace and Service). Such activities may concentrate on the micro-level building of 'social capital' through inclusive forums or the training of local conflict-resolution activists; macro-level support to diplomatic negotiations or creating opportunities for the leaders of opposing groups to meet on an informal basis; or both levels simultaneously. They can be neutral and impartial- helping all parties to meet and have an open discussion- or informed by a political analysis that distinguishes perpetrators from victims and provides support only to the latter.

At the present time there are voices in favour of all these strategies. The dictum of "do no harm" (Anderson 1998) has been especially well-developed in arguing that NGOs should adopt a carefully-analytical approach which places a high priority on ensuring that humanitarian aid is not captured by warring factions. While such incidents are well-documented in the relief literature, ODI (1998:3) argue strongly that-at worst-support to armed groups 'has probably been slight'. In contrast, some donor agencies (including, DFID in the UK) have encouraged NGOs to engage not only with relief and development but also with the active promotion of social and political processes that contribute to peace-building and/or foster conflict resolution. Whether such an approach represents good practice or simply "an increasingly selective and conditional approach by some donors in their funding of NGO humanitarian activity" is debatable (ODI 1998). What is clear is that most NGOs lack the capacity to conduct the strategic analysis necessary to success in these areas, especially in the complex and contingent environments in which they operate. While the codes of practice and evaluation studies that are presently being promoted may foster operational effectiveness and efficiency in NGO relief activities, only limited numbers of NGOs have the analytical skills and detailed local knowledge that are needed to judge the impact of NGO activity on the complex social, economic and political processes that underpin violent conflict.

Humanitarian Action: New Directions

Any credible analysis of the role of NGOs in humanitarian and conflict resolution work reveals that networking and influencing strategies are required to have any significant impact on reducing the suffering that occurs in complex political emergencies. Direct action may achieve laudable humanitarian gains but is likely to operate only at a token scale in relation to aggregate levels of suffering. A number of options emerging, but only a small number of NGOs have begun to explore their potential:

⇒ Influencing national governments to operate in ways that go beyond "realist" foreign policy considerations (e.g. monitoring the UK's "ethical foreign policy" and questioning why the US has no ethical foreign policy at all).

⇒ Monitoring the effectiveness of regional forces in peace-making to judge whether they are an excuse for Northern countries to avoid more wide-ranging military action.

⇒ Examining how the UN might regain is credibility and develop the capacity to engage effectively in peace-making, and co-ordinate the activities of its constituent parts.

⇒ Exploring strategies through which national and global

civil societies could move beyond their current responses to complex political emergencies (charitable donations and/or public disengagement), to mobilise governments to react to emerging conflicts early in their life-cycle (not-as today- "too little, too late").

⇒ Overseeing the private sector so that businesses who gain from war economics find that the pursuit of such profits can result in social sanctions (such as consumer boycotts or local media coverage that challenges their management decisions). Examples include traders in Angola, diamonds in Sierra Leone, timber in Liberia, the manufacturers of land mines, and international 'security' companies.

Underlying all these strategies is the need for NGOs to put their own house in order by reducing dysfunctional competition in relief funding and operations; working more closely with Southern groups to build up their relief and peace-building capacity, and widen the current Northern-centric humanitarian policy dialogue; making a reality of codes of conduct by institutionalising accountability, including to beneficiaries; and developing 'peace audits' to evaluate the impact of their activities on the processes that lead to conflict (Goodhand and Hulme 1998b). NGOs have an important role to play in responding to the threefold challenge of 21st century insecurity (Edwards, 1999): a more systematic engagement in long-term peace-building and equitable development; stronger international political action on the causes of suffering; and responding more effectively with developmental relief when crises of break out. However, if they wish to gain more influence over other actors in pursuing these roles, then NGOs will need to invest in their own credibility and legitimacy by becoming more knowledgeable and transparent about the achievements of their existing humanitarian and peace-building work.

Organisational Implications

The changing global context sketched out above suggests four key challenges for NGOs in the next 15-20 years:

⇒ how to mobilise a genuinely- inclusive civil society at every level of the world system ?

⇒ how to hold other institutions accountable for their actions and ensure that they respond to social and environmental needs ?

⇒ how to ensure that international regimes are both implemented effectively and work to the benefit of poor people and poor countries ?

⇒ how to ensure that gains made at the global level are translated into concrete benefits at the grassroots.

These challenges raise major questions about how NGOs organise themselves to work in more global and strategic ways in the future. Four areas of organisational change seem especially important: roles, relationships, capacities, and- underlying all these things- the thorny issues of legitimacy and accountability.

NGOs Roles

Clearly, NGOs operate in so many contexts and at so many levels that generalisation is hazardous. However, some trends can be identified in relation to the need to think and act globally. It is difficult to see how NGOs could re-shape the costs and benefits of global change through stand-alone projects at the local level, funding, or the delivery of basic social and economics services. Instead they must build outwards from concrete innovations at grassroots level to connect with the forces that influence patterns of poverty, prejudice and violence: exclusionary economics, discriminatory politics, selfish and violent personal behaviour, and the capture of the world of knowledge and ideas by elites. In a sense this is what NGOs are already doing, by integrating micro-level action in their project and advocacy activities but the changing global context challenges us to make this our natural way of working instead of something bolted on to mainstream activities as an optional extra. Moving from development as delivery to development as leverage is the fundamental change that characterises this shift, and it has major implications for the ways in which NGOs organise themselves, raise and spend their resources, and relate to others.

Despite the changing context, many NGOs appear reluctant to shed their traditional roles. Some Northern NGOs continue to be operational on the ground, and even where they work through "partners", many tend to dictate the scope and pace of work through their control over funding and procedures (Fowler 1998, Wallace 1997). There is little real evidence that Northern NGOs are handing over local-level activities to Southern groups and limiting their roles to those most appropriately played in the North. Building constituencies for international co- operation has been relegated to the margins of NGO activity. Development education is largely out of fashion; "public education" is skewed in favour of advertisements for emergencies and child sponsorship; and very few agencies try to communicate complex development messages through the media. Yet it is the media that shapes and forms opinions for all generations; the use of the media for fund-raising instead of education will be detrimental to organisation that seek an active supporter base in the years to come.

In the South, some NGOs have developed a strong and independent funding base, but most remain dependent on external resources. Their roles are determined as much by donor fashion and demands as by needs and the causes of need. While some do pioneering work in confronting inequalities at every level, many still confine themselves to a limited role as deliverers of development according to ideas and designs imposed or imported from outside. In future, NGOs will need to find better ways of building constituencies for their work at every level; methods of working together through strategic partnerships that link local and global processes together; and a much effective methods of identifying barriers to change and points of average where their combined experience gives them authority and voice. By sinking roots into their own societies and making connections with others inside and outside civil society, NGOs can generate more potential to influence things where it really matters because of the multiplier effects that come from activating a concerned citizenry to work for change in a wider range of settings.

NGOs have always been confused about their identity-part market institution providing a cost-effective service against alternative providers, part social actor pushing for more fundamental change. The mixing together of these roles is inherently problematic, and though it can be managed more or less effectively (and can be a positive force in injecting co-operative values into the competitive world), it will eventually demand that NGOs make a clearer choice about who they are and what they want to do. Founded as charities to channel money from rich countries to poor countries, it is hardly surprising that NGOs find it difficult to adapt to a world of more equal partnerships and non-financial relationships. We think that those that fail to adapt will eventually go to the wall, or slip quietly into anonymity.

Relationships

Competition for resources in an ever-more tightly-constrained funding environment is characteristic of NGO sectors in all countries. Much NGO advertising, media work and lobbying is driven by the need to gain a higher profile in the market-place in order to ensure a continued flow of resources from both the public and official donors. Donor requirements drive many of the changes that are being made in systems and procedures, passed down the aid-chain from Northern to Southern NGOs, and on to community-based organisations. Participatory approaches could be a countervailing force to these trends, but they are often used as a tool to involve communities in NGO-driven agendas: few NGOs have developed structures that respond to grassroots demands. Although NGOs talk constantly of "partnership", control over funds and decision-making remains highly-unequal.

This picture is a familiar one, but it is also partial, and

the changing global context opens up a world of possibilities for NGOs to relate to each-other in different and healthier ways: alliances among equals, genuine partnerships, and synergistic networks that come together and then break apart, can replace the asymmetries of power and voice that have characterised North- South relationships for so many years. Information technology helps this process along by enabling less hierarchical modes of organisation and communication- advantages already well-exploited by the business community, but not yet by NGOs. Peter Senge (1998) argues that the most successful organisations of the 21st century will look more like "democratic societies than conventional corporations". Rather than trying to generate order out of chaos world (and making things more complex in the process), they will try to generate order out of chaos through non-authoritarian relationships between people who are genuinely interested in helping one-another to develop new learning and capacities. Jonathan Kotter (1998) likens this model to a "smaller mother ship with many more satellites and fewer organisational boundaries".

These structural innovations are especially important in relation to NGO activities that stretch across national borders- like lobbying- but thus far conflicts of interest and the need for profile have retarded their development. Friction continues over who speaks for whom and on what basis: No them NGOs still prefer to go to international forums themselves to present the case for change "on behalf of" others; Southern NGOs may "speak for" communities who are unaware of the campaign or unsure of its benefits. The move to embrace advocacy has to go hand-in-hand with alliances that can ensure that changes at the macro- level are actually translated into gains for people on the ground. The new global agenda requires, not only that NGOs link with each-other in different ways, but also that they forge relationships with other groups in civil society which can reach further and deeper into the mainstream of politics and economics- like trade unions, consumer groups, the women's and environmental movements, universities and think-tanks, and the news media- eventually creating a global movements for sustainable development. We need new ways of talking and relating to different sections of the public, especially young men and women, and we must loosen or manage the relationship between NGOs and official donors so that the "piper (s) do not call an inappropriate tune" for organisations that claim to respond to the voices of the people they serve.

Capacities

To support these roles and relationships, NGOs will need to develop a range of new skills and competencies in learning, bridging, mediation, dialogue and influencing. NGOs current focus on narrow management issues (often borrowed uncritically from the corporate sector), acquiring skills valued by donors, and traditional concepts of lobbying, need to be replaced by a broader base of capacities which include the ability to listen to, learn from, and work with others at both local and global levels, and outside the development sector; a more strategic understanding of how and where global issues "bite" on the NGO agenda; and how organisations need to change in order to respond to new demands. NGOs need to develop ways of working that are less focused on promoting their own profile, and more concerned with building alliances, working with others, and dividing up roles and responsibilities in a collaborative way. More openness to new ideas and a greater willingness to learn will be essential in the context of new actors and problems; fast-moving and unpredictable change; the entry of corporations, churches and trade unions into development debates; and the increasing sophistication of information technology (Edwards 1997).

These developments will challenge NGOs to develop a more sophisticated understanding of the changing context for their work, recognise the implications for their practice, and select the alliances and strategies required to address them on a continuous basis. Innovations in markets and economics will demand much greater detail from NGOs in their analysis and proposals, without losing the power of grassroots testimony and straightforward protest. Finely-nuanced judgements in complex political emergencies will require more highly-developed information-gathering and analytical skills. NGOs are unlikely to be able to succeed in these tasks without help from the research community, demanding a rapid expansion of academic- practitioner collaboration and new forms of co- working across institutional boundaries. Combined with the rise of civil society in the South, the absence of simple answers to sustainable development dilemmas challenges traditional approaches to NGO advocacy. Engaging with others over the long term in a process of mutual learning and innovation becomes more important than claiming that NGOs have the answers and merely wish to convert others to their point of view. This will be a major challenge to organisations who have grown used to occupying the moral high ground. In addition, the emergence of short-term conflicts of interest between groups of poor people in different parts of the world (especially in global trade) underscores the importance of building capacities across the board so that everyone can share equally in negotiating a fair deal in the regimes of the future, instead of pretending that "win-win" solutions can be plucked out of the air by NGO thinkers in North or South.

Legitimacy and Accountability

Underlying these changes are more fundamental questions about NGO legitimacy and accountability, for above all it is this area- the right of NGOs to do what they do and say what they say- that is being challenged by world events and the changing climate of ideas. The legitimacy of NGOs (especially those based in the North) is now an accepted topic of public debate. Much of the criticism that is emerging in newspapers and elsewhere is superficial, motivated more by ideology than intellectual rigor and in serve danger of "throwing the baby out with the bath-water". However, it looks set to continue, especially around the key issue of representation as global regimes mature in more pluralistic fashion. Claiming the right to speak out simply because an NGO has projects or contacts on the ground is unlikely to be acceptable to a sceptical audience in the media, among other observers, and- most importantly- a more critical local population. Southern NGOs are questioning the right of Northern NGOs speak for them; women are questioning the right of male-dominated NGOs to represent them; and as access to technology grows, communities feel they can speak for themselves through video and the internet as well as more traditional arenas such as marches and demonstrations. A recent internet conference in preparation for a UN meeting on women in Addis Ababa found that - in contrast to most internet discussion groups - over 40 percent of contributors were women from Africa, even though they are the groups most excluded from resources and technology. As poor people find more ways to access information and find a louder voice in global debates, the legitimacy of Northern-based, male-dominated organisations to appropriate the voices of others will disappear completely. They will have to learn to stand aside, make space for others, and share their rich financial and technological resources, and access to power, in more democratic networks.

To answer this growing chorus of criticism, NGOs must be good civic actors themselves; otherwise they will be unable to encourage co-operation and accountability in other institutions; nor will they be considered legitimate participants in an emerging international civil society. However, few NGOs have democratic systems of governance or accountability. As service-providers they do not need them; as social actors they certainly do. The legitimacy of a social actor comes from their rootedness in their own society, from a more engaged and supportive domestic constituency, and from the alliances they develop with other parts of civil society. NGOs will have to become more open and transparent in an age when institutional accountability is a condition for a seat at the negotiating table. The tradition of hiding controversial issues behind closed doors, and a persistent failure to convert NGO rhetoric about equity and participatory management into institutional practice, is hardly a good basis for persuading others of the need for reform. If NGOs are to become social actors in a global world, pushing for justice, equity, democracy and accountability, then clearly these characteristics need to be reflected in their own systems and structures.

The current balance of power in the NGO world is very hard to shift-as we found when organising this conference. Channels of communication and networking are far more open to those in the North, and to well-resourced NGOs in the South. Few are prepared, it seems, to back their support for broader participation with the financial resources required to promote the voices of smaller organisations and marginalised groups. Unless this changes, public questioning of NGO legitimacy and accountability will continue to mount, fatally undermining the credibility that NGOs will need if they are to play a part in global debates.

Conclusion

Against such a huge and complex canvass, it would be unrealistic to expect any consensus to emerge from three days of discussions in Birmingham. However, the participants in the conference do represent a wide cross-section of origins and backgrounds, and bring a huge richness of ideas and experiences to the table. At the very least, our discussions will provide an opportunity to exchange ideas about civic action in the 21st century, take stock of our successes and failures in a critical yet supportive atmosphere, and identify areas for common action, research and learning.

In this process of dialogue and experimentation, civic

values take centre stage. NGOs are unlikely to agree on the details of how to confront globalisation and issues of conflict and humanitarian action, still less on their implications for NGOs as organisations However, they would probably all agree that certain (non-market) values are crucial to our common future-co-operation, non-violence, respect for human rights and democratic process- however these things are defined and played out in different cultural contexts. Whether these are understood as "civic" or "social" values, or just values that all sectors of society can support and represent, is less important than working together to make them the bottom line in decisions over economics and the environment, social policy, and politics. NGOs must be leaders in cultivating a global moral order which finds poverty and violence unacceptable. They must be exemplars of the societies they want to create, and work much harder to mainstream civic values into the arenas of economic, social and political power.

This is clearly an agenda for radical change. At present, NGO may sense the need for such a change but are wary of the institutional consequences, so most try to defend the values-based approach of a global social movement inside an operational framework that drives the organisation further into the market place (Edwards 1998a, 1998b). The result is an unsurprising muddle, and a great deal of internal tension. It may be that these tensions are simply too great for large, aid-dependent NGOs to resolve, in which case new organisations will emerge around and alongside them-one can't "change a super-tanker into a white-water raft" as Chris Roche remarked of Oxfam. The leading NGOs of today may come to be regarded as useful but temporary creations of a particular moment in history, to be gradually replaced by new forms of civic organisation more attuned to the needs and characteristics of the 21st century. The best of the NGO world will have the courage, imagination and room-to-manoeuvre to make a successful transition between the two; the rest will gradually slip from public attention, with no great loss to humankind.

The fundamental question facing all NGOs is how to move from our current position-as unhappy agents of a foreign aid system in decline-to where we want to be-as vehicles for international co-operation in the emerging global arena. Every NGO will interpret this challenges in a different way, and they will occupy their own distinctive niche in the patterns of civic action that develop. This does not matter, so long as NGOs are transparent and accountable for what they do. Their constituencies (public and private) can then decide whether they are worthy of their support in the radically different world context that is emerging. Our contention is that global trends challenge all NGOs to re-think their mandate, mission, and strategies. Although this will demand major organisational changes and a degree of self- sacrifice in the short term, it will be a force for liberation in the longer term, both at the broad level of societies and at the narrow level of organisations and their staff. In a global future, NGOs have the world at their feet. We must seize our chance.

11

Funding of An NGO

Guidelines For Department of Family Welfare Supported NGO Schemes

In this chapter we have compiled funding schemes for the benefit of the NGOs; some of the ministries and institution and their formats and forms for getting funds for various purposes for running the NGOs.

Population stabilisation is important for sustainable development. This requires that family planning and reproductive health care is accessible to all. It also means increasing outreach of primary and secondary education, extending basic amenities including sanitation, safe drinking water and housing, providing transport and communication. To make these meaningful, it is critical that women are empowered, have equal opportunities and can assert their rights in all spheres-health and reproductive health, nutrition, education, employment, etc.

The National Population Policy (NPP) 2000 emphasises the commitment of the Government of India (Gol)to voluntary and informed choice in family planning and reproductive health care services.

The NPP 2000 provides strategies for addressing the reproductive and child health needs of the people and achieve net replacement levels (TFR = 2.1) by the year 2010.

The purpose is to increase access and coverage of a comprehensive package of reproductive and child health services, including family planning. To achieve this purpose, the government, the corporate sector and the voluntary and non-government sector are expected to work together in partnership.

The NPP 2000 lists partnership with NGOs as one of the strategic themes. The Action Plan mentions the objectives of the collaboration. The work of NGOs is essentially supplementary and complementary in nature to that of the government. NGOs have a comparative advantage of flexibility in procedures, and a rapport with the local population. The GoI therefore proposes to involve NGOs in using strategies for expanding access to health services.

Guidelines For Mother NGO (MNGO) Scheme

The Department of Family Welfare in the Ninth Five Year Plan (1997-2002) introduced the Mother NGO scheme under the Reproductive and Child Health Programme. Under this scheme, the DoFW identified and sanctioned grants to selected NGOs called Mother NGOs in allocated districts/s. These MNGOs, in turn, issued grants to smaller NGOs, called Field NGOs (FNGOs), in the allocated district/s. The grants were to be used for promoting the goals/objectives as outlined in the Reproductive and Child Health (RCH) Programme of GoI.

The underlying philosophy of the Mother NGO scheme has been one of nurturing and capacity building. Broadly the objectives of the programme are:

⇒ Addressing the gaps in information or RCH services in the project area.

⇒ Building strong institutional capacity at the state, district / field level.

⇒ Advocacy and awareness generation.

At the time of preparing these Guidelines, 105 MNGOs were participating in 439 districts, through approximately 800 field NGOs. In keeping with the philosophy of capacity building, four NGOs had been identified as Regional Resource Centres (RRCs) to provide technical support to the MNGOs.

The lessons learnt over the past three years have indicated that modifications need to be made in the existing guidelines of the scheme. These are in terms of decentralisation, simplification of fund disbursal process, rationalisation of jurisdiction, and interface with local government bodies. Additionally, it was found that involving the NGOs in service delivery and addressing gender issues cross cutting the RCH service areas would be required to make the programme more effective. The Guidelines of the MNGO Scheme were accordingly revised to make the programme more effective and user friendly.

Guidelines

In addition to capacity building and nurturing small NGOs, the scheme focuses on addressing the unmet RCH needs. This is possible by involving NGOs in delivery of RCH services, in areas which are under ***served*** **or** ***un-served**** by the government infrastructure. Accordingly, NGOs are expected to move from exclusive awareness generation to actual delivery of RCH services. This will be done by utilising and strengthening the existing government infrastructure and human resources and not creating a parallel structure.

⇒ ***Un-served and under served*** areas are those socio-economic backward areas, which do not have access to health care services from the existing government health infrastructure, especially urban slums, tribal, hilly and desert areas including SC/ST habitations.

In specific terms these areas are: where the post of MO, ANM & LHV have been vacant for more than 1 years; the PHC is not equipped with minimal infrastructure; performance on critical RCH indicators is poor.

Additionally, interventions are expected to address gender issues. Proposed interventions must seek to enhance male involvement and partnership in improving the reproductive health status of women and children. The interventions must also include adolescent population. Community needs to be adequately mobilised to generate demand for RCH services.

Greater emphasis on service delivery means that the service providers are able to measure outcomes concretely.

Therefore the revised guidelines focus on development of clear outputs and measurable indicators at the project proposal stage by the MNGO. The role of MNGO becomes one of an active facilitator and manager of the project and not only a fund distributor.

A decentralised approach is adopted in the management and implementation of the MNGO Scheme. This means, starting from identification of NGOs, recommending NGO proposals for GoI approval, the State RCH Society takes responsibility for implementing the scheme. The MNGOs are members of the District RCH Society.

The role of Government of India is one of policy guidance, approvals, funding and technical support.

In order to optimise results, the NGO is expected to complement and supplement the government health infrastructure and not substitute it. The NGOs' efforts are more effective by developing linkages with local governments, related government departments, and establishing networks with technical and resource institutions.

Rationalisation of jurisdiction is done with a view to enable the NGOs to provide in-depth service in the project areas and optimise resources. The project duration of three years is extendable to five years, which facilities long term planning and stable implementation.

Role of MNGOs and FNGOs

FNGOs under the MNGO Scheme are involved in

service delivery, in addition to advocacy and awareness generation.

The key service delivery areas under the MNGO Scheme are:

⇒ Maternal and Child Health

⇒ Family Planning

⇒ Adolescent Reproductive Health

⇒ Prevention and Management of RTI

Indicative service delivery guidelines for the above mentioned RCH components are presented in Part Three of this Guidebook.

⇒ Some MNGOs have expertise in various aspects of development but limited expertise in the health sector. In order to provide hands on experience in implementing RCH service delivery interventions to MNGOs, the scheme provides funds to MNGOs for implementation of demonstrative service delivery projects in the allotted areas. The scope and scale of the project is comparable to that of the FNGO project.

  To facilitate implementation of service delivery projects by FNGOs, the MNGOs must have a dedicated team of staff including project Director with project management experience (preferably with regard to health/ RCH), and qualified trainers.

⇒ The MNGO cannot simultaneously apply as a Service NGO (SNGO) since these are two distinct functions

The role of the MNGO include the following functions:

⇒ Identifications of un-served and under served areas

⇒ Release of advertisement, identification and selection of FNGOs

⇒ Motivate NGOs, CBOs, SHGs and other local level bodies in case of non-availability of suitable FNGOs

⇒ Development of baseline data through Community Needs Assessment (CNA) and end line project data

⇒ Impart project orientation to FNGOs

⇒ Development of proposal with output and process indicators for approval

⇒ Provision of IEC materials to FNGO

⇒ Capacity building of FNGOs

⇒ Technical support to FNGO for induction and in-service training of project staff

⇒ Ensure that qualified staff in appointed by FNGO according to the job requirement and support their search for the same through development of TOR, information on resources

⇒ Wherever possible, inclusion of programmes/ groups such as Mahila Samakhya, NYK, Swa-Shakti in the FNGO orientation and frequent interaction

⇒ Liaise, network and coordinate with state and district health services and Panchayati Raj Institutions, linkages with other NGOs and technical institutions

⇒ Moniter performance of FNGOs and progress of the project through supportive supervision

⇒ Exchange and share learning and experiences with other MNGOs in the state and region

⇒ Work closely with RRCs and State NGO Coordinator

⇒ Document best practices

⇒ Submit quarterly financial and project progress reports to State RCH Society and District RCH Society

⇒ Submit statement of expenditure & utilisation certificates as per MoU

The role of FNGOs include the following functions:

⇒ Conduct Community Needs Assessment

⇒ Develop proposal based on baseline data

⇒ Provision of RCH services as proposed

⇒ Interaction for convergence with ICDS, rural development and anganwadi initiatives

⇒ RCH orientation to PRI members, members of Mahila Samakhya, NYK, Swa Shakti, Mahila Swasthya and others

⇒ Share information on the type of services that can be availed from the government health infrastructure

⇒ Create conductive working environment for the ANM

⇒ Facilitate the monthly RCH camps conducted by the PHC through mobilisation of community

⇒ Timely submission of quarterly progress reports, utilisation certificates etc. as per agreement to the MNGO

⇒ Documentation and maintenance of records and registers.

Institutional Framework

The revised guidelines of the MNGO Scheme are expected to add value to the scheme as it exists and to improve accountability at all levels. These guidelines are applicable within the Institutional framework as laid out below.

GoI

Government of India provides support through policy

guidelines, approvals and release of funds to State RCH Society. Grants-in-Aid Committee, (GIAC) approves the MNGO project recommended by the NGO Selection Committee. The NGO Selection Committee is constituted at the state level for the purpose of MNGO selection and is chaired by the Joint Secretary, Department of Family Welfare, GOI. Its function is to recommend MNGO proposals for approval by the GIAC, which is chaired by the Secretary. Family Welfare, and has representation of Financial Advisor and Planning Commission.

Regional Resource Centres (RRCs)

Technical support for NGO capacity enhancement, documentation of best practices, induction and in-service training, liaison with the state government, updating data base on RCH issues and development of MIS is provided by Regional Resource Centres and other technical institutions as found necessary. This is expected to complement the technical support decisions made by the State RCH Society.

Apex Resource Cell (ARC)

Located within the NGO division, the ARC will coordinate the activities of all the RRCs, manage budgets, and facilitate RRC coordinate and interaction with state governments.

Regional Director (RD)

⇒ Receive all applications from MNGO applicants and conduct pre-scrutiny/ desk review of all applications, based on checklist

⇒ Provide the collated information on the NGO applications

to the State RCH Society and convene the meeting of the State NGO Committee till the State NGO Coordinator is identified and placed

⇒ Participate in the review of applications as a member of the State NGO Committee

⇒ Participate in the final selection of MNGO as a member of NGO Selection Committee

⇒ Undertake field visits if required and submit tour reports to State Secretary (FW) & copy to NGO Division, GoI.

NGO Selection Committee

The selection of MNGOs will be carried out by the NGO Selection Committee, chaired by the Joint Secretary, FW, GoI. This Committee will be constituted at the level of each state for the purpose of selection of MNGOs. The other members include the State Health & Family Welfare Secretary, Regional Director, RRC Representative, Project Director RCH Society/director (FW) as Member Secretary and 1-2 co-opted members.

The selection of MNGO will be based on desk review reports and field appraisals of the eligible NGOs conducted by the RRCs. After selection of the MNGO, the NGO selection Committee will place the recommendation to the GIAC for approval.

State RCH Society

The State RCH Society constitutes a technical NGO Committee, called the State NGO Committee and ensures the placement of State NGO Coordinator. From selection of

MNGOs, recommendation of projects for GoI approval, fund disbursement, capacity building, training, monitoring to evaluation, is the responsibility of the State RCH Society.

State NGO Committee

The State NGO Coordinator convenes the meeting of the State NGO Committee, chaired by the Secretary (FW) or his nominee. Till the time the State NGO Coordinator is identified and gets placed, the Regional Director convenes the NGO committee meetings. The presence of GoI representative, RD and State NGO Coordinator is mandatory The RRC and Director (FW) are also members of the Committee.

The Primary responsibilities of the State NGO Committee are:

⇒ Examine findings of the desk review and identify eligible NGOs

⇒ Get field appraisal of eligible NGOs done by the RRCs

⇒ Coordinate training of selected MNGOs

⇒ Release of grant-in-aid as per MoU

⇒ Monitoring of MNGOs

⇒ Organize meetings to review the MNGO performance from time and ensure timely release of funds

⇒ Commission MNGO evaluation through external evaluating agency

⇒ Send utilization certificates to GOI

⇒ Act as arbitrator in case of dispute

For review of NGO applications:

⇒ On receiving the pre-scrutiny/desk review reports from the RD's office, the State NGO Committee convenes a meeting for review of NGO applications and prepares agenda

⇒ Invite Secretary (FW) and other members of the committee to attend the meeting

⇒ Prepare minutes and decision taken. Communicate the same to GoI and respective NGOs.

State NGO Coordinator

⇒ The full time NGO coordinator is responsible for management of the DoFW supported NGO schemes, including the MNGO Scheme

⇒ The roles and responsibilities of the NGO coordinator are liaising, coordinating and supporting the MNGOs

⇒ Towards this, the coordinator works closely with the State RCH Society, communicates government RCH and health policies to MNGOs, undertakes periodic field visits, develops terms of reference and participates in the evaluations, ensures timely submission of reports by the MNGOs, timely release of funds and maintains necessary records

⇒ The State NGO Coordinator functions as a coordinator point between the MNGOs and the RRCs and other technical resource institutes for meeting the technical needs of the NGOs under the MNGO Scheme

⇒ The State NGO coordinator is a part of the State RCH Society, and reports to Secretary (Family Welfare).

District RCH Society

The District RCH Society constitutes a technical committee called District NGO Committee for selection and approval of FNGOs and recommendation of MNGO projects.

The District RCH/FW officer convenes the District NGO Committee. Other members include, state NGO Coordinator, RRC representative, MO, PHC, ANMs of the concerned project area and an NGO (who is not a grantee) nominated by the district collector.

Functions:

⇒ Select and approve FNGO projects

⇒ Approve and recommend the MNGO project proposal based on FNGO projects

⇒ Facilitate the signing of MoU between the MNGO and the District RCH Society

⇒ Send the signed MoU to State RCH Society for Release of funds and inform GoI

⇒ Undertake review meeting to access performance of FNGOs and MNGO.

Appraisal and Evaluating Agencies

The Regional Resource Centres conduct the field appraisals prior to MNGO selection. There is a panel of identified and trained evaluating agencies at the regional and state levels that conduct the subsequent mid term and final evaluations. The state can request any of these agencies to evaluate the MNGO project. The agencies also obtain feedback from the State RCH Society and the District RCH

Society who are responsible for periodic monitoring of the MNGO projects.

Inter- Departmental Linkages

NGOs under the MNGO scheme are expected to network with PRIs, women's groups including self-help groups, youth networks, teachers, parents and other members in the community.

Guidelines for MNGOs

The following two sections - 1.4 & 1.5 - provide detailed guidelines for MNGOs and FNGOs in terms of Procedural and Process Guidelines. Procedural Guidelines spell out the criteria that applicant NGOs must fulfill in order to apply for funding. Process Guidelines spell out the processes involved in selection, sanction and monitoring of projects.

Procedural Guidelines for Submission of Application

NGOs applying for MNGO status must fulfill the following eligibility criteria. The criteria have been grouped into four sections. These are criteria for Registration, Experience, Assets and Jurisdiction.

Registration

⇒ NGO should be registered under the Indian Societies Registration Act/ Indian Trust Act/ Indian Religious and Charitable Act/ Company Act or their state counterparts for more than three years.

⇒ NGOs applying for MNGO status in a State other than that of its registration, should have State specific chapters registered. Alternatively, branches affiliated to a national level federation/organisation can be registered with the parent body.

Experience

⇒ Proven experience of working for three years in Health & Family Welfare, and the social sector (e.g. education, women's empowerment, rural development)

⇒ Implemented preferably a field project in Health or Reproductive and Child Health (RCH)

⇒ Scale of operation during the previous three years should be comparable to the funding sought

⇒ Field presence for at least two years in the district for which the NGO is seeking MNGO status

⇒ Experience in capacity building, organising training in health / RCH, gender and other social sectors is preferred

⇒ An NGO blacklisted or placed under funding restriction by any Ministry or Department of the Government of India (GoI), State Government or CAPART is not eligible for applying under the scheme.

Assets

⇒ Minimum fixed assets of Rs 2 lakhs in the name of the NGO, in the form of land and / or building. This should be reflected in the latest audited balance sheet of the NGO and should be retained during the length of the project

⇒ Office premises in the district where it wants to operate.

Jurisdiction

⇒ Each MNGO is allotted only two districts to work

⇒ Only one MNGO can work in a district

⇒ Preference is given to NGOs, which seek to cover un-served and underserved areas in the district. The NGO identifies these areas in consultation with the District RCH Officer.

NGOs who wish to apply for the MNGO status must fulfill the eligibility criteria as mentioned above. A transparent and participatory process of selection is followed for identifying suitable NGOs for implementing projects under the scheme.

Process Guidelines for Selection. Funds Release and Monitoring

Below are the guidelines for a stepwise selection of MNGOs.

Selection Process of MNGOs

⇒ Advertisement is given in two leading state level daily newspapers for the un-allotted/ surrendered districts (under the MNGO Scheme)

⇒ Completed applications (See Format and Checklist) are received at the office of the Regional Director (RD) Health Services

⇒ The office of the RD conducts desk review based on checklist (See Checklist)

⇒ GoI is informed of the status of applications received till the cut off date by the office of the RD. This is copied to the state government

⇒ A meeting of the State NGO Committee is convened normally within one month. The findings of the desk review are discussed here. The Committee identifies NGOs that have fulfilled the eligibility criteria

⇒ The State NGO Committee informs rejected applicants. This is copied to GoI & State Government

⇒ A field appraisal of all eligible applicant NGOs is conducted by the RRCs within a defined time frame (See Part 4 for Format)

⇒ A meeting of the NGO Selection Committee is convened under the Chairpersonship of JS (FW), GoI, for selection of the MNGO based on desk review reports and field appraisal reports of all eligible NGOs

⇒ The NGO Selection Committee recommends the proposal to the GIAC for approval of MNGO. Decision of GIAC is informed to State RCH Society

⇒ Selected MNGOs go through induction training within 4-6 weeks of selection by the RRCs. The focus of the orientation is on the relevant aspects including management (technical and financial) of the MNGO scheme. (See Checklist)

⇒ Following the induction training, the MNGOs use their skills for identifying suitable FNGOs in the unserved and underserved areas (See Checklist). The MNGO is expected to use the initial grant of Rs 1 lakh during this preparatory phase. The MNGO identifies FNGOs in consultation with the District RCH Society (See FNGO selection process)

⇒ Within our weeks of completing the selection of FNGOs, the MNGO is expected to develop a consolidated project proposal based on the collected data and the indicators from the FNGO proposals

⇒ The MNGO's consolidated proposal is then placed for consideration of District NGO Committee, which communicates the recommendation to the State RCH

Society. The State RCH Society recommends the MNGO project proposal to GoI for the final approval of GIAC and release of grants of the State RCH Society

⇒ The selected MNGO signs a Memorandum of Understanding (MOU) with the District RCH society

⇒ Copy of the signed MOU is sent to the State RCH Society for release of funds. A copy is sent to GoI and RRCs for information.

Duration of Grant

The MNGO is sanctioned a project for a period of three years. Retention of the MNGO status is based on the evaluation, which is to be conducted at the end of Year One and Year Three.

Fund Flow

The flow of funds is from the GoI to the State RCH Society. The State RCH Society is responsible for release of funds of the MNGOs.

GoI to State RCH Society

⇒ GoI releases the 1st installment to the State RCH Society for each district allocated under the MNGO scheme. This is done in the first quarter of the financial year

⇒ Release of the 2nd installment is based on request from State RCH Society.

State RCH Society to MNGO

⇒ State RCH Society releases a grant of Rs.1 lakhs for the preparatory phase to the MNGO. This is primarily for conducting Community Needs Assessment/ baseline survey, identification of FNGOs, orientation of FNGOs, getting FNGO proposal and preparing a consolidated proposal with indicators for submission. If found required, some parts of the found may be used for nurturing/ preparing SHGs/youth groups who could eventually become FNGOs

⇒ MNGOs get an annual allotment of approximately Rs. 5-15 lakhs per district. The budget is based on the number of FNGOs (to whom the grants will be given by the MNGOs) and the nature of the proposed interventions

⇒ MNGOs are allowed to retain 20% of the total project cost (i.e. Rs. 5-15 lakhs). This is in the range of Rs. 1-3 lakhs for administrative cost, which includes capacity building cost

⇒ A non-recurring grant of a maximum of Rs 1.5 lakhs is permitted for purchase of assets during the first 6 months of the project. This expenditure is allowed as a one-time expenditure in the life of the project for clinical equipment and training materials as required by the project. Office equipment can include office furniture such as, table, chairs, storage, cabinets, computer, printer

⇒ An emergency-rolling fund of Rs 1 lakh can be made available to the MNGO to meet exigencies such as non-receipt of drugs, vaccines and contraceptives. This is however subject to a no objection certificate from the District RCH Officer.

⇒ On receipt of the sanction letter and signed MoU from the District RCH Society, the State RCH Society releases grants to the MNGO in the following stages:

* 1st release - for a period of 18 months
* 2nd release - next 16 months and based on favourable

evaluation report by the empanelled evaluating agency and utilisation certificate (UC) for the first 12 months or the end of the financial year, whichever is earlier

* 3rd release**- the final grant of 2 months is released on receiving all completed UC and audited statement of accounts along with project completion report

⇒ The MNGO claims reimbursement of the last installment after submission of the final reports.

⇒ In order to facilitate project continuation, the release of funds will not be totally stopped on account of non submission of UCs by one or two FNGOs with valid reasons (e.g: natural calamities). In such cases, the fund will be released proportionately for those FNGOs who have submitted the UCs, and the MNGO is required to submit the UCs for the complete project before the end of the financial year

In case of default, no further grant will be released. The State RCH Society evaluates the performance and if there is violation of any norms, blacklists the NGO.

Monitoring

A system of periodic reporting and ongoing monitoring is in place for assessing the NGO's performance.

⇒ The MNGO submits reports (financial and performance) every quarter to the State NGO Coordinator and District RCH Society

⇒ The MNGO monitors the work of FNGOs on a monthly basic, and also undertakes field visits and review meetings as per appropriate checklist

⇒ It is mandatory for the State RCH Society to have half yearly review meetings in which the District RCH Society is also represented. The MNGOs makes a presentation to the State RCH Society on their performance (project & financial), during the period based on the activity plan for the year

⇒ The State NGO Coordinator shares the half yearly reports of the MNGOs with the RRCs, to identify areas requiring technical inputs.

Performance Indicators

Retention of MNGO grant and the funds release is based on performance of the NGO.

⇒ The MNGO clearly identifies output and measurable indicators at the project proposal stage. The MNGO also encourages the FNGO to identify these when the FNGO submits its proposals to the MNGO. These are to be identified in consultation with the corresponding tier of Family Welfare Administration and related sectors of Social Development.

⇒ The MNGO supports the FNGO to conduct a baseline survey before the commencement of any activity in the project area. An end line survey is also to be conducted to assess the improvements in service delivery in a given area of intervention.

⇒ The MNGO must be able to demonstrate qualitative and quantitative improvement in meeting the RCH needs of the community in the project area.

⇒ The MNGO assesses progress of FNGO against a cluster of service delivery indicators selected by the FNGOs. The progress of the MNGO is in turn assessed based on the indicators spelt out by it in its consolidated proposal.

Evaluation

⇒ The MNGO performance is evaluated at the end of year one and year three by an external evaluating agency.

⇒ The State RCH Society commissions the evaluation.

Reporting

⇒ The MNGO submits six monthly reports to the State RCH Society with copies to the District RCH Society.

⇒ The State RCH Society shares the 6 monthly reports with Regional Resource Centres and the GoI

⇒ The utilisation certificates for the funds are submitted by the states to GoI

⇒ At the end of the project, the MNGO submits a project completion report to the State RCH Society.

Guidelines for FNGOs

Procedural Guidelines for submission of Application

NGOs applying for FNGO grant must fulfill the following eligibility criteria. The criteria have been grouped into four sections. These are criteria for Registration, Experience, Assets and jurisdiction.

Registration

⇒ NGO should be registered under the Indian Societies Registration Act/ Indian Trust Act/ Indian Religious and Charitable Act/ Company Act or their State counterparts for a minimum of two years.

Experience

⇒ Proven experience of working for two years in Health

and Family Welfare and in social sector (e.g. education, women's empowerment, rural development)

⇒ Preferably implemented a field project in Health and Reproductive and Child Health (RCH)

⇒ Scale of operation during the previous two years should be comparable to the funding sought

⇒ Field presence for at least two years in the geographical area for which it is seeking a grant

⇒ Experience in capacity building, organising training in gender and other social sectors is preferred

⇒ An NGO blacklisted or placed under funding restriction by any Ministry or Department of the Government of India (GoI), respective State Government or CAPART is not eligible for applying under the scheme.

Assets

⇒ Minimum fixed assets of Rs 1 lakh in the name of the NGO, in the form of land and / or building. This should be reflected in the latest audited balance sheet of the NGO and should be retained by it during the length of the project

⇒ The NGO has office premises in the district / block where it wants to operate.

Jurisdiction

⇒ Jurisdiction of FNGOs is linked to the service area of the health sub center

⇒ Field NGOs are expected to provide RCH service delivery in the un-served and under served areas.

Process Guidelines for Selection, Funds Release and Monitoring

Selection of FNGOs

NGOs who wish to apply for the FNGO grant must fulfill the eligibility criteria as mentioned above. A transparent and participatory process of selection is followed for identifying suitable NGOs for implementing projects under the Scheme.

⇒ MNGO undertakes field visits to identify under served and un-served areas in the district, in consultation with the District RCH officer.

⇒ MNGO calls for applications from NGOs through open advertisement based on eligibility criteria

⇒ MNGO screens applications. Based on scrutiny of documents and field visit the MNGO identifies suitable FNGOs

⇒ MNGO provides orientation to selected FNGOs on baseline and /or Community Needs Assessment (CNA), MNGO orients FNGOs on how to develop a project proposal

⇒ MNGOs provide input and guidance to FNGOs in carrying out the baseline and /or CNA in the identified geographical areas. (See Checklist)

⇒ FNGOs submit to MNGO project proposals thus developed

⇒ District RCH/ FW Officer convenes the meeting of the District NGO Committee for approval of FNGO project proposals.

Duration of Grant

The FNGOs work for a period of three years. The project is evaluated annually by the MNGO.

Funds Flow

Funds flow from MNGOs to FNGOs. MNGO disburses grants in the following stages:

⇒ 1st release - for a period of 18 months

⇒ 2nd release - next 12 months and based on favourable report by the MNGO and utilisation certificate (UC) for the first 12 months or the end of the financial year whichever is earlier

⇒ 3rd release- for a period of 4 months and based on the Utilisation Certificate (UC) of the next 12 months and supported by report from MNGO

⇒ 4th release**- The final grant of 2 months is released on receiving completed UC and audited statement of accounts along with project completion report.

** The FNGO claims reimbursement of the last installment after submission of the final reports.

Monitoring

⇒ FNGOs submit quarterly reports (financial and performance) to the MNGO with copies to the District RCH Society

⇒ MNGO conducts monthly monitoring visits to the FNGOs.

Performance Indicators

Retention of grant and funds release is based on performance of the NGO.

⇒ The FNGO identifies output level indicators when submitting its proposals to the MNGO. These are identified in consultation with the corresponding tier of Family Welfare Administration and related sectors of Social Development

⇒ A baseline survey is conducted by the FNGO before the start of any activity in the project area. An end line survey is also conducted to assess the improvements in service delivery in the area of intervention

⇒ The FNGO is able to demonstrate qualitative and quantitative improvement in meeting the RCH needs of the community in the project area

⇒ The MNGO assesses progress of FNGO against a cluster to service delivery indicators selected by the FNGOs.

12

Guidelines For Service NGO (SNGO) Scheme

NGOs with an established institutional base and delivery infrastructure are encouraged to complement the public health system in achieving the goals of the RCH programme. Any NGO that is engaged in directly providing integrated services in an area co-terminus to that of a CHC/ block PHC with 1,00,000 population (approximately 100 villages or more) is called a Service NGO.

Service NGOs are expected to provide a range of clinical services directly to the community. For example, services for safe deliveries, neo-natal care, treatment of diarrhoea and ARI, abortion and IUD services, RTI/STI etc. These services must reach out to make and female population in all age groups. In order to provide these services effectively, the applicant NGO must have appropriate staff, infrastructure such as clinic/ hospital, ambulance, etc.

Non-clinical services could include documentation and surveillance of data, health data management, training of dais, village health committees, SHG leaders and micro credit groups, PRIs among others. The purpose of training, for example, dai training or training of VHCs, will clearly be to improve the access and quality of clinical services. In order to impart these skills, the NGO must have the appropriate infrastructure base and a training center/ institute recognised by the government. A non-recurring, one time grant can be provided to SNGOs for strengthening their existing infrastructure base, in case there is a requirement. Applicants for the SNGO scheme must have staff with demonstrated experience and skills, and credible referral linkages and network for providing outreach services.

This NGO Scheme, called the Service NGO Scheme, is expected to promote the achievement of the RCH objectives in the areas which are un-served or under served** by the public health services and infrastructure and complement the MNGO Scheme. SNGOs differ from MNGOs in terms of their scope and coverage of work. SNGOs can provide a range of clinical and non-clinical services, directly to the community while the MNGOs provide through the FNGOs. While FNGOs can take up a particular service delivery area, SNGOs are expected to provide an integrated package of RCH services. The SNGO may be provided with a non-recurring one-time grant for infrastructure improvements as required whereas FNGOs are not eligible for this.

Un-served and under served areas are those socio-economic backward areas, which do not have access to health care services from the existing government health infrastructure, especially urban slums, tribal, hilly and desert areas including SC/ST habitations. In specific terms theses areas are: where one of the posts of MO, ANM & LHV have been vacant for more than 1 year; the PHC is not equipped with minimal infrastructure: performance on critical RCH indicators is poor.

The SNGOs provide the following comprehensive range of clinical and non-clinical services in the following RCH areas:

The SNGOs implement large-scale projects in the key RCH service areas covered under the MNGO Scheme viz. Family Planning (such as setting up of IUD clinics), Adolescent Reproductive Health, Maternal and Child Health, and RTI. Additionally, SNGOs can take up other areas such as MTP services, and Dai Training. SNGO proposals for service delivery in emerging RCH areas such as Gender based Violence, and Male Participation will be encouraged. Gender and community mobilisation processes are expected to be cross cutting in all aspects of service delivery. Community needs to be adequately mobilised to generate demand for RCH services.

The above is an illustrative list only. Indicative guidelines for these RCH service delivery areas are presented in Part Three of this Guidebook. The SNGO can propose interventions in other service areas. The SNGO must provide a clear justification for this and it must be a felt need in the community.

Greater emphasis on service delivery means that the service providers are able to measure outcomes concretely. Therefore the guidelines focus on development of clear outputs and measurable indicators at the project proposal stage by the SNGO.

This will be done by utilising and strengthening the existing government infrastructure and human resources and not creating a parallel structure.

Institutional Framework

A decentralised and participatory approach is adopted in the management and implementation of the SNGO Scheme.The SNGO guidelines are provided to ensure accountability at all levels. These guidelines are applicable within the Institutional framework as laid out below.

GoI

Government of India provides support through policy guidelines, approvals and release of funds to State RCH Society. Grants-in-Aid Committee (GIAC) approves the MNGO project recommended by the NGO Selection Committee. The NGO Selection Committee is constituted at the state level for the purpose of SNGO selection and is chaired by the joint Secretary, Department of Family Welfare, GoI. Its function is recommend SNGO proposals for approval by the GIAC, which is chaired by the *Secretary, Family Welfare*, GOI, and has representation of *Financial Advisor and Planning Commission.*

Regional Director (RD)

⇒ Receive all applications along with letter of interest and concept paper from NGO applicants and conduct pre-scrutiny of all applications, based on checklist

⇒ Provide the collated information on the NGO applications to the State RCH Society and convene the meeting of the State NGO Committee till the NGO coordinator is identified and placed

⇒ Participate in the review of applications as a member of the State RCH Society

⇒ Participate in the final selection of SNGO as a member of the NGO Selection Committee

⇒ Undertake field visits if required and submit tour reports to State Secretary (FW) & copy to NGO Division, GOI.

Regional Resource Centres (RRCs)

Technical support for NGO capacity enhancement, documentation of best practices, induction and in-service training, liaison with the state government, updating data base on RCH issues and development of MIS is provided by Regional Resource Centres and other technical institutions as found necessary. This is expected to complement the technical support decisions made by the State RCH Society.

Apex Resource Cell (ARC)

Located within the NGO division, the ARC will coordinate the activities of all the RRCs, manage budgets, and facilitate RRC coordination and interaction with state governments.

NGO Selection Committee

The selection of SNGOs will be carried out by the NGO Selection Committee, chaired by the Joint Secretary, FW, GoI. This Committee will be constituted at the level of each state for the purpose of selection of SNGOs. The other members include the State Health & Family Welfare Secretary, Regional Director, RRC Representative, Project Director RCH Society/ director (FW) as Member Secretary and 1-2 co-opted members.

The selection of the SNGO will be based on desk review

reports and field appraisals of the eligible NGOs conducted by the RRCs. After selection of the SNGO, the NGO Selection Committee will place the recommendation to the GIAC for approval.

State RCH Committee

The State RCH Society constitutes a technical NGO Committee, called the State NGO Committee and ensures the placement of State NGO Coordinator. From identification of SNGOs, placing SNGO proposals for final approval by GoI, fund disbursement, capacity building, training, monitoring to evaluation, is the responsibility or the State RCH Society.

State RCH Committee

The State NGO Coordinator convenes the meeting of the State NGO committee, chaired by the Secretary (FW) or his nominee. Till the time the NGO coordinator is identified and gets placed, the Regional Director convenes the State NGO committee meeting. The presence of GoI representative, RD and State NGO Coordinator is mandatory. The RRC and Director (FW) are also members of the Committee.

For review of applications:

⇒ On receiving the pre-scrutiny/desk review reports from the RD's office, the State NGO Committee convenes a meeting for review of NGO applications and prepares agenda

⇒ Invite Secretary (FW) and other members of the committee

⇒ Prepare minutes and decision taken, Communicate the same to GoI and respective NGOs

The primary responsibilities of the State NGO Committee are:

⇒ Examine findings of the desk review and identify eligible NGOs

⇒ Get field appraisal of eligible NGOs done by the RRCs

⇒ Coordinate training of selected SNGOs

⇒ Release of grant-in-aid as per MoU

⇒ Monitoring of SNGOs

⇒ Organize meetings to review the SNGO performance from time and ensure timely release of funds

⇒ Commission SNGO evaluation through external evaluating agency

⇒ Send utilisation certificates to GOI

⇒ Act as arbitrator in case of dispute.

State NGO Coordinator

⇒ The full time State NGO Coordinator is responsible for management of the DoFW supported NGO schemes, including the SNGO Scheme

⇒ The roles and responsibilities of the State NGO Coordinator are liaising, coordinating and supporting the SNGOs

⇒ Towards this, the State NGO Coordinator works closely with the State RCH Society, communicates government RCH and health policies to SNGOs, undertakes periodic field visits, develops terms of reference and participates in the evaluations, ensures timely submission of reports by the SNGOs, timely release of funds and maintains necessary records

⇒ The State NGO Coordinator functions as a coordination point between the SNGOs and the RRCs and other technical resources institutes for meeting the technical needs of the NGOs under the SNGO scheme

⇒ The State NGO Coordinator is a part of the State RRC Society, and reports to Secretary (Family Welfare).

District RCH Society

⇒ The District RCH Society constitutes a technical committee called the District NGO Committee, for recommending SNGO project to State RCH Society. The District RCH/ FW officer convenes the meeting of the District NGO Committee to be chaired by the District RCH Officer. Other members include, state NGO Coordinator, RRC representative, MO, PHC, ANMs of the concerned project area and an NGO (who is not grantee) nominated by the district collector

Functions:

⇒ Review SNGO projects and recommends to state RCH Society

⇒ Facilitate the signing of MoU between the SNGO and the District RCH Society

⇒ Send the signed MoU to State RCH Society for release of funds and inform GoI.

Appraisal and Evaluating Agencies

The Regional Resource Centres conduct the field appraisals prior to SNGO selection. There is panel of identified and trained evaluating agencies at the regional and state levels that conduct the subsequent mid term and final evaluations. The state can request any of these agencies to evaluate the SNGO project. The agencies also obtain feedback from the State RCH Society and the District RCH Society on the SNGO projects.

Inter- Departmental Linkages

Service NGOs are expected to liaise with, as well as complement and supplement the government work at the district and block levels. Service NGOs liaise with PRIs at appropriate the elected members in RCH and planning for activities in sectors requiring extension of services.

Service NGOs are expected to work with diverse networks at the local level. These could include self- help groups, DWCRA groups, Mahila Swasthya Sanghas, programmes like Mahila Samakhya-Swa Shakti and youth groups such as Nehru Yuvak Kendras.

Procedural Guidelines for Submission of Application

Eligibility Criteria

NGOs applying under the SNGO Scheme must fulfill the following eligibility criteria. The criteria have been grouped into four sections. These are criteria for Registration, Experience, Assets and Jurisdiction.

Registration

⇒ The NGO should be registered under the Indian Societies Registration Act/ Indian Trust Act/ Indian Religious and Charitable Act/ Company Act or their state counterparts for more than five years.

⇒ NGOs applying for SNGO in the state other than that of

its registration, should have state specific chapters registered. Alternatively, branches affiliated to a national level federation/ organisation can be registered with the parent body.

Experience

⇒ Proven experience (in the last three years) in implementing field projects in Health and Reproductive and Child Health (RCH) and social sector (education, women's empowerment, rural development, etc.). Proven expertise in provisioning of services, and training is required

⇒ Scale of operation during the previous three years is comparable to the funding sought

⇒ SNGO has the necessary human resource base with RCH and social sector qualification and experience. The NGO has qualified professionals such as medical doctors, paramedics, counsellors and accountants

⇒ An NGO blacklisted or placed under funding restriction by any Ministry or Department of the Government of India (GoI) or CAPART is not eligible for applying under the scheme.

Assets

⇒ Minimum fixed assets of Rs 5 lakhs in the name of the NGO, in the form of land and / or building. This should be reflected in the latest audited balance sheet of the organisation and should be retained by the NGO during the life of the project

⇒ Office premises, service delivery center/s, training institute in the district where it wants to operate.

Jurisdiction

⇒ Minimal area serviced by the SNGO is equivalent to the service area of the CHC/ block PHC as appropriate. For SNGOs providing clinical services, the minimum geographical area is co-terminus to that of PHC and those providing referral services, will cover an area co-terminus to that of CHC

⇒ The maximum geographical area covered by a SNGO providing training is not more than one district

⇒ The SNGO can implement the programme in convergence with the intermediary organisations. (SHG, PRI, NYK, DWC, MSS, Mahila Samakhya). However, the NGO cannot sub contract to other NGOs or bodies in the project area.

Process Guidelines for Selection, Funds Release and Monitoring

Selection of SNGO

⇒ Advertisement is given in two leading State level daily newspapers by the State RCH Society, inviting a letter of interest/concept note on the desired area of intervention

⇒ Completed applications including letter of interest/ concept paper (See Format and Checklist) are received at the office of the Regional Director (RD), Health Services. The concept paper is not a project proposal. It is to show the intent and the contents should reflect why such a project is required

⇒ The office of the RD conducts desk review with the State NGO Coordinator based on checklist. (See Checklist)

⇒ GoI is informed of the status of applications received till the cut off date by the office of the RD. This is copied to the state government

⇒ A meeting of the State NGO Committee is convened normally within one month. The findings of the desk review are discussed here. The Committee identifies NGOs that have fulfilled the eligibility criteria

⇒ The State NGO Committee informs rejected applicants, with copy to GoI and state government

⇒ A field appraisal of all eligible applicant NGOs is conducted by RRCs within a defined time frame

⇒ A meeting of the NGO selection Committee is convened under the Chairpersonship of js (FW), GoI, for selection of the MNGO based on desk review reports and field appraisal reports of all eligible NGOs

⇒ The NGO Selection Committee recommends the proposal to the GIAC for approval of MNGO. Decision of GIAC is informed to State RCH Society

⇒ The SNGO prepares the detailed project proposals and submits within 6 weeks to the District NGO Committee/ District RCH Society for consideration

⇒ District RCH Society communicates the recommendation to the State RCH Society. The State RCH Society places the final recommendation to GoI for the approval of GIAC and release of grants to the State RCH society

⇒ The SNGO signs a Memorandum of Understanding (MoU) with the District RCH Society

⇒ Copy of the signed MoU is sent to the State RCH Society

for release of funds. A copy is sent to GoI and RRCs for information.

Induction Training

⇒ Through RRCs, GoI organises induction training within 6-8 weeks of sanction of NGO project

⇒ The orientation focuses on the relevance of the scheme, expectations, finance and accounting information, programme implementation processes and reporting.

Project Duration

⇒ Each SNGO proposal covers initially a three year term. Based on the evaluation, the grant may be cancelled if the performance is found to be sub optimal. If favourable, the project duration is extended for another two years.

Funding Pattern

⇒ The scale of funding depends on the nature of intervention proposed. The SNGOs can get an annual allotment of approximately Rs. 10-15 lakhs per CHC/block CHC area towards recurring and non-recurring expenses. In order to determine the range of funding that can be proposed, a set of illustrative financial guidelines relating to the service delivery areas has been presented in Part Three of this Guidebook

⇒ In order to make judicious use of existing primary health infrastructure, in the urban and rural areas, the service NGO networks where ever and to the extent possible with such infrastructure. This has direct implication on costing of services.

Release of Funds

The flow of funds is from the GoI to the State RCH

Society. The State RCH Society is responsible for release of funds to the SNGOs.

GoI to State RCH Society

⇒ GoI releases 1st installment to the State RCH Society under the SNGO scheme. This is done in the first quarter of the financial year

⇒ Release of the 2nd installment is based on request from State RCH Society.

State RCH Society to SNGO

⇒ On getting approval from the State RCH Society based on the field appraisal, the SNGO prepares a project proposal. The State RCH Society releases a grant of Rs. 1 lakh for conducting base line survey and development of detailed project proposal

⇒ The SNGOs get an annual allotment of approximately Rs. 10- 15 lakhs per CHC/ block CHC area towards recurring and non-recurring expenses

⇒ The SNGOs are allowed 20% of the total project cost for administrative cost, which includes capacity building cost

⇒ A non-recurring grant of a maximum of Rs. 1.5 lakhs is permitted for purchase of assets during the first 6 months of the project. (List provided below). This expenditure is allowed as a one-time expenditure in the life of the project.

-- Purchase of land or building is not permitted.

-- Clinical equipment required for the implementation of the proposed project.

-- Office equipment: Office furniture such as, table, chairs storage cabinets, computer, printer.

⇒ SNGO may be provided with a one time non recurring grant for infrastructure improvements (civil works) as required. This will be roughly equivalent to one third of the grant amount. (PPC guidelines to define the exact % of grant allowance for infrastructure development may be looked at)

⇒ An emergency rolling fund of Rs. 1 lakh can be made available to the SNGO to meet exigencies such as non-receipt of drugs, vaccines and contraceptives. This is however be subject to a no objection certificate from the District RCH Officer

⇒ On receipt of the sanction letter and signed MoU from the District RCH Committee, the State RCH Society releases grants to the SNGO as under:

* 1st release- for a period of 18 months

* 2nd release- next 16 months and based on favourable evaluation report by the empanelled evaluating agency and Utilisation certificate (UC) for the first 12 months or the end of the Financial Year, whichever is earlier

* 3rd release**- the final grant 2 months is released on receiving all completed UC and audited statement of accounts along with project completion report.

⇒ The NGO claims reimbursement of the last installment after submission of the final report.

Monitoring

A system of periodic reporting and on going monitoring is in place for assessing the NGO's performance.

⇒ The SNGO submits reports (financial and performance)

every quarter to the State NGO Coordinator and District RCH Society

⇒ The State NGO Coordinator undertakes half yearly field monitoring visits to SNGOs

⇒ It is mandatory for the State RCH Society to have half yearly review meetings in which the District RCH Society is also represented. The SNGOs make a presentation to the State RCH Society on their performance (project & financial), during the period based on the activity plan for the year.

⇒ The State NGO Coordinator shares the half yearly reports of the SNGOs with the RRCs, to identify areas requiring technical inputs

Performance Indicators

Retention of grant and the funds release is based on performance of the NGO.

⇒ The SNGO clearly identifies output and measurable indicators at the project proposal stage. These are to be identified in consultation with the corresponding tier of Family Welfare Administration and related sectors of Social Development

⇒ The SNGO conducts a baseline survey before the commencement of any activity in the project area. An end line survey is also to be conducted to assess the improvements in service delivery and results in a given area of intervention

⇒ Project proposal clearly indicates the To Rs of the project and specific benchmarks against which the progress of the project can be evaluated. The progress of service NGO is measured against a cluster of indicators selected and included in their project proposal

⇒ The SNGO must be able to demonstrate qualitative and quantitative improvement in meeting the RCH needs of the community in the project area.

Evaluation

⇒ The SNGO performance is evaluated at the end of year one and year three by an external evaluating agency.

⇒ State RCH Society commissions the evaluation.

Reporting

⇒ The SNGO submits six monthly reports to the State RCH Society with a copy to the District RCH Society

⇒ The State RCH Society shares the 6 monthly reports with Regional Resource Centres and the GoI

⇒ The Utilisation Certificates for the funds are submitted by the status to GoI

⇒ At the end of the project, the SNGO submits a project completion report to the State RCH Society.

13

Service Delivery Guidelines

The achievement of the goals of the National Population Policy 2000 is possible only by increasing access and quality of RCH services. A great deal of effort has gone in raising awareness at the community level regarding small family, care during pregnancy, infant care, prevention and management of childhood diseases, prevention of unwanted pregnancy, among other RCH issues. However, this has not been matched by increasing the availability of FP products, information and services, and quality RCH care by the existing governmental health infrastructure, especially in remote and far-flung areas.

The MNGO scheme as implemented in the last three years has indicated that a number of FNGOs have been providing para-clinical and non-clinical RCH services. Their capacity can be enhanced to be included in the pool of service providers. Therefore the revised guidelines place emphasis on service delivery by the FNGOs.

Additionally, there are a number of NGOs who are not part of the scheme, but with capacity and resource to provide

RCH services. These NGOs can be considered for support under the Service NGO Scheme.

The gap in services could be reduced if the capacity of the NGOs is combined with that of the government and complements the existing services.

FNGOs, MNGOs and SNGOs function in two kinds of scenarios.

(a) Where the government infrastructure is present and functional with staff, supplies and service capacity. In such areas, the NGOs complement the service delivery by enhancing and sustaining the demand for RCH services at community level and by collaborating with the government system.

(b) Where the government infrastructure is not in place, or available but with poor service quality. In such areas, the NGOs complement the service delivery by strengthening the government system, providing services and sustaining the demand for RCH services at community level, as the need may be.

In both scenarios, the service providing NGOs can draw upon central government schemes (e.g: National Maternity Benefit Scheme, fund for referral transport for emergency obstetrics care from PRI) and state government schemes for funds, technical support, training, IEC materials etc.

Service delivery areas for interventions under the MNGO Scheme are as follows:

* Maternal and Child Health
* Family Planning Services
* Adolescent Reproductive Health

* Prevention and Management of RTI

In addition to the above, the service delivery areas for interventions under the SNGO Scheme are as follows:

* MTP Services
* Dai Training
* Violence Against Women
* Male Involvement

Detailed guidelines for project development has been provided for each of the above-mentioned RCH components in this section of the NGO Guidebook. The concluding part of this section presents some financial guidelines specific to service delivery. The NGOs must refer to these broad financial guidelines when planning their intervention and budget.

Detailed Guidelines for RCH Components

Maternal and Child Health

a) RCH Context

Both the RCH programme and the National Population Policy (2000) place importance on achieving the policy goals of reducing maternal, infant and child mortality and morbidity. Several programmes have been introduced to reduce the Maternal Mortality Rate (MMR). It is estimated that India accounts for nearly 20% of maternal deaths worldwide. The maternal mortality ratio is defined as the number of maternal deaths (during pregnancy, child birth, and the puerperal period) per 100,000 live births. This situation is due to poor reach of health care delivery network in rural areas.

Infant Mortality Rate (IMR) refers to the possibility of an infant surviving up to the age of one year. The Infant Mortality Rate declined in India from 101 per thousand live births during 1978 to 72 in 1998. However, this reduction is not the same in all states. In UP, MP, Orissa, Rajasthan, Bihar and some other parts of the country, the IMR continues to range between 80-103 per thousand live births. The Child Mortality Rate (CMR) (deaths of children 1-4 years age group per thousand children) has also shown similar uneven decline. Mortality risks are higher among infants born to women under age of 20 and where birth intervals are less than 24 months. Studies show that infant mortality rates are higher in rural areas than in urban areas. IMR declines sharply with increasing education and awareness of the mother.

Gender inequalities hamper access to health services. Even when services are available, the utilisation of services can be inadequate. This is due to ignorance or prevalent socio-cultural practices reinforced by the low status of women. Early marriage, childbearing and early motherhood increase the risk of maternal morbidility and mortality, and infant mortality.

Maternal and child health is also severely affected by repeated pregnancies. Child mortality rates are higher among girls that among boys. Neglect of the girl child's health is often due to socio-cultural reasons such as son-preference.

Maternal and child health programmes should address such gender biases and inequalities.

b) Coverage

A population of 25-30,000 spread over 30-40 villages

and preferably co-terminus with area of a PHC could be covered by the NGO. The NGO will be expected to provide a basic package of MCH services in the area. It will also establish linkage with referral services, especially with basic and comprehensive emergency obstetric care facilities, either in public or in private sector. Adolescent mothers will also be included.

c) Measurable Output

The NGO should be able to demonstrate a measurable/describable change in maternal and child (0-6 yrs) health status in the community. Following illustrative indicator/s can be considered at the output level:

⇒ % reduction in maternal death

⇒ % increase in women and men getting married after attaining the legal age of marriage

⇒ % increase in the birth interval by all women in reproductive age group

⇒ % of deliveries assisted by skilled personnel (including TBAs)

⇒ % of new born initiated breast feeding within 1/2 hours of birth

⇒ % of girls and boys in 12-23 months age group completely protected with immunisations

⇒ % of girls and boys in 0-6 yrs given rational management of diarrhoea

⇒ % of girls and boys reduced by 50% from several grades of malnutrition.

d) Strategic Interventions

In order to achieve the outputs, the NGO must identify key strategic intervention areas. A gender perspective must be duly incorporated in its project design and in identifying strategic interventions and activities. NGOs can consider the following strategic interventions:

⇒ Access to quality Ante Natal Care services

⇒ Institutional deliveries through skilled attendant at delivery

⇒ Essential neo-natal care

⇒ Access to quality child survival interventions

⇒ Community action for safe motherhood and child survival

⇒ Any other.

If necessary, the NGO must conduct a baseline to assess current MCH needs. This could be done for both preventive and promotive MCH services. If a supportive environment already exists in the community, the NGO should strengthen the same from a MCH perspective. In case the supportive environment is lacking, the NGO should invest in strengthening the same.

The NGO proposing to provide access to MCH services must have the capacity and infrastructure to do so. The NGO must avoid duplication. It must play a complementary role in strengthening the existing health care delivery system for addressing gaps in service delivery. Wherever the existing health care delivery system lacks the capacity, the NGO can identify appropriate referrals, and prepare budgets accordingly.

e) Activities

In each strategic intervention area, the NGO can undertake several different types of activities. The NGO is expected to establish verifiable indicators for each of the strategic intervention areas.

Given is an illustrative list of activities in the strategic intervention areas:

Strategic Intervention 1: Access to quality ANC

⇒ Increasing knowledge on danger signs during pregnancy and delivery, early prediction of complications, weight monitoring, completion of immunisation, appropriate nutrition and nutrition supplements

⇒ Development of a birthing plan and ensuring availability of skilled birth attendant

⇒ Any other

Strategic Intervention 2 : Institutional deliveries

⇒ Appoint qualified nurses to conduct normal deliveries with back up transport for referral in case of complications

⇒ Mobilise community support for transport for referral in the event of complications

⇒ Any other

Strategic Intervention 3 : Essential neo-natal care

⇒ Communication and education on components of essential neo-natal care

⇒ Provision of essential neo-natal care in home deliveries

⇒ Any other

Strategic Intervention 4 : Access to quality child survival interventions

⇒ Establishing depot holders for ORS and co-trimoxazale tablets

⇒ Scheduling immunisation services once a month in each village. (Hepatitis B vaccination can also be included in the package)

⇒ Counselling of parents for improved care seeking behaviour

⇒ Nutrition rehabilitation centres for grade III & grade IV children (As day care centres)

⇒ Any other

Strategic Intervention 5 : Safe motherhood and child survival

⇒ Advocacy with PRIs and other stakeholders on improved care-seeking behaviour, social audit of maternal and infant deaths and getting these issues discussed in Panchayat meetings

⇒ Train the functionaries of community based agencies such as PRI, SHGs, ICDS, Health, etc. in developing an emergency transport plan, and in developing accounting and reporting systems for operating the same. Focus should be on encouraging the community to use the transport for reaching the EOC services

⇒ Developing a Community Nutrition fund for severely malnourished children and pregnant women

⇒ Any other.

Based on the facilities of undertaking activities, existing health care infrastructure (both in public and private sector), and ICDS, a work plan and budget needs to be prepared.

Family Planning Services

a) RCH Context

Family planning is an important RCH component. The National Family Health Survey II (NFHS) data shows 98% awareness regarding general family planning (male and female sterilisation). However, knowledge regarding spacing methods is inadequate and limited. Moreover, the increased awareness has not been matched by increase access to family planning products and services. The NFHS II estimates unmet needs for contraception at around 30%. It indicates that the unmet demand for both limiting and spacing continues to remain high in many states. In rural areas, dependable sources of contraceptive supplies (oral pills, condoms) and follow up care for acceptors are not easily available. Alternative service delivery systems such as commercial, social marketing, and community based distribution system are yet to take roots in rural areas.

An understanding of gender issues in the family planning services is important for effective service provision. Lack of information/ services, prevailing myths and misconceptions regarding contraception and care during pregnancy, and poor quality of available family planning services result in unwanted and repeated pregnancies and unsafe abortions.

Male participation in acceptance of temporary or permanent methods is negligible. According to NFHS II data, 34.2% acceptors of family planning methods were for female sterilisations and 1.9% for male sterilisations. There are socio cultural beliefs that influence the choice of methods- for example that men are at the risk of losing their virility if they undergo vasectomy resulting in resistance to use of condoms. The project interventions should place emphasis on bringing attitudinal change among men about temporary and permanent methods of family planning as is in the case of women.

Women contra-indicated for sterilisation, often have few other contraceptive options. For example, sterilised women often cannot insist on condom use by their husbands. They are therefore exposed to the risk of sexually transmitted infections (STI). Health concerns, limited options, and husband's opposition are important reasons for non-use. Poor reproductive health and high pregnancy loss lead to limited use of temporary methods. Non-availability of a wide range of reversible methods to suit varying needs can lead to reliance on abortion as a method for spacing births. A significant proportion of unmet need can be met through provision of quality contraceptive services. However, the lack of inter- spousal communication leads to non-use of contraception.

The National Population Policy 2000 recognises the rights of men and women to be informed and have access to safe, effective, affordable and acceptable methods of family planning of their choice. The number of unintended pregnancies can be reduced through adoption of appropriate family panning methods.

This will reduce the number of times a women is exposed to the risk of child bearing under adverse circumstances. It is important to ensure that family planning products and services are available and accessible to both men and women. This also includes those in the reproductive age group including adolescent boys and girls. Special attention is to be given in areas which are un-served or under served by the existing government health infrastructure.

b) Coverage

Approximately 800-850 eligible couples are expected to live in a sub-centre area and 6000 eligible couples at the PHC level (the number will vary incase of tribal/desert area). The NGO should provide comprehensive Family Planning counselling and contraceptive services and establish linkages with other relevant RCH services. Focus should also be on unmarried young adults.

c) Measurable Output

The NGO should be able to define outputs that can be measured. The following indicators may be considered:

⇒ % of reduction in unmet demand for contraception by the end of the project period

⇒ % of couples in the reproductive age group who know about FP methods and source of availability

⇒ % increase in boys and girls postponing their marriage

⇒ % increase in eligible couple postponing birth of first child

⇒ % of eligible couples reporting current unmet need

⇒ % increase of men using condoms

⇒ % of villages having assured supplies of non-clinical spacing contraceptives

⇒ % increase in couple protection rate, client continuation rates for OCPs and condoms

⇒ % of facilities reporting regular IUD insertion,

⇒ % of PHCs/ CHCs reporting sterilisation (male and female) cases every month, ratio of male and female sterilisation

⇒ % reduction in women resorting to unsafe abortion

⇒ % of FP/RH camps held in the district as planned

⇒ % of private practitioners providing contraceptive services

⇒ % Number of workers trained in counselling skills.

d) Strategic Interventions

In order to achieve the output/s, the NGO must identify key strategic intervention areas. The NGO must have clarity on what gender issues need to be addressed. I' must plan how to address them through selection of appropriate strategies and activities. The following are 3 suggested strategic intervention areas in which the NGO could undertake activities.

⇒ Demand generation in the community for services through awareness, information, products

⇒ FP services for eligible couples and young adults including counselling, natural, temporary and permanent methods, and referral

⇒ Community based distribution of contraceptives

⇒ Any other.

If is has not already undertaken, the NGO must conduct a baseline study in order to assess the needs of eligible couples and young adults in terms of knowledge, attitudes, practices and access to FP services. If a supportive environment already exists in the community, the NGO should strengthen the same. The NGO may like to undertake advocacy interventions for informing people about contraceptive choices. The NGO proposing to provide access to FP services must have the capacity and infrastructure to do so.

e) Activities

In each strategic intervention area, the NGO can undertake several different types of activities. Given below is an illustrative list only:

Strategic Intervention 1 : Demand generation

⇒ Orientation programmes for various stakeholders such as eligible couples, young male and female, teachers, community leaders, PRI members, women's groups, ICDS, NYKs on composite FP products and services

⇒ Designing communication plan/ activities for men/ women/ adolescent girls and boys for addressing biases/barriers relating to FP

⇒ Health education/ training for women's groups

⇒ Mobilising eligible couples, individual men and women, to participate in FP and RCH camps

⇒ Training of providers (of NGO) for all methods on IPC skills and for providing gender sensitive services

⇒ Any other.

Strategic Intervention 2: Clinic based FP programmes

⇒ Establishing clinic days for offering contraceptive services

⇒ Providing an expanded range of quality contraceptives

⇒ Clinical and gender training of service providers (of NGO) for all methods

⇒ Training of lady health supervisors / ANMs (of the NGO) in IUD insertions and in use of guidelines from a gender and quality of care perspective

⇒ Any other.

Strategic Intervention 3: Community based distribution of contraceptives

⇒ Establishment of depot holders in each village for easy availability of FP services

⇒ Training of depot holders/ volunteers in non-clinical spacing contraceptives, gender and counselling skills

⇒ Initiatives to promote linkages of women's groups with the health system

⇒ Any other

Based on the above, a work plan and a budget plan will be prepared.

Adolescent Reproductive Health

a) RCH Context

The RCH Programme draws on a life-cycle approach. Adolescent Reproductive Health (ARH) is an important RCH component. In India, nearly 40% of the population comprises of adolescent and young adults. They are in the reproductive age group. Despite being such a significant group, their special needs have not been addressed.

Sexual and reproductive decision making by adolescents is affected by factors relating to age and gender. Young boys and girls have poor understanding of pubertal changes and have very little access to counselling and services. Service providers often tend to be judgmental while catering to the needs of adolescents. There are few existing programmes providing information on sexual health and sexuality to adolescent girls and boys.

Adolescent girls have little choice on whom and when to marry. They are usually not in a position to negotiate contraceptive use. Almost 75% of marriages in rural India among adolescent girls is below the age of 16. The first child is born even before the girl is 18 years of age. Infants born to teenage mothers are at higher risk of low birth weight, pre maturity and still born. Incidence of obstetric complications is also high among the adolescent mothers. Poor personal hygiene, myths and misconceptions about sexual and reproductive health lead to complications in pregnancies and maternal mortality. Often young girls do not get information on physiological implications of menstruation. Instead they are subject to taboos during menstruation such as, solation, not permitted to cook/or mingle in the family.

The magnitude of adolescent sexual activity is significant. It is higher in boys than girls. Most adolescents seek information from friends and peers on sexual and reproductive issues. These tend to be misleading or inaccurate. Girls are not encouraged to know about their bodies and about reproduction till they are married.

However, gender norms expect boys to be sexually experienced well before marriage. This results in risky sexual behaviour on the part of many young men. Young people are at a greater risk of contracting sexually transmitted diseases including HIV/AIDS. This is due to early onset of sexual activity, reluctance/ ignorance to use prevention methods and frequent partner change.

For unmarried adolescent girls, access to contraception and to MTP is very difficult. This is largely due to social pressures and biases of service providers. This puts unmarried adolescents at risk of unsafe abortions. Girls are not expected to be informed about contraception before marriage. There is pressure to bear the first child immediately after marriage. As a result there is near absence of contraception in the 15-19 age group. This also means that adolescent girls run greater risks related to STIs. Early pregnancy carries with it higher risks of maternal mortality.

In the past, both health and family welfare programmes have neglected the adolescent groups. Some interventions focused on married adolescents. It is important to understand age and gender specific reproductive health needs of adolescents. Increase in opportunities for awareness and access to affordable RH products and services will have positive impact on the lives of adolescents and their health status.

b) Coverage

Approximately 750-800 adolescent boys and girls in the age group (10-19 years) are expected to live in a sub-centre area (the number will vary incase of tribal/desert area). The NGO will be expected to provide comprehensive Adolescent Reproductive Health (ARH) education for increasing the knowledge on RH issues (family planning RTI/ STI, personal hygiene, anaemia, teenage pregnancy and age at marriage), and services. Focus will be on both in school and out of school, married and unmarried adolescent girls and boys. Interventions could cover mixed or exclusive group.

c) Measurable Output

The NGO should be able to define measurable outputs. It is expected that the NGO should be able to measure progress in terms of:

⇒ % of adolescent girls and boys gained knowledge on RH leading to improved behaviour/practice

⇒ % of improvement in utilisation of RH services

⇒ % reduction in teenage pregnancies

⇒ % of adolescent girls and boys coming for voluntary counselling and treatment of RTI/STI

⇒ % of girls and boys getting married after reaching 18 and 21 years of age respectively

⇒ % number of peer educators per 100 adolescents available to impart nutrition and health education and reproductive hygiene

⇒ % of adolescent girls who adopt hygienic practices during menstruation/ reproduction

⇒ % of boys who observe penile hygiene

⇒ % of adolescents who use condom during their last sexual act

⇒ Qualitative changes as depicted through process documentation, case studies etc.

d) Strategic Interventions

In order to achieve the output/s, the NGO must identify key strategic intervention areas. There are differences in the needs and concerns of adolescent girls and boys. The strategies for working with girls would vary from that of working with boys.

Working with mixed groups of girls and boys must be attempted. Invariably, all adolescent interventions must have support of parents and guardians. The NGO must have clarity on what gender issues need to be addressed. It must plan how to address them through selection of appropriate strategies and activities.

The following are three suggested strategic intervention areas in which the NGO could undertake activities:

⇒ Supportive environment in the community for addressing ARH

⇒ Access of adolescent girls and boys to knowledge and counselling/ clinical services related to ARH

⇒ Enhancing life skills opportunity for adolescent girls and boys (personality development skills such as self-awareness, self-confidence, self-esteem, problem solving, negotiation skills, ability to analyze)

⇒ Any other

The NGO must conduct a baseline study in order to assess the needs of adolescent girls and boys in terms of knowledge, attitudes, practices and utilisation of services. If a supportive environment already exists in the community, the NGO should strengthen the same from the ARH perspective.

The NGO proposing to provide access to ARH services must have the capacity and infrastructure to do so. ARH is a relatively new aspect. It is therefore important that the NGO networks and links with institutions which the required experience, both from public and private sources.

e) Activities

In each strategic intervention area, the NGO can undertake several different types of activities. Given below is an illustrative list.

Strategic Intervention 1 : Supportive Environment

⇒ Orientation programmes for various stakeholders such as parents, teachers, parent-teachers association, community leaders, PRI members, women's groups, ICDS, NYKs etc. on adolescent health issues

⇒ Capacity building of teachers to take up the role of guide/ counsellor and communicate messages related to adolescent health

⇒ Mobilising community for identifying appropriate social space for imparting information and counselling

⇒ Mobilising and enhancing the knowledge and skills of adolescent girls and boys to participate in this process

⇒ Any other

Strategic Intervention 2 & 3: Access to services & life skills development

⇒ Orient service providers, including private practitioners (formal and informal) on ARH and selected health issues

⇒ Co- curricular activities with ARH and selected health messages

⇒ Capacity building of a number of students (boys and girls) in each school or in each village as peer educators for adolescent health

⇒ Conducting family life education camps and life skills and leadership development training for adolescent girls and boys

⇒ Provision of counselling services for adolescent girls and boys on ARH and sexuality issues.

⇒ Training selected teachers, peer educators, and health workers as counsellors

⇒ Checklist based RTI/ STI during health camps

⇒ Diagnosing anaemic girls and providing IFA tablets

⇒ Linking adolescent clinic with monthly RCH camps conducted by PHC

⇒ Any other

Based on the above, a work plan and a budget plan will be prepared.

Prevention and Management of Reproductive Tract Infections (RTI)

a) RCH Context

Reproductive Tract Infections (RTI) including Sexually

Transmitted Infections (STI) are being recognised as a major problem. This has been brought into the reproductive health agenda. Many RTIs are sexually transmitted. The emergence of HIV and identification of STIs as a facilitating factor for transmission of HIV/ AIDS has led to efforts of designing appropriate programmes to address unmet needs for RTIs / STIs.

Young people are at a greater risk of contracting sexually transmitted diseases including HIV/AIDS, due to early onset of sexual activity, reluctance/ignorance to use preventive methods and frequency of partner change.

The common causes of RTI among women include infections due to inadequate medical procedures such as unsafe abortions, unclean deliveries, and other diagnostics, and therapeutic procedures, infections associated with inadequate personal, sexual and menstrual hygiene practices and sexually transmitted infections. Men also experience RTI in the form of uretheritis and genital infections.

Though both men and women get infected, the prevalence and the consequences are much more severe for women.

Women hesitate to discuss the issue of RTI since it is related to sexual activity. Untreated RTI/ STI create complications resulting from spread of infection to other part of reproductive tract or other organs of the body. Major complications include, infertility, ectopic pregnancy, and cervical cancer resulting in mortality or psychological problems for women. Some infection may cause fetal wastage, pre-term delivery, low birth weight babies or infecting the newborn during the delivery.

Treatment of women for STD and RTIs without the cooperation of men is an area of concern in the management of RTIs and STDs. Self-reporting of gynaecological problems is low. This is because it is associated with a sense of embarrassment and shame. This effects chances of being diagnosed and treated. Extra marital sexual behaviour of male partners contributes to the problem. Lack of negotiating ability of women in the practice of unsafe sex by partners also contributes to the problem. Treatment options available to the women are limited by a number of factors. These include a symptomatic nature of these diseases in women , their access to services, non-availability of female doctors, cultural resistance to internal examinations, and lack of availability of non-stigmatising treatment in public sector. Patients find it easier to use the quality of service offered by unqualified quacks though the quality of service is poor. These is need to increase the availability of quality services to people to meet their unmet needs for the management of RTI.

b) Coverage

A population of 25-30,000 spread over 30-40 villages and preferably coterminus with the area of a PHC can be covered by the NGO. Since these services are yet to be introduced in many CHCs, such services can be expanded to include the entire block. The NGO will be expected to establish linkage with referral services for treatment failure or reoccurrence cases. It should also linkages of RTI/STI with the other service components of RCH.

c) Measurable Output

The NGO should be able to demonstrate measurable change in terms of reducing prevalence of RTIs/STIs (i.e. self reported prevalence). Examples of specific output indicators could be:

⇒ % of male/female in 15-49 yrs age group reporting RTIs/STI on the basis of household survey

⇒ % of male/ female/ couples/ partners who complete treatment.

d) Strategic Interventions

The NGO must be able to duly incorporate a gender perspective in its project design and in identifying strategic interventions and activities. The NGO must have clarity on what gender issues need to be addressed. It must plan how to address them through selection of appropriate strategies and activities.

To achieve this output, following strategic interventions can be considered:

⇒ Behaviour change communication (BCC) and social mobilisation

⇒ Promoting condom as a method of dual protection

⇒ Case Management of symptomatic individuals

⇒ Orientation of the private practitioners

⇒ Any other.

If it has not already undertaken, the NGO must conduct a baseline study in order to get the estimates on current patterns of treatment sought. If a supportive environment already exists in the community, the NGO should strengthen the same from the HIV/ AIDS prevention perspective. In case the supportive environment is lacking, the NGO should invest in strengthening the same.

The NGO proposing to provide access to RTI/STI services must have the capacity and infrastructure to do so. It is important that the NGO networks and links with institutions having the required expertise and experience, both from public and private sources. Most medicines used for the RTIs/ STIs cannot be prescribed by anyone other than a qualified allopathic doctor. Services of a medical doctor should be hired. Partnership with private sector should be fully explored.

e) Activities

In each strategic intervention area, the NGO can undertake several different types of activities. Activities should be chosen keeping in mind the ground realities as mentioned above. Given is an illustrative list of activities in the strategic intervention areas:

Strategic Intervention 1: Behaviour change communication and social mobilisation

⇒ Planning local area level communication strategy for BCC, with a focus on community members, especially women to protect themselves from RTI/ STI and HIV infection

⇒ Implementation of the communication plan for emphasising preventive behaviour

⇒ Orientation programmes (for both private and public sector providers) for sensitisation to gender issues and issues of partner management, compliance, condom use and counselling for avoiding risky behaviour

⇒ Outreach programmes for community based groups, PRIs, TBAs and adolescents

⇒ Any other

Strategic Intervention 2: Promoting dual protection

⇒ Depot holder providing quality condoms for dual protection in all villages having more than 500 populations

⇒ Provision of quality condom supplies on a regular basis

⇒ Communication activities by depot holder for prevention of STIs in the village

⇒ Any other

Strategic Intervention 3: Case Management of Symptomatic Individuals

⇒ Setting up mobile clinics, attached with small lab setup, for the purpose of enhancing sensitivity of syndromic approach for the vaginal discharge patients. Simple lab tests e.g., RPR, Grams staining, Ph test, KOH test and wet mount can be designed in such a manner that the same village is visited again after seven days for the follow up

⇒ Provision of lab equipments and reagents, drugs and medicines

⇒ Any other

Strategic Intervention 4: Orientation of private practitioners

⇒ Organise orientation programmes for raising awareness

on causation, transmission and prevention of RTI /STIs including HIV/AIDS, early diagnosis and immediate treatment of RTIs

⇒ Related issues including partner management, compliance, condom use and counselling for avoiding risky behaviour

⇒ Any other

Based on the facilities of undertaking activities, existing health care infrastructure (both in public and private sector), a work plan and budget needs to be prepared.

MTP Services

a) RCH context

In India, unwanted pregnancies are common. Abortion is one of the major causes of maternal mortality and morbidity. It is estimated that about 9% of maternal deaths in 1998 were due to unsafe abortions. The prevalence rate of abortion in India is unknown. However, the most widely cited figures suggest that around 7 million abortions take place annually. As per GoI service statistics, about 1 million abortions are performed annually under the Medical Termination of Pregnancy (MTP) Act. Around 6 million abortions are performed by practitioners, many of whom are unqualified and untrained. They induce pregnancy termination at uncertified places and use dubious methods. The health impact of unsafe abortions is a major public health concern. Post-abortions care and management of post-abortion complications is an essential service at the PHC, CHC, and district hospital levels.

Induced abortion is carried out to terminate unwanted

pregnancies. There can be many reasons for seeking abortion services. These include non- use of spacing method, lack of information, fear of side effects, limited accessibility of quality services, and contraceptive failure. Male domination can restrict a woman's control over her body and fertility. Abortion can also be due to non-consensual sex within or outside marriage; sexual violence , including sexual abuse and rape of adolescent girls.

In a society like India, son preference is very common. This induces women to go for abortion of female foetus even though it is illegal in India. Second trimester abortions are usually high due to sex selective abortions. Easy availability of prenatal diagnostic techniques has resulted in increased use of sex determination tests even among the rural poor. Many private clinics offer both sex determination and sex selective abortion services. The education and counselling should focus on men as well as women regarding social implications of sex selective abortions, equal opportunity for girls children for survival and growth, safe sex and promotion of use of condoms/ pills and other temporary methods.

Unmarried women who get pregnant find it difficult to seek MTP services. This is due to fear of social discrimination. Abortion services are also costly for many women, especially rural women. Women therefore often seek unsafe practices through quacks or through consumption of harmful indigenous substances. Abortion complications sometimes are quite severe. This can lead to infertility and RTI. Service providers may be biased and male partners may not be supportive. All these factors affect women's access to safe and legal abortion services.

b) Purpose of Support

The NGO should not promote abortion as a method of family planning. It should aim to reduce unwanted pregnancy. This can be through expanded and improved family planning services. Support will be provided to NGOs to:

(i) Prevent, manage and treat the complications of spontaneous or unsafely- induced abortions; and

(ii) Provide safe and legal abortion services, post- abortion counselling and family planning. Access to quality family planning information and services will be an essential part of post-abortion services.

c) Coverage

The NGO is expected to provide clinic-based FP and MTP services to a population located in a block covering approximately 200 villages. Women in reproductive age groups, including partners, will be the main clients for the services. The comprehensive services will include couple counselling, provision of FP products and services, safe and legal abortion and MTP services, post-abortion counselling, and temporary and permanent methods of contraception. Emphasis will be on providing quality and affordable services. The facilities can provide services for termination of pregnancy up to eight weeks of gestation by the MVA method. These services should be set up as per the guidelines of GoI. A copy of these guidelines can be obtained from the district health office.

d) Measurable output

The NGO should be able to define measurable outputs

in terms of :

⇒ % of abortion related complications reported at the facilities in the area

⇒ % of repeat abortions

⇒ % of abortions as per age distribution (including adolescent girls)

⇒ % of MTP clients who have received post abortion contraceptive counselling and FP services

⇒ % of girls and boys getting married after attaining the legal age of marriage.

e) Strategic Interventions

To achieve the output/s, the NGO must identify key strategic intervention areas. The following are 3 suggested areas in which the NGO could undertake activities:

⇒ Inform the community about safe and legal abortion services

⇒ Increase access to safe and legal clinic facilities and improved quality care

⇒ Follow up services.

The NGO proposing to provide access to safe and legal abortion services must have the capacity and infrastructure to do so.

f) Activities

In each strategic intervention area, the NGO can undertake several different types of activities. Given below is an illustrative list.

Strategic Intervention 1 : Demand generation for quality services:

⇒ Community orientation for eligible couples, SHG members, PRI, anganwadi, teachers, ANM, NGOs including FNGO/ MNGOs, adolescent boys and girls IEC on complications of unsafe abortions and availability of safe and legal services

⇒ IEC on MTP and PNDT (Pre-natal Diagnostic Techniques Act)

⇒ Develop network with related service providers such as pharmacies, chemist shops, private practitioners, dais, sub centres, ANM, PHCs, depot holders in the villages, other NGOs involved

⇒ Any other.

Strategic Intervention 2 : Increase access of safe and legal clinic facilities and improved quality care.

⇒ Hiring of qualified staff as per guidelines

⇒ Identification of proper premises for the clinic as per MTP Act and related guidelines

⇒ Orientation and training of the staff on social dimensions of FP and MTP issues, legal implications, gender biases, government policies, quality service, developing a client centred approach, and counselling skills.

⇒ Equipment and supplies

⇒ MIS

⇒ Any other

Strategic Intervention 3 : Follow up services:

⇒ Availability of effective counselling services

⇒ Post- abortion FP services
⇒ Establish a follow up net work within the community
⇒ Maintenance of records and documentation
⇒ Any other.

Based on the above, a workplan and a budget plan will be prepared.

Training of Traditional Birth Attendants (TBA)/ Dai

a) RCH context

One of the main goals of National Population Policy 2000 is to reduce maternal mortality and morbidity. Unsafe deliveries and practices are often conducted at home by relatives and untrained Traditional Birth Attendants (TBA) or commonly known as 'Dai'. This can lead to high maternal mortality and morbidity. About 74% deliveries in the country take place outside formal health institution. Data on safe deliveries (institutional deliveries and deliveries conducted by trained personnel) is available from the rapid household surveys for 496 districts. This data shows that only 123 districts have more than 70% safe deliveries; 240 between 30-70% while in 142 districts safe delivery rates are less than 30%.

All deliveries should be conducted by trained health functionaries. However, presently the health care system is not in a position to provide services of a trained health functionary at the time of delivery. It is therefore important to ensure that the Dais are trained. The Dais or the traditional birth attendants (TBAs) have been conducting deliveries using traditional methods, handed down to them over generations. Most of them are illiterate, poor and do not have adequate skills in conducting safe deliveries in identifying high-risk cases among pregnant women during the ante-natal period. Lack of proper skills and absence of aseptic techniques in their work lead to high morbidity and mortality. The services of the Dai need to be better utilised in the rural areas. This can be ensured by providing them with the necessary training and promotion of aseptic delivery practice.

b) Coverage

Pregnant women in a sub district area, covering approximately 100-120 villages will be served by the trained dais. The NGO will be expected to provide the basic training to dais, provide certification, moniter their performance, release the payment and do follow up work. The training will be comprehensive to enable the Dai to provide support to pregnant mothers from early registration stage till safe delivery. This will include nutrition counselling, antenatal check up, identification of high risk cases, identification of danger signals during delivery and make appropriate referrals.

The number of dais to be trained will be calculated based on the institutional delivery capacity available (30 beds/ 50 beds hospital) in the project area and the need in the community. At least one trained Dai plus a backup should be available in each village in the project area. It is important that dais are given hands on training to acquire skills.

This means that the NGO has adequate infrastructure to train the dais as per the Gol curriculum and for hands on training. The SNGO must have trained personnel with experience to provide the training. The SNGO should be clear on the certification and competency criteria for TBA/ dais (after how many deliveries conducted independently, the certificate will be given to them).

The SNGO will develop appropriate mechanism to ensure that the dai will be able to link with the referral net work and her cases will be accepted on priority basis by these institutions. Monitoring mechanisms will be established to ensure that the Dai actually applies her skills in the project area. The training should enable the dais to provide support for safe delivery at home. They should also support those who wish to have institutional delivery.

c) Measurable Output

The NGO should be able to demonstrate the usefulness of Dai training in measurable terms. This should reflect in terms of :

⇒ Changes in the practices related to care during pregnancy.

⇒ Increase in the number of deliveries by trained persons in the project area.

To achieve the output, at the end of the training the Dai should be able to:

⇒ Understand the profile of the women who can safely deliver at home and those who require hospital care.

⇒ Monitor and mange first stage of labour

⇒ Conduct normal delivery of baby and placenta, including newborn care using the right techniques.

⇒ Understand the importance of aseptic techniques during delivery

⇒ Understand the five principle (clean hands, clean surface, clean blade, clean cord tie, and clean cord stump) and clean perineum.

⇒ Recognise the complications during the second and third stages of labour and link up with appropriate referral.

⇒ Know why to refer, when to refer, where to refer and how to refer

⇒ Advice women on dangers of unsafe abortions, availability of MTP and help in their referral as required.

d) Strategic Interventions

In order to achieve the output the following strategic interventions may be considered.

⇒ Demand generation in the community through awareness, information and service of dais.

⇒ Providing quality care. Ensure mechanisms are in place for continued use of services or Dai in the project area.

⇒ Any other.

e) Activities

It is important that the NGO has the capacity and infrastructure to provide Dai training and follow up. Since most of the Dais are illiterate or neo literate, the NGOs should be able to understand their requirements. They should have sufficient knowledge about the project area including existing pregnancy care and delivery practices. The NGO must conduct a baseline. The activities may include:

Strategic Interventions 1 : Demand generation

⇒ Development of a data base for the availability of safe institutional facilities and the number of trained and potential dais in the project area.

⇒ Development of criteria for the selection of trainees

⇒ Community orientation for utilising the services of the trained Dais for simple cases

⇒ Any other.

Strategic Interventions 2 : Providing quality care and ensuring sustainability

⇒ Orientation of trainers

⇒ Ensure availability of Disposable Delivery Kit (DDK) and weighing machines

⇒ Linkage with private hospitals and the government infrastructure for referrals

⇒ Linkage with other NGOs (FNGOs/ MNGOs) engaged in MCH interventions in the project area for providing Dai support

⇒ Development of simple and user friendly IEC and training materials

⇒ Development of checklist for enabling the Dai to collect her fee

⇒ Provision of certificate along with some form of identity to each trained Dai (a photo identify card or a distinctive badge).

Based on the above a work plan and a budget plan will be prepared.

Reference: Contents of Dai Training

The Dai training guidelines of Government of India are given for reference.

⇒ Definitions of Asepsis and Sepsis, Sterilisation Techniques and how to sterilise scissors or blade if necessary

⇒ Discussion on physical signs of pregnancy, antenatal care, importance of early registration in the PHC, rest, IFA tablets, and TT immunisation

⇒ Identification of Danger Signals during pregnancy, labour and postnatal period:

* *During pregnancy*- bleeding, swelling of face and hands, severe headache, breathlessness at rest, twin pregnancy and anaemia.

* *Labour*- Mechanism of normal labour, labour pain of more than 12 hours without progress in primi-paras.

* *Postnatal*- severe bleeding, fever with chill and rigour and foul odour from genital tract.

⇒ Care of mother and newborn after delivery.

⇒ In addition, the ethical and legal issues involved in the practice of sex selective foeticide and infanticides must form a part of the curriculum

⇒ Dais will be oriented on availability of funds for referral transport with the Panchayats and how to access the fund when needed. This should be done in areas where referral transport scheme is in operation.

Violence Against Women

a) RCH Context

Violence against women and girls is a human rights

and a public health issue. In the Indian context, violence begins even before a girl child is born (e.g.; sex selective abortions) or soon after birth (female infanticide). It continues to affect women throughout their lives. Women face nutritional, educational and recreational deprivation. They also face dowry related violence, rape, physical and mental abuse and many other forms of violence. Ninety percent of domestic abuse, with or without visible violence, requires medical, psychological, and public health treatment. There are many causes for violence against women. These can be socio-cultural (son- preference and gender biases), economic deprivation, lack of control over resources, health related (infertility), non-recognition of women's labour and male superiority.

Women rarely come forward to register a case of violence. They hesitate to even discuss the issue openly due to lack to adequate support mechanisms both within the household and outside. In the rural areas, health workers are often the only point of contact with public services.

Health care providers can play an important role by (a) enhancing the awareness of the family and community members and (b) identifying victims of violence and linking them with medico-legal or medico-social support services.

Violence against women has a direct negative impact on several important RH issues. These are safe motherhood, family planning, and the prevention of sexually transmitted diseases and HIV/ AIDS.

b) Purpose of Support

NGOs will be supported for:

⇒ Increasing levels of awareness among the community and health care providers on violence against women and its RH consequences

⇒ Providing services for prevention and management of health and RH consequences of violence against women.

c) Coverage

The NGO will be expected to identify and focus on a set of population starting from a block level. The NGO should adopt a comprehensive approach to the issue of violence against women in the context of RH. The NGO should establish linkage with other relevant RCH services.

d) Measurable Output

The NGO should be able to define measurable outputs in terms of :

⇒ % of reported cases of gender based violence by victim/ witnesses/others

⇒ % of women victims of violence accessing/provided timely health services/referral support

⇒ % of women and young girls accessing counselling services

⇒ qualitative changes as depicted through process documentation, case studies, etc.

e) Strategic Intervention

To achieve the outputs, the NGO must identify key strategic intervention areas. The following are 3 suggested areas in which the NGO could undertake activities:

⇒ Supportive environment in the community for addressing violence against women.

⇒ Identifying institutional and community based mechanisms to address violence against women

⇒ Access to services (information, counselling referrals) for managing RH consequences of violence.

⇒ Any other

If necessary, the NGO must conduct a baseline study. This is to assess the prevalence of violence, its causes, and existing mechanisms for prevention and management of violence. If a supportive environment is already existing in the community, the NGO should strengthen the same from a gender perspective. The supportive role of men and young boys in preventing and managing the RH consequences of violence must be emphasised.

The NGO should have the capacity and infrastructure and avoid any duplication with the existing health care delivery system. It must play a complementary role and sensitise/ strengthen the existing health care delivery system for addressing the RH consequences of gender-based violence. Wherever the existing health care delivery system is found to be weak, the NGO can identify appropriate referrals and prepare budgets accordingly.

f) Activities

In each strategic intervention area, the NGO can undertake several different types of activities. Given below is an illustrative list.

Strategic Intervention 1 & 2 : Supportive environment & community based mechanisms

⇒ Sensitisation programmes for various stakeholders such

as adults, couples, young adults, teachers, community leaders, PRI members, village health committees, women's groups/ SHGs, ICDS, NYKs on gender based violence and RH consequences

⇒ Community mobilisation for identifying appropriate social spaces. This is to provide information and services for addressing the issue

⇒ Male mobilisation activities for addressing the issue (*sammelans*)

⇒ Set up CBOs/ women's groups as community surveillance/ vigilance groups on gender based violence

⇒ Legal literacy camps

⇒ Institutionalise innovative community initiated responses to violence, such as, Nari Adalat, Nari panch.

⇒ Any other

Strategic Intervention 3 : Service support

⇒ Checklists for screening women victims of violence developed and used by service providers

⇒ Training of health care providers on identification and management of RH consequences of violence against women

⇒ Establish counselling centres with community outreach facilities and referral linkages

⇒ Selection of partner NGOs, counsellors, location and development of counselling protocols

⇒ Establish information and surveillance systems for addressing the issue

⇒ Any other.

Based on the above, a work plan and a budget plan will be prepared.

Male Involvement

a) RCH context

Male involvement refers to the various ways in which men participate in improving the health and reproductive health status of women and girls. Men also have their own health needs and concerns.

They are often misinformed about sexual and reproductive health issues. Family Welfare clinics are generally viewed as female places. Logistic constraints, such as lack of male staff or convenient hours, also make it difficult for men to access services. Male involvement in RCH programmes aims at promoting joint decision-making on issues of sexual and reproductive health.

Evidence also suggests that promoting safe/ responsible sexual behaviour among men has positive results. Women and men can as a result make informed reproductive choices. The National Population Policy 2000 (NPP 2000) too brings men to the forefront in population and reproductive health programmes.

b) Purpose of Support

NGOs will be supported to increase male participation for improving the reproductive health status of women and men. This means that men support women in their access to reproductive health services. It also means that men assume responsibility for their sexual and reproductive behaviour.

Men will offer their support for safe, voluntary and satisfying sexual relationships, participate in family planning, provide support to their partners during pregnancy, assist women during both normal and difficult deliveries, and participate meaningfully in children's well being. Male participation enhances cooperation and respect between sexes based on shared roles and responsibilities.

c) Coverage

NGOs will be expected to identify and focus on a set of population starting from a block level. Male involvement will be defined in relation to family and household members-men as partners, fathers, and brothers as well community/religious leaders, managers and service-provider, and as clients. Focus will also be on young boys for their future roles as partners and fathers. Eligible couples will also be covered.

d) Measurable Outputs

The NGO must define measurable outputs in terms of:

⇒ % of eligible couples covered by contraception, especially by temporary and permanent male contraceptive methods.

⇒ % of couples utilising other RH services.

⇒ % of males attending group communication activities conducted in villages.

⇒ % of men aware of causation, transmission and prevention of RTIs/STIs.

⇒ % of men aware of different components of ANC, etc.

⇒ Qualitative changes as depicted through process documentation, case studies, etc.

e) Strategic Interventions

To achieve the outputs, NGOs must identify key strategic intervention areas. The following are 3 suggested areas in which NGOs can undertake activities:

⇒ Build a supportive environment among men and community leaders through information, advocacy and behaviour change communication (BCC.)

⇒ Provide community outreach services with a focus on men and couples.

⇒ Improve access to sexual and reproductive health services for women and men.

⇒ Any other.

f) Activities

In each of the strategic areas the NGOs for their own and their partners sexual and reproductive health.

⇒ Involvement of experienced people as community advocates for addressing myths and misconceptions and changing discriminative norms around gender issues.

⇒ Sensitisation programmes on male involvement issues among religious/ panchayat leaders and adult women.

⇒ Use of existing male spaces, for examples, markets, taxi stands, sport arenas, youth clubs etc for creating a supportive environment

⇒ Any other.

Strategic Intervention 2 : Community outreach services

⇒ Male group activities for participatory community diagnosis of health service needs, concerns of women, and obstacles to men's involvement in RCH.

⇒ Mass media activities that highlight health information/ communication.

⇒ Sexuality and gender education for school boys and other youth.

⇒ Outreach health melas and other innovative ways of involving men.

⇒ Work on gender-based violence prevention with focus on men.

⇒ Work with organised groups of men at work place, trade unions, farmer/ dairy co-operatives, migrant workers for RH services/referrals and promotion of male methods of contraception.

⇒ Any other.

Strategic Intervention 3: Access to Sexual and Reproductive Health Services

⇒ Adapting clinic timings to meet men's needs.

⇒ Using couple approach in counselling for safe sex, partner treatment for RTIs/ STDs, HIV/ AIDS, and infertility

⇒ Provide space/ time for couple counselling or having separate timings for men.

⇒ Community-based distribution of contraceptives aimed at men

⇒ Training of male community-based distribution workers

⇒ Training of private and public health paramedics in counselling and contraceptive methods

⇒ Set up telephone hotlines to provide confidential counselling

⇒ Screening, clinical diagnosis and treatment

⇒ Integration of HIV prevention with FP during counselling and educational activities.

⇒ Counselling services for adolescent boys

⇒ Any other.

NGOs providing services for addressing the sexual and reproductive health needs of men must have the capacity and infrastructure to do so. It must avoid duplication with the existing health care delivery system. It must add preventive and promotive services for men without restricting ongoing services for women. It must ensure integrated services for men within existing services instead of establishing independent services. The NGO must ensure that the programme does not contribute to reinforcing gender inequalities.

Based on the above, a work plan and a budget plan will be prepared.

Financial Guidelines Specific to Service Delivery

NGOs will refer to the following financial guidelines specific for service delivery.

Funds availability

Funds will be made available to NGO according to the proposed interventions for: Base line studies, conducting *Community Needs Assessment*, staff salaries and honorarium, conducting IEC activities, induction and in service training for the staff, community orientation, development of mass media campaigns, various types of camps, MCH clinics, provisions purchase of FP supplies, essential drugs (according to list) to meet situations where government supplies are not available, purchase of clinical equipment, consumables required for the clinics/ camps, setting up of depots hiring of space for clinic/ meetings, monitoring visits- travel and DA, referral transport, documentation, relevant records, registers and formats, follow up on referral cases, administrative and contingency.

Limitations

⇒ The salary component of the budget will not exceed 35 % of the total budget.

⇒ Contingency of 10% of the total cost less the salaries's permissible.

⇒ Charges such as rented space, TA and DA for the staff will be according to existing government norms. A list will be provided as annexure for other items such as dai fee, where existing government norms will be adhered to. Any deviation will be approved after scrutiny by the RCH society.

⇒ Funds will not be available for construction of building and purchase of vehicles.

Budget modification

The NGO will incur expenditure as per the approved budget. Flexibility will be available to make adjustments among the budget heads up to 10% without prior approval. Additional changes between the budget heads will be permissible with prior approval by the State RCH Society.

1. Indicative Rates for Medical and Para Medical Government Staff

Sl. No.	Category of Staff	Maximum permissible
1. (i)	Doctor (full time) -MO level	Rs. 10000/-
(ii)	Doctor - Per visit (as per GoI schemes)	Gynae- Rs. 800/- Anaesthetist-Rs.1000/-
2.	ANM- full time	Rs. 5000/- per month (Varies from State to State)
3.	Staff Nurse (graduate)	Rs. 7500/- per month
4.	Dai	Rs 25/- per delivery (As applicable under scheme for FAG States)
5.	Community Health Workers full time	Rs. 1000/- per month

2. Training cost per training

S.No.	Details	Cost (in rupees)
1.	TA	Rs. 50/-
2.	DA	Rs. 50/- per day
3.	Material and Admn.expenses	Rs. 50/- per candidate
4.	Honorarium for resource persons	Rs 300/- per day

3. I.E.C.

Rs. 5000 per-centre (for handouts, street plays, wall painting etc.) Stationery and Register : Rs. 2500/-

Appendix

Formats and Checklists

Following are some indicative Formats and checklists that can be used under the MNGO Scheme and the SNGO Scheme. The checklists highlight some key criteria. These can be further adapted to local needs and based on the nature and scale of interventions by different categories of NGOs viz. FNGO, MNGO and SNGO.

Project Proposal Format

A. Organisational Profile

* Name of the Organisation :
* Address :
* Street, Distt., State :
* Pin Code :
* Ph. & Fax no. (with STD code) :
* E-mail :
* Name & designation of Chief Functionary :

*	Name of other Office bearers, with contact numbers & address	:
*	Registration details	:
	Act under which registered	:
	Date of registration	:
*	FCRA no. (if available)	:
*	Banking details (Account no., name and address of bank)	:
*	PAN No.	:
*	Fixed assets (land & building) as per Audited balance sheet	:
*	Number of full & part time staff	:
*	Details of Technical Staff	:

B. Project Profile

Brief resume of work done in Health including RCH, and Social Sector/s by NGO in the last 5 years/ 3 years/ 2 years (as applicable for SNGO/ MNGO/ FNGO respectively), as below:

Year	Source of Funds	Amounts of funds (Rs)	Name of Project	Objectives & Key strategies	Geographical area & beneficiary

* Project proposal will specify proposed coverage area based on a situational analysis of the proposed district/ block,

with respect to information on key RCH indicators, quality & equity issues viz gender and socio-economic profile.

⇒ Based on the above, the organisation will specify its competencies and strengths to address these issues.

C. Attachments to be Furnished

(TO submit 2 copies of the proposal and enclosures.)

⇒ Registration Certificate

⇒ Bye laws and Memorandum of Association

⇒ Annual report for each of the previous last 5 years/ 3 years/ 2 years (as applicable for SNGO/ MNGO/ FNGO respectively)

⇒ Audited statement of Accounts for the last 5 years/ 3 years/ 2 years (as applicable for SNGO/ MNGO/ FNGO respectively)

⇒ Latest list of Executive members along with contact address and year of election

⇒ Details of Health & Family Welfare infrastructure, medical and non-medical personnel available with the organisation along with their designation, qualification and experience.

Below is an illustrative Checklist for preparation of proposal by MNGO, based on the approved FNGO proposals, by the district level committee.

⇒ Situational analysis clearly indicating the RCH status in the district.

⇒ Goals and Objectives

⇒ Proposed intervention strategies and activities

⇒ Quantitative and qualitative, verifiable indicators

⇒ Monitoring and evaluation plan

⇒ Documentation

⇒ Reporting mechanism

⇒ Organisation structure

⇒ Financial management structure

⇒ Action plan year wise and activity and fund flow chart for the first year

⇒ Attach proposals from FNGOs.

Format or field appraisal for NGOs

Field Appraisal Reports will scrutinise the Organisational Profile, Profile and Attachments. For ease of reference these are mentioned below as well. Any information not available or unsatisfactory will be high lighted in the field appraisal.

A. Organisational Profile

⇒ Name of the Organisation :

⇒ Address :

⇒ Street, Distt., State :

⇒ Pin Code :

⇒ Ph. & Fax no. (with STD code) :

⇒ E-mail :

⇒ Name & designation of Chief Functionary :

⇒ Name of other Office bearers, with contact numbers & address :

⇒ Registration details :

⇒ Act under which registered :

⇒ Date of registration :

⇒ FCRA no. (if available) :

⇒ Banking details (Account no., name and address of bank) :

⇒ PAN No. :

⇒ Fixed assets (land & building) as per Audited balance sheet :

⇒ Number of full & part time staff :

⇒ Details of Technical Staff :

⇒ Does the NGO have experience of working with CBOs ? Provide details if any :

⇒ Details of NGOs presence & net-working in the district for which grant is sought :

⇒ Has NGO been evaluated by any independent agency ? If yes, attach report :

⇒ Has a Government Department/ Ministry ever blacklisted or imposed funding restrictions on the NGO ? (Please provide details, if yes) :

⇒ Brief resume of work done in Health including RCH, and Social Sector/s by

NGO in the last 5 years/ 3 years/ 2 years (as applicable for SNGO/ MNGO/FNGO respectively), as below:

Year	Source of Funds	Amounts of Funds (Rs)	Name of Project	Objectives & Key strategies	Geographical area & beneficiary

⇒ Please indicate specific experiences in RCH related issues, clearly indicating areas of specialisation if any.

⇒ Situational analysis of the proposed district/ block, with respect to information on key RCH indicators, quality & equity issues viz. gender and socio-economic profile.

B. Attachments to be Furnished

(To submit 2 copies of the proposal and enclosures.)

⇒ Registration Certificate

⇒ Bye laws and Memorandum of Association

⇒ Annual report for each of the previous last 5 years/ 3 years/ 2 years (as applicable for SNGO/ MNGO/ FNGO respectively)

⇒ Audited statement of Accounts for the last 5 years/ 3 years/ 2 years (as applicable for SNGO/ MNGO/ FNGO respectively)

⇒ Latest list of Executive members along with contact address and year of election

⇒ Details of Health & Family Welfare infrastructure, medical and non-medical personnel available with the organisation along with their designation, qualification and experience.

C. Broadly the Field Appraisal Report should Focus on the Items Listed below in the Checklist.

Management

⇒ Statement of goals and objectives of the organisation and whether the proposed project fits into that framework.

⇒ Extent of involvement of members of the board/ Governing Body in guiding/ review of the work carried out by the organisation.

Organisation Staffing

⇒ Organisation organogram - assessing structure of the organisation

⇒ Clearly defined roles and responsibilities of staff at different levels

⇒ Length of service of core staff proposed in the organisation-examining staff turnover

⇒ Examining the reporting structure and the teamwork that exists

⇒ Assessing the staff morale, motivation and involvement.

Experience of the Organisation in Project Management

⇒ Management of RCH/ health project

⇒ Management of social sector/community development project.

Financial Management System

⇒ Details of number of staff, their qualifications and years of experience in the Accounts department of the NGO

Accounting system being followed:

⇒ Are the primary books of accounts, voucher, cashbook and ledger being maintained ?

⇒ Examining the voucher-contents and process, including preparation, authorisation and acknowledgement of receipt.

⇒ Maintenance of cashbook and how frequently it is balanced.

⇒ Posting into the ledger and correlation of entries in the other books.

⇒ Process of preparation of receipts and payments account and annual balance sheet.

⇒ Examining the single largest project handled and the adequacy of the systems and other infrastructure to determine the capacity of the organisation to handle the proposed project - assessment of fund handling capacity.

⇒ Process of the bank reconciliation and its periodicity.

⇒ Any internal audit system and notes of the auditors if any.

Inventory Systems

⇒ Are their stock maintenance systems providing physical inventory ?

⇒ Are there periodic monitoring to track inventory and plan for purchase ?

⇒ Is there any inventory of capital assets and what form is it maintained in ?

⇒ What are the purchase policies and procedures available within the organisation ?

⇒ Are the inventory records updated and maintained ?

Project Planning & Monitoring Systems (especially for SNGO/ MNGO)

⇒ How is planning done for each project in terms of human resources, financial resources and other resources within the organisation ?

⇒ What experience does the NGO have in conducting Community Needs Assessment, Baseline and Endline Survey ?

⇒ Is there any mechanism by which they are able to identify strengths and weaknesses and measure the same through indicators ?

⇒ Is the process of planning a participatory one ?

Information Systems (especially for SNGO/ MNGO)

⇒ What is the system that is being adopted to monitor the projects ?

⇒ How effective has been the system in identifying bottlenecks, achievement of objectives and in planning and reporting ?

⇒ Is the system adequate to meet the requirements of the MNGO programme ?

⇒ What are the improvement areas ?

⇒ Credibility of the Organisation based on community feedback ?

Assessment of Liaisoning & Networking (especially for SNGO/ MNGO)

Capacity of the organisation to forge relationships with:

⇒ Central Government

⇒ State government

⇒ Other NGOs/ donors

⇒ Private sector / public sector

⇒ Community

A FNGO is assessed on its capacity to mobilise the community and to liaise and network with local level health system and community groups.

Overall Assessment

⇒ Evaluation of the organisation's potential

⇒ NGO's presence in the community

⇒ Areas requiring capacity building

⇒ Primary areas requiring attention

⇒ Level of transparency of information in the organisation

⇒ If blacklisted by any Government body or Donor ?

Criteria for Rejection during Pre- Scrutiny at the RD Office

⇒ Insufficient fixed assets

⇒ Insufficient registration details

⇒ Late applications

⇒ Any other

Identification of Un-Served & Underserved Areas

Checklist for identifying un-served and under served areas

⇒ Collect secondary data from District Health Department

⇒ Have discussions with CMO, District RCH officer, ANM & other Health Administration officials

⇒ Prepare a map of the district, clearly identifying the un-served and underserved areas.

⇒ Listing of NGOs functioning in the area.

Checklist for conducting Community Needs Assessment by FNGO, supported by MNGO

⇒ MNGO will guide the Community Needs Assessment process

⇒ A group consisting of the following will conduct Community Needs Assessment:

Mandatory : FNGO, PRI representative, Teacher, Anganwadi Worker / ANM.

Desirable : Members form DWCRA groups, other SHGs, MSS, Mahila Samakhya.

Induction Training for MNGOs will Focus on

⇒ Relevance of the MNGO scheme, expectations

⇒ Conducting CNA/ Baseline Survey

⇒ Management of RCH Service Delivery Project with measurable indicators

⇒ Project proposal development

⇒ Project implementation and management, including Financial Management

⇒ Reporting and Documentation

⇒ Supportive supervision

⇒ Monitoring

⇒ Evaluation.

Orientation of FNGOs by the MNGO will Focus on

⇒ Identification of RCH issues in the community

⇒ Relevance of involvement of FNGOs in RCH service delivery

⇒ Conducting Community Needs Assessment

⇒ Project proposal development

⇒ Project implementation and management processes, including financial management

⇒ Reporting and Documentation.

How To Write A Proposal ?

Components of a project proposal are:

⇒ Covering Letter

⇒ Proposal

⇒ *About the Organisation.* Appendices attached. Annual Report of last three years, Statement of Income and Expenditure for the last three years, list of Governing Board or committee members, list/ profile of the core members, CEO, Project Director for this particular project, copy of the newsletter.

Contents of the Project Proposal

⇒ *Title* - The Title of the project must be attractive and self- explanatory in itself, that means, it must mention What you are going to do, for Whom, Where. For example, A Day Care Centre for Senior Citizens in Bombay.

⇒ *Executive Summary* - An executive summary of the entire proposal should be presented along with the detailed proposal. The summary would give an overview of the proposal in brief and is a one page summary.

⇒ *Rationale / Conceptual Framework-* After the title, would come the rationale of the project, stating the purpose of the project, the need for beginning the programme. The rationale could be broad based talking about the general status to a specific area of the problem *or* start with an incident to more general focus about the issue (could be supplemented with facts and figures). Information based on objective research, not subjective impression, should be provided to justify the need or problem. The rationale should be written in a way that would lead to objectives.

⇒ *Objectives-* Objectives of the project should be minimum 3 in no maximum 5 in no. Preferably, not to separate them into long and short term objectives and the objectives must be clear and there should be a central focus/ common link in all the objectives. The objectives should be such that it would lead to the action/ activities.

⇒ *Activities-* To clearly state tasks or action the NGO would take to achieve the objectives. The activities must be specific, clear and in point from and must flow naturally from problems and objectives.

⇒ *Target Group / Beneficiaries-* The project proposal must mention the criteria for selecting a particular target group and the number, eligibility of the beneficiaries.

⇒ *Location of the Project-* Precise geographical location of the project.

⇒ *Project Duration-* If possible, to mention the period phase wise, that is, in 1st phase- outreach will a certain no, 2nd phase- will cover more people or areas depending on the first phase. Phases could be divided into pilot or experimental phase.

⇒ *Organisational Manpower*- Manpower required from within or outside the NGO to carry out the project, hierarchy, committee or any either way of functioning and qualifications of the personnel.

⇒ *Implementation Plan / Project Management and implementation*- A detailed process, step by step or stage wise execution plan to be incorporated in the project proposal.

⇒ *Infrastructural Requirements*- needed for the project, for example, space, vehicle or equipment.

⇒ *Monitoring Mechanism*- Mechanism by which an NGO would check or periodically review the project. This portion must contain information as to who would monitor - internal or external monitoring, which area would be monitorised or focus/ thrust area of monitoring. Monitoring of the programme and of financial aspect in the project proposal in order to rectify the project at a specific stage and improvise on the same at a given moment.

⇒ *Evaluation*- To mention the objectives of evaluation and how it will be carried out. Helps to understand whether data of records is kept or there is documentation on the project. Evaluation is conducted periodically or concurrently as the project is being implemented or at the end of the project. Evaluation aids in improvising the future projects so that the errors are not repeated and more precaution and foresight is integrated in the project proposal.

⇒ *Sustainability & Follow- up / Direction for the Future-* This aspect is very important to ensure the running of the project or to decide viability of the project in the long run once funding stops. For example, in an income generation project for the senior citizens, the latter would take over the project by forming an association.

⇒ *Budget-* Budget is a tentative estimate or statement of income and expenditure. Thus, it shows where the money is coming from and where is it going through.

Bratislava Declaration on Tax Treatment of NGOs

The participants in the Round Table on "Tax Treatment of NGOs" which was organised by the Europhil Trust (France) and SAIA-Service Centre for the Third Sector (Slovakia) with the assistance of the Information and Documentation Centre on the Information and Documentation Centre on the Council of Europe (Bratislava) and of Kluwer Law International (The Haque, London), bringing together in the City of Bratislava on 16 an 17 December 1996 fifty women and men from nineteen countries: layers, tax specialists, university professors, politicians, national and international civil servants and NGO officers.

⇒ ***Recognising*** that non-governmental organisations (NGOs) play a vital role in the life of the community at all levels-local, national, regional and global- and in every field of human endeavour.

⇒ ***Reaffirming*** their commitment to the freedom of association and peaceful assembly, and the freedom of expression which are fundamental human rights.

⇒ ***Noting*** that money, time and talent, voluntarily donated, constitute the lifeblood of genuine NGOs.

⇒ ***Considering*** that international solidarity between people, nations and generations is an essential feature of the civil society and that many NGOs conduct activities abroad and receive donations form legal and physical persons residing abroad.

⇒ ***Emphasising*** the responsibility of the commercial sector towards the community and the importance of corporate citizenship.

⇒ ***Recalling*** that through the tax policy and legislation many countries acknowledge the significance of the activities benefiting the community by NGOs and their donors, and encourage them to continue doing so in the future.

⇒ ***Regretting*** that the international dimension of philanthropy is not always taken sufficiently into account in national legislations and that cross-border action by and giving to NGOs is sometimes handicapped by administrative obstacles.

⇒ ***Recalling*** Recommendation 656 (1972) of the Parliamentary Assembly of the Council of Europe on equal tax treatment of non-profit organisations, which has been inspired by a proposal for the conclusion of a European convention formulated by Interphil at its 1970 Round Table in Strasbourg.

⇒ ***Paying tribute*** to those countries which have incorporated in their tax policies and laws rules providing for recognition of the legal status and equal tax treatment of foreign or international NGOs.

⇒ ***Believing*** that those rules can serve as useful models for a general international tax regime in favour of NGOs.

⇒ ***Bearing*** in mind the documentary work of (1) the International Bureau of Fiscal Documentation in Amsterdam, carried out at the behest of a working group set up by The Europhil Trust and resulting in the publication of " Tax Treatment of Cross- border Donations" (1994, and updates), of (2) the International Institute of Association and Foundation Lawyers in Washington DC, whose series of voluntarily contributed country reports is being published by Kluwer Law International under the title "International Charitable Giving: Laws and Taxation" (1994 and updates), and of (3) the Union of International Association Brussels, whose "Yearbook of International Organisations" is an indispensable source of information on NGOs of every category and orientation.

Recommend Governments

(i) to provide in their domestic law for favourable tax treatment of NGOs and their activities and of their benefactors,

(ii) to provide in their domestic law for recognition of the legal personality of foreign and international NGOs and to become parties to the 1986 Convention No 124 of the Council of Europe on that subject,

(iii) to grant foreign and international NGOs active in their territory and persons resident in their territory donating to those NGOs abroad at least benefactors,

(iv) to include favourable tax treatment of NGOs and their benefactors in treaties on avoidance of double taxation.

Recommend Intergovernmental Organisations

i. to promote within their respective fields of competence and circle of member and observer States favourable and equal tax treatment of all NGOs whose work is beneficial to the community, as well as of their donors.

ii to draw up a multilateral framework Convention on favourable and equal tax treatment of NGOs and in so doing to take account of the experience available through all appropriate NGOs.

Invite The Europhil Trust

to initiate, in co-operation with other competent NGOs and experts from all regions of the world, the drawing up of fundamental principles and international standards for favourable and equal tax treatment of NGOs and their benefactors.

